Wicker Basketry

Flo Hoppe

Sterling Publishing Co., Inc.
New York

ACKNOWLEDGMENTS

I want to thank all those who have helped this book become a reality. I especially want to mention:

My husband, Don, for his patience and confidence in me, his willingness to go along with me to many basketry events, and most of all for putting up with the fact that I hate to do housework and cook;

My children, Tyson, Bronwen, Jason, and Nathan, for their patient understanding of their housework-disabled mother and for their willingness to do the work in exchange for a more "interesting" life;

My mother, Priscilla Fries, for exposing me to the arts at an early age;

Virginia Juergensen, for the encouragement to write this book and for technical assistance with the illustrations;

My photographer, John Keys, who has patiently taken pictures of my baskets for years under unusual and sometimes very trying circumstances;

Judy Olney, for her thorough, meticulous, and sensitive editing of the manuscript and illustrations;

Roger Olney, for all of his wonderful custom photo work and his patience with my last-minute requests;

Allen Keeney, of Allen's Basketworks, for providing the pictures of rattan processing in Indonesia;

Jim Widess, of The Caning Shop, for cheerfully shipping me six pounds of information on rattan;

Theresa Ohno, for the use of her beautifully made baskets in this book;

Sandy Webster, for the arrow border;

The Wazes, for their computer expertise and the use of their IBM-compatible computer;

My super friend, Nora Santaferrara, for always being there;

And all my students, who have encouraged and challenged me over the last sixteen years.

Illustrations by Ann Sabin and Flo Hoppe
Cover and production by Linda Seals, B. Vader Design
Photography by John Keys, unless otherwise credited
Cover photo by Joe Coca

Published 1999 by Sterling Publishing Company, Inc.
 387 Park Avenue South, New York, N.Y. 10016
Originally published by the Interweave Press
© 1989 by Flo Hoppe

Sterling ISBN 0-8069-1991-4

10 9 8 7 6 5 4 3 2 1

Distributed in Canada by Sterling Publishing
 C/o Canadian Manda Group
 One Atlantic Avenue, Suite 105
 Toronto, Ontario, Canada M6K 3E7

Distributed in Great Britain and Europe by Cassell PLC
 Wellington House, 125 Strand
 London WC2R 0BB, England

Distributed in Australia by Capricorn Link (Australia) Pty Ltd.
 P.O. Box 6651, Baulkham Hills, Business Centre
 NSW 2153, Australia

Dedicated with love to my husband, Don

CONTENTS

PREFACE

I wish this book had been available when I was learning wicker basketry. For years, my only teachers were books. Most of these publications were very old and the baskets they showed were outrageously old-fashioned. But I was so hungry for information that I was glad to have them, outdated as they were. By gathering bits and pieces of information from each book and by years of experimentation, I acquired the skills I sought.

After several years of making baskets on my own, I wanted to share my fun with others. So I began teaching, and continued to learn because students have a wonderful way of challenging and pushing a teacher to her limits. Soon writing became another way of communicating my ideas and techniques.

My own work has evolved from the strictly traditional to more experimental container forms, but I always come back to the traditional techniques and shapes to regroup my thoughts. The most important advice I can give you is to get a good grounding in traditional techniques, then practice and practice until they become so much a part of you that you don't consciously think about them when designing or making a basket. This experience will free you to be truly creative and develop a unique style of your own.

If at all possible, take a class from an experienced teacher, whose help with the techniques can save you much time and effort. A class also offers the opportunity to share ideas and perspectives with other students. It's exciting for me to teach a class because I derive these same benefits. Every time I teach I learn something new.

I have been an enthusiastic basketmaker for almost two decades. I hope you will enjoy it as much as I do. Happy basketing!

HOW TO USE THIS BOOK

Remembering my own frustrations and quest for answers, I have tried to write in a way that will make the information helpful and interesting to beginners as well as to more experienced basket-makers. This book can be used both as a reference work and as a tutorial.

Read the Introduction, Chapters 1 and 2, first, for an understanding of the type of basketry we are discussing, the materials used in the examples, and the necessary tools.

The second section, Techniques, Chapters 3 through 8, gives detailed information on weaves, bases, preparing to weave the sides, borders, and handles, and color in baskets. This information will supplement the instructions for specific baskets in the third section, and will be a resource for your own designing. Skim this material, then come back to individual points when you need them.

The third section, Patterns and Designing, Chapters 9 through 11, can provide a self-study program or an outline for a series of basketry classes. Chapter 9 contains patterns for fourteen basic baskets, beginning with a series of six baskets that are graded for beginners. These six introductory designs are presented with step-by-step photos. Chapter 10 gives instructions for another ten baskets, these incorporating color patterns. Chapter 11 offers pointers for developing your own designs. The book ends with a glossary, an extensive bibliography, and information on suppliers and basketry guilds. Throughout the book, reference figures are indicated in the text like this: (3.5). Photos and drawings are numbered sequentially, so the first number (3) tells you which chapter the figure is found in, and the second (5), tells you that you want the fifth illustration in that chapter.

If you are a beginner, choose one of the six easy baskets and start weaving, referring to the reference section for more detailed information if you need it. If you are experienced, scan the entire volume, and then copy my designs or incorporate my ideas into your own baskets. The reference section includes more techniques than are demonstrated in the sample baskets, because I would like to encourage you to learn from the traditional forms and techniques, and then push beyond into more contemporary and individual designs of your own.

A Hint for Left-Handed Basketmakers

I'm a leftie, too. If my left-handed students are having trouble with instructions, I usually suggest that they photocopy the diagrams and tape them to a window, with the printed image toward the glass, and then follow the reversed picture. In a pinch, the book can also be propped up in front of a mirror.

Introduction

CHAPTER 1
Wicker Basketry

Wicker basketry includes a broad series of techniques for making baskets primarily from round materials, like reed. Each basket consists of a rigid framework for the bottom and sides, which is horizontally interwoven with pliable materials. The pieces which are fashioned into the framework are called *spokes* and the pieces which hold them together are called *weavers*.

The interweaving makes the basket hold together and establishes its shape. Interweaving can be carried out in many different ways, resulting in a variety of patterns and textures throughout the basket.

The word *wicker* is derived from the Anglo-Saxon *wican,* meaning "to bend," and the Swedish *viker,* meaning "willow twig or wand." Today, the term applies to any round, flexible material that can be interwoven in a rigid framework. This distinguishes it from splints, which are flat and flexible, and other basketry techniques, like coiling, which do not include a rigid framework.

The most common materials used for wicker basketry are round reed and willow, but other commercially available materials, such as vine rattan, seagrass, twine, and paper twist, can add interest to wicker baskets. (A few of the designs in this book also incorporate flat materials, for a change in texture.) Naturalists can use the same techniques to weave with vines, roots, twigs, and other gathered materials.

For several reasons, this book will concentrate on the use of commercially available reed. First, it's easiest to see what's happening in the structure of a basket if the materials are smooth and regular. Second, reed is readily available. Third, the

fine points of shaping and of color use take precedence when the materials are not heavily textured. Of course, you can use gathered natural materials to make baskets with the techniques described in this book; the bibliography tells you where to find more information on other types of materials.

Since basketry is an amalgamation of techniques derived from many cultures, there's bound to be some confusion with terms and definitions. For instance, the word *cane* can mean "chair cane," or "reed," or "nine-foot sticks of rattan that measure at least 20mm in diameter." The word *rattan* can mean "reed" or else "the palm from which reed is derived," and *vine rattan* is not a rattan at all, but a flexible vine that lookes like grapevine. Although these ambiguous terms cannot be completely avoided, I will clarify the ways in which I am using the words and have provided a glossary to which you can refer.

RATTAN

The rattan or cane palm is the source of reed, one of the most popular materials for basketmaking because of its strength, flexibility, and uniformity. Unprocessed rattan vines have a thick base and run to a narrower tip. Processed reed is completely uniform in diameter throughout its length, and has no readily discernible base or tip. Rattan (from the Malayan word *rotan*) is a vine-like plant which grows in the jungles and rain forests of tropical countries from Madagascar to Taiwan. The best plants for basketmaking come from Malaysia and Indonesia.

Processing rattan for the furniture and

basketmaking markets is an industry which employs half a million people. It requires a great deal of skill. Since the material comes to us in neat little coils we don't realize the time and labor involved in its preparation. Processing one's own materials, like honeysuckle or grapevine, can give a hint of the procedure.

Rattan of the genus *Calamus* is the most important source of commercial rattan. This climbing, vine-like palm has a tough, thorny outer bark. T. C. Whitmore, in *The Palms of Malaya*, describes it as a "climbing, horribly prickly" palm. It commonly grows to a length of 200 to 300 feet with an average diameter of about one inch. A young rattan plant will grow across the dense undergrowth on the jungle floor before attaching itself to a tree with its long, thorny leaf tip. It continues to push its way upward, trying to grow through the heavy forest canopy. Because the rattan plant is top-heavy, the branches supporting it can break and send the whole coil to the ground. It's not unusual to see huge coils of rattan on the jungle floor.

Harvesting is a problem because of the thorns and the tangled manner in which the rattan grows. The harvesters cut off the mature stems near the ground with a *parang*, or jungle knife, then leave them to dry. Later, to remove the outer bark, they twist the rattan and pull it around a nearby tree, or draw it through a fork or notch in a tree. At the jungle site, the rattan is cut into canes twelve to thirty feet long, which are then bent and tied into bundles. Bundles designated for export are carried out of the forest on the backs of the harvesters and sent to processing centers in Singapore and Hong Kong. Rattan intended for local use is left to dry in the sun.

Rattan for commercial use is classified by size. The term **cane** refers to material 20mm in diameter or larger *(chair cane,* used for weaving seats and backs of chairs, is a different item and is described along with rattan). Cane is used for such sturdy items as walking sticks, handles, and furniture frames, and is sold in bundles of nine-foot lengths.

Cane must be cured within fifteen days of harvest or it develops a black mold which affects its color and flexibility. Curing consists of boiling the cane in diesel oil to bring out the water and resins. Then the cane is rubbed with sand or sawdust to remove the resins. Finally it is dried, graded again, and rebundled for export.

The second classification, **rattan,** includes anything under 20mm in diameter. Rattan is usually sold in bundles of 100 strands, each measuring between sixteen and thirty feet in length

and bent double. When rattan reaches the processing centers, it is carefully graded and sorted into bundles of uniform size, weight, color, and hardness. The leaf nodes or joints are smoothed, and the hard skin is removed. The rattan is soaked in water, straightened, and rubbed with sand or coconut fiber to bring out the beauty of its smooth glossy surface. It is dried in the sun, then bleached and disinfected with sulfur fumes.

At processing centers in Hong Kong and Singapore the rattan is cut into **chair cane** and **reed.** Chair cane comes from the glossy outer skin of the rattan. Machines are used to peel off this skin and cut it into pieces of uniform width and thickness. The tough, fibrous core that remains is processed with specialized machinery to make different types of reed. When flat and flat oval reed are cut, the pole is first made round. The curved outer part of the pole is cut into flat oval reed and the rest of the pole is cut into different widths of flat reed. (Reed has a definite grain, just like wood. The outer surface of the pole is smooth and the inner surface is rough.)

When round reed is cut, the pole is put through a die which has several circular knives of different sizes, so that every bit of the core is used. The very center is frequently oval and is either sold as oval-oval or is split for flat oval. Waste from the cutting process is called **rattan wool** and is used for packing material or as upholstery padding.

Although on first inspection reed looks quite predictable and uniform, the more you work with it the more you will discover that grading does not guarantee consistency. There are over 200 species in the *Calamus* genus alone, each with its own characteristics, and the package of reed you take from the supplier's shelf may contain strands from several of these species. Reed from the different species varies in quality, and the best grade comes from a species that has always been in short supply because of over-harvesting. An attempt has been made to code the different grades by placing colored ties on the coils, but this system has not proved reliable.

If the quality cannot be completely consistent, can you at least expect that the sizing will be? No; the size designated turns out to be a useful guideline, not a guarantee. Reed is all cut to metric measurements, but in some American suppliers' catalogs measurements are given in inches. Therefore, the measurements you read will be approximate. To further confuse matters, there are separate European and American numbering systems, and within each system there are discrepancies because the reed originates in different countries. Different basketry books and suppliers vary slightly on which American designation equals which European size. Add to this the language barriers between exporters and buyers, and the result is a regular stewpot of problems. It's not uncommon for a supplier to receive whole bales of reed that are completely mislabeled.

Despite these problems, your first baskets will be successful because reed is a flexible material and precision is not essential. By the time you become more proficient, you will be more familiar with the range of variations and you will compensate for them as you work.

Reed is usually sold by the pound, either in coils or in straight bundles. Some suppliers carry the "Continental coil," which weighs three-quarters of a pound. In the descriptions of baskets in Chapters 9 and 10, I have specified the amounts of reed you will need in each size by weight; you won't need to weigh out your materials, but this will help you tell how many baskets you can make from a coil or bundle of reed. It's easier to "guesstimate" this way than by trying to measure linear feet of reed.

Different qualities of reed have different names, and these labels are established by the suppliers. For example, one supplier uses "Indonesian" for the best quality, and "first quality" for the next grade down. Become familiar with each supplier's terminology so you'll know what to order.

Whole rattan is another category of basketmaking materials in the rattan family. *Datu, kooboo* (or kubu), and *puloet* are three types of rattan which have the glossy bark left intact. Datu is light tan in color and ranges from 2¼mm to 4½mm in diameter. Puloet is slightly larger, 3mm to 5mm, and is more reddish. Kooboo is the largest, ranging from 5mm to 8mm, and is also light tan. These three varieties are always ordered by name, not by size. Each has a range of sizes within a pound because the rattan strands haven't been trimmed to a uniform diameter.

Datu, kooboo, and puloet look very "natural" because of the bark and leaf joints, but they can be more difficult to work with than standard reed because of their stiffness and variations in diameter. Before they can be used, these types of rattan must be soaked for an hour, and then mellowed in a damp towel overnight.

Smoked reed is a chocolate brown color. It was originally produced in Sumatra by a special process using heat and ammonia; the reed was colored all the way through. Now it is just a lower-quality reed which has been dyed. Be aware that smoked reed can be unusually flexible and

easy to weave while it is wet, but it becomes quite brittle when dry.

OTHER COMMERCIALLY AVAILABLE MATERIALS

Seagrass is a two-ply twisted grass. There are two types, Hong Kong and Taiwanese. Seagrass is greenish tan in color and varies in texture; Hong Kong is not as smooth as Taiwanese and may be tough on the hands.

Seagrass is a nice accent in a basket. Weave with it dry; when it is wet, the ends will unravel. After weaving and trimming a basket, you can apply craft glue to the ends of the seagrass to prevent fraying.

Seagrass is available in the following sizes: #0 (⅛"), #1 (⁵⁄₃₂"), #2 (¹¹⁄₆₄"), and #3 (³⁄₁₆").

Vine rattan is another material sometimes used as an accent. It is not a rattan at all, but a very flexible vine that has the look of grapevine. It is sold in one size only, but varies in diameter and texture within the coil. It is available in its natural color, or smoked.

PREPARATION AND STORAGE

When you are ready to begin one of the basketry projects described in Chapters 9 and 10, your materials must be prepared for use. The strands of reed have to be sorted according to strength and flexibility. Strands to be used for spokes should be sturdy. Weavers should be flexible; if they are too brittle they will snap and break when handled. You may be able to guess which strands will be more flexible when the reed is dry, but be aware that each strand's true nature will be revealed only when you have soaked it.

Spokes provide the vertical framework of the basket, and must be firm and strong. For spokes, the best sizes of reed to use are #4, #5, and #6 (a specific size will be suggested for each project). Overly flexible strands in these sizes can be saved to use as weavers on very large baskets.

Weavers are the long strands worked horizontally through the spokes. Sizes #2 and #3 make good weavers, and all but the most brittle strands can be used. The brittle ones should just be thrown out; using them leads to both frustration and inferior baskets.

To sort the reed, soak one end of the coil or bundle in warm water for a few minutes to determine the flexibility of each strand. Because reed is a natural material, each strand will have its own unique character. When wet, some will be stiff, while others will feel like cooked spaghetti. Use the most flexible for the parts of the basket, like the base, where the weaver will have to turn lots of corners in a tight space. Save the less pliable strands for broader, less intricate areas.

When you are ready to work, the strands you will be using need to be completely wet in order to have maximum pliability. Soak a selection of reed in lukewarm water, about five minutes for #1 through #4 reed, or up to ten minutes for #5 through #10. Soaking reed too long may cause it to bring up "hairs" when you are weaving; poor quality reed is "hairy" whether it is wet or dry.

The reed you plan to use for spokes will be curved from being stored in a coil, and after you cut the spokes to length you need to soak them until they are completely straight before you start to work. Spokes must be kept thoroughly dampened throughout the weaving process. They need not be as wet as the weavers, but never let them become bone-dry. Dry reed will be difficult to

shape and can break easily. Dry spokes are stubborn and will fight you; wet ones will do what you want them to do.

Once you have made a few baskets, you will be able to tell how much reed to soak for a working session. However, it's easy to soak a few more strands if you see that you will be running out soon.

If you have wet reed left over when it's time to quit, allow it to dry thoroughly, then keep it in a cool, dry, well-ventilated area. Since reed is a natural fiber, it will easily support the growth of mold if it is put away damp. Excessive humidity also can cause reed to mold, so don't store your supplies in sealed plastic bags or in a damp basement.

Removing mold from reed or a basket is difficult, but a dilute bleach solution scrubbed in with a small brush will eliminate most of the stain. Dyeing the stained reed or basket in a dark color may obscure minor mold marks.

Round Reed Sizes

Round reed is the primary material used to construct the baskets in this book. Reed is measured most accurately in millimeters, but most basket suppliers' catalogs in the United States refer to the American sizes. For this reason, American sizes are used throughout this book.

The following chart gives the equivalent American and British round reed sizes, based on the metric measurements. The existing system of sizing reed is not completely consistent. For instance, depending upon the supplier you are dealing with, an American #4½ may be 3mm or 3.25mm. The chart gives the range of sizes found by comparing various suppliers' lists. So you can follow me as easily as possible, the American sizes are listed in boldface type, as are the equivalents

which I am using. *When in doubt, buy reed by its metric measurement.* And remember that reed is a natural material and variations in sizing are to be expected.

While a large number of sizes of reed are available, I don't use anything larger than an American #6 (4.5mm) for spokes, because the heavy sizes become too hard to handle. For large baskets, I use #6 (4.5mm) for the framework (spokes), and make the body with weavers up to #5 (3.5mm). The large baskets are strong because I use a lot of spokes, placed close together.

Sizes 11 through 19 are also available (approximately 8.00 through 10.00mm), but are not used for the baskets in this book.

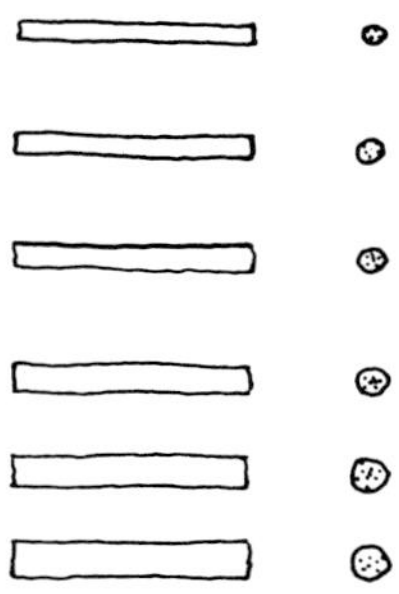

	American	British	Metric diameter
	00	0000000	**1.00** mm
	—	00000	1.125 mm
	0	0000	**1.25** mm
	—	000	1.375 mm
	1	00	**1.5** mm
	—	0	1.625 mm
	2	1	**1.75** mm
	—	2	1.875 mm
	2½	3	**2.00** mm
	3	4	**2.25** mm
	3½	5	**2.5** mm
	—	6	2.625 mm

4	7	**2.75** mm
4½	8	3.00-**3.25** mm
5	9	3.25-**3.50** mm
—	10	3.375 mm
5½	11	3.50-**4.00** mm
—	12	3.75 mm
6	—	4.00-4.50 mm
—	14	4.25 mm
6½	15	**4.50** mm
7	16	**5.00** mm
7½	—	5.50 mm
8	—	5.75-**6.00** mm
8½	—	6.00-**6.50** mm
9	—	6.50-**7.00** mm
9½	—	7.00-**7.50** mm
10	20	7.50-**8.00** mm
12	—	**10** mm

Flat Reed Sizes

Flat reed is used as an accent in some of the baskets.

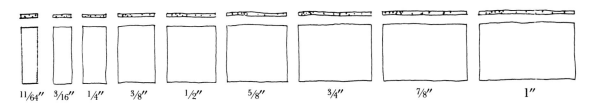

11/64″   3/16″   1/4″   3/8″   1/2″   5/8″   3/4″   7/8″   1″

Cane Sizes

Carriage	1.5 mm	Medium	3.0 mm
Superfine	2.0 mm	Common	3.5 mm
Fine-Fine	2.25 mm	Narrow Binder	4 mm
Fine	2.5 mm	Medium Binder	5 mm
Narrow Medium	2.75 mm		

Wide Binder   6 mm

Slab Rattan   8-10 mm

CHAPTER 2
Tools

If this is your first attempt at basketry and you don't want to invest much money in equipment, you can get along with a few essential tools. In a pinch, you can make the Interwoven Base Basket with just a good pair of sturdy scissors or diagonal cutting pliers and a tape measure. For general purposes, I recommend a minimum tool kit including heavy duty cutters, diagonal cutting pliers, roundnose pliers, needlenose pliers, an awl (you can substitute an ice pick or sturdy knitting needle), a knife, and a tape measure.

The comprehensive list below includes these basics as well as more specialized tools that you might want to acquire as you need them. Sources for these tools are given in the "Suppliers" section at the back of the book.

1. **Cutters:** Large, sturdy spring-loaded cutters can be used on larger sizes of reed, or several smaller strands held together. The shears pictured are seven-inch fruit and flower shears (see Goldblatt Tool Company in Suppliers). Similar cutters are available from basketry suppliers or stores that carry garden supplies.

2. **Sewing scissors:** These are useful for cutting or tapering flat reed. They are not generally strong enough for cutting round reed or pointed enough for trimming. They are available at fabric shops and many discount stores.

3. **Diagonal cutting pliers:** These are also known as wire cutters, side cutters, or dikes. They're used for cutting individual strands of reed and for trimming. The pair I like best is spring-loaded and is manufactured for trimming plastics (see Dianne Stanton in Suppliers). They are available at hardware or building supply stores.

4. **Platoshear diagonal cutters:** This little pair of pliers is also spring-loaded and is terrific for trimming (see The Country Seat in Suppliers). Because the blade is very short, it's not good for general cutting. Similar cutters are available from other basketry suppliers.

5. **Japanese trimming shears:** Because of their length, these are great for trimming ends inside a basket. They have comfortable plastic handles and a long shank with small sharply pointed tips. They are available from basketry suppliers.

6. **Roundnose pliers:** These are essential for pinching spokes so they can be bent without breaking. Roundnose pliers crush the fibers in only a very narrow area, unlike flatnose pliers, which produce a broad crunch—and therefore a sloppier, less precise bend. Available from Rio Grande Albuquerque in Suppliers, as well as from jewelry and electronics suppliers.

7. **Flat or needlenose pliers:** These are good for pulling short ends of reed through small openings. Try to get the kind without serrated grip surfaces. Available from Rio Grande Albuquerque in Suppliers, as well as from jewelry and electronics supply houses.

8. **Awls:** These are needed for splitting spokes and opening spaces in the weaving. Although you can get along with one, there are four kinds which I find work well and you will want to discover them if you plan to make lots of baskets:

a) *Large awl:* I use this to open a space for a large handle, and use a home-made one. You can do without, but if the resources for making one are available you can duplicate mine. Begin with a ⅜" steel rod about 10" long and a file handle, both of which can be found at a hardware store. Put the handle on one end of the rod, then point the other end with a grinder.

b) *Medium awl:* I use this for bi-spoking (adding spokes as the basket increases in size) and for opening spaces for small handles. In the United States, you can go to a hardware store and buy a scratch awl with a 5-inch shaft. My favorite medium awl was made in Great Britain by Dryad; it's called a bodkin, rather than an awl, but is the same tool, with a 5-inch shaft and a comfortable 4½-inch handle (available from English Basketry Willows in Suppliers).

c) *Small awl:* I use this to split base spokes and to make spaces for inserting weaver ends. A Stanley awl with a 2⅝-inch shank is good. It has a comfortable rounded handle and is available in hardware stores. Similar awls can be obtained from basketry suppliers.

d) *Bone awl:* This broad, flat awl, made of bone, opens spaces where a round awl may leave an indentation (available from Connecticut Cane & Reed in Suppliers). You may find it useful when weaving borders or wrapping handles.

9. **Tape measure:** Use a flexible tape measure, of the type available in fabric shops.

10. **Yardstick:** This is for measuring spokes, and so forth. The handiest one I've found is the kind that folds in thirds. Yardsticks are available at hardware stores and fabric shops.

11. **Knife:** A sharp single- or multi-bladed knife is handy. I like one called sheep's foot blade, because the cutting edge is straight. It's available in sporting goods shops.

12. **Twist-ties:** I use these for marking spokes and spaces. The vinyl-covered wire ties that come in a roll are most convenient; paper-covered ties may transfer their color to wet rattan. They are available from hardware stores, garden shops, or office suppliers.

13. **Brass gauge:** This is a good tool for figuring the actual sizes of reed, in inches or millimeters, if you find that information is important to you (see The Country Seat in Suppliers).

14. **Plastic dishpan:** I find this a good size for soaking materials and baskets. The rectangular kind is handier because it accommodates both materials and a basket in progress. Available from drug stores or variety stores.

15. **Spray bottle:** If your basket is too big for the dishpan, you can keep things damp by spraying water on the sections you're working.

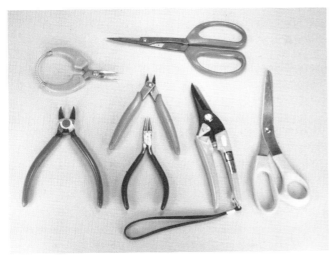

Scissors, diagonal cutting pliers, needlenose and round-nose pliers.

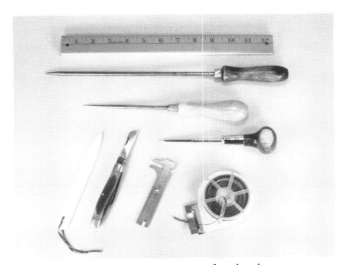

Ruler, awls, knife, brass gauge, and twist ties.

Techniques

CHAPTER 3
Weaving Techniques

We have defined wicker basketry as a broad series of techniques for making baskets from round materials. Weaving techniques produce the fundamental fabric of a basket; there are many ways that the "pliable materials" can be worked onto the rigid framework. Each distinct weave plays both a structural and a design role in a basket. Some weaves are strong; others are highly decorative. A few combine both qualities.

This section covers several general categories of weaves—*over-and-under, Japanese, pairing, waling, braiding,* and *diamond*—and a number of variations. It includes information on appropriate ways to use each weave, things to watch out for, and design potential. It also offers techniques for joining weavers and a guide to avoiding problems with joins, and concludes with pointers on the final task in the weaving of the basket: trimming the ends of the weavers to produce a smooth surface.

OVER-AND-UNDER WEAVES

All over-and-under weaves call for the weaver to move over one spoke and under the next (in one case over two, under two), repeating around the basket. When you count rows on weaves in this category, you can count the over-strokes singly on two adjoining spokes or by twos on one spoke (3.1).

Randing

The simplest and most basic weave is called randing (3.2). It also goes by the names *simple weave, plain weave,* and *in-and-out;* if someone speaks in shorthand of *over-and-under weave,* this is the technique under discussion. It is probably the easiest weave to understand, but can be challenging to do perfectly.

The easy part of randing: in its simplest form, you weave with only one strand of reed, and it moves over one spoke and under the next, repeating this all the way around the basket. Worked in this way, it requires an uneven number of spokes, so on each row the weaver will go under the spokes it went over on the previous row, and vice versa. There are several variations, which allow you to use even numbers of spokes and to create other patterns while maintaining the "over-and-under" rhythm.

The hard part of randing: other weaves, with different patterns and multiple weavers, control the spokes better—for example, pairing or waling, which will be described later. Pairing and waling catch each spoke with every stroke and lock it in place with a twist of the weavers, whereas randing goes behind every other spoke with no locking. As a result, randing is not as good a weave to use for shaping a basket.

To maximize your control when you want to shape with randing, use weavers of the same stiffness and you will have an easier time keeping the spokes correctly aligned (3.3). If one weaver is stiffer than the other, the spokes will shift position slightly and your basket will develop a ridged or corrugated appearance (3.4).

Because it exposes the spokes, randing is called a **transparent** weave. It can be used to best advantage for textural contrast with a more solid weave, such as waling. Waling is not a transparent weave; it completely covers the spokes on the outside of the basket, creating a dense appearance.

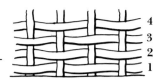

3.1 Counting rows of an over-and-under weave

3.2 Randing

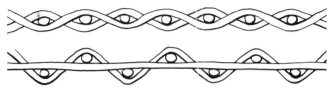

3.3 (above) Spokes correctly aligned: Woven with weavers of the same stiffness

3.4 (below) Spokes not correctly aligned: Woven with one weaver stiffer than the other

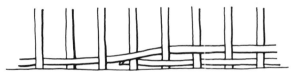

3.5 Randing: Woven over an uneven number of spokes so that rows alternate

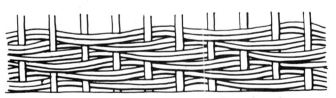

3.6 Spiral slewing: Woven over a number of spokes divisible by 4 plus 1

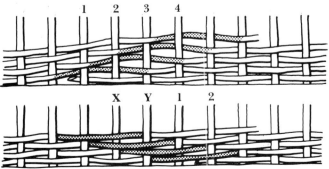

3.7 (above) Indian weave: Adjusted at the beginning of each row by weaver going behind two spokes

3.8 (below) Indian weave: Adjusted at the beginning of each row by weaver going in front of two spokes

We'll start with a description of the most basic form of randing: using only one weaver and an uneven number of spokes. Place the weaver behind a spoke (3.5), then weave it in front of the next, behind the next, and so on around the basket. Because of the uneven number of spokes, the position of the weaver on each row will automatically alternate with its position on the previous row.

Spiral Slewing

The next variation of the over-and-under weaves, spiral slewing, is a fast-moving weave which creates a bold, spiral pattern (3.6). It requires two weavers, although the two weavers work as one. Two strands are used to give the pattern definition. It is woven over a number of spokes divisible by four, plus or minus one—for example, 17 spokes or 15 spokes (16 is divisible by four, then plus or minus one).

Hold the two strands together and weave over two spokes and under two spokes, working from left to right. When you use the correct number of spokes (divisible by four, plus or minus one), a spiral ridge forms. The spiral moves to the left if you choose "plus one" and to the right if you choose "minus one."

When you begin this weave or make joins, the bulky cut ends of the doubled weavers can interrupt the flow of the pattern. A technique for staggering the ends is shown in illustration 3.11.

Indian Weave

Indian weave is randing worked over an even number of spokes. There is one weaver. As we noted above, the weaver alternates its position on adjacent rows only if there is an *uneven* number of spokes. Indian weave takes this into account by requiring a slight adjustment at the beginning of each row, which causes the rows to alternate. As the weaver reaches the beginning of a new row, it goes either behind two spokes (3.7) or in front of two spokes (3.8).

This maneuver, which arises out of necessity, also creates a design element. The adjustment creates a spiral ridge on either the inside (under two spokes) or the outside (over two spokes) of the basket.

Chasing Weave

Chasing weave is another type of over-and-under weave. It is worked with two weavers over an even number of spokes (3.9); the weavers work independently. You weave one row with the first weaver, then a row with the second, and so forth.

Mark any two adjacent spokes with twist-ties. Begin by inserting a weaver behind spoke 2, then weave in front of the next spoke, behind the next, and so on, until you come back to the beginning. Add a second weaver behind spoke 1 (to the left of spoke 2) and weave in front of the next, behind the next, and so on around.

Continue in successive rounds, making your transitions between rounds like this: as you complete a round, stop the working weaver two spokes to the left of the resting weaver and then pick up the resting weaver, which is on the right, for the next round. When you have completed your work with this technique, end the section of chasing weave with the two weavers behind their beginning spokes.

Double Chasing

Double chasing or *slewing* is yet another type of over-and-under weave (3.10). It's woven with four weavers, in two sets; each set contains two weavers held together and worked as one. Stagger the cut ends of the weavers at the beginning and end points, as shown in 3.11 and described below, to produce a smoother transition between rows.

To work this pattern, begin by marking any two consecutive spokes with twist-ties. For the staggered beginning, insert weaver A behind spoke 2. Weave in front of spoke 3, then behind spoke 4, where you add weaver B on top of A. Hold these two weavers together and weave around until you come to within a few spokes of the beginning.

Weavers A and B rest for a round while you begin weavers C and D. Insert weaver C behind spoke 1, weave in front of spoke 2 and behind 3, then add weaver D on top of C. Hold weavers C and D together and weave a round.

Work an even number of rows, alternating AB and CD as working weavers. End the first set of weavers with weaver B behind spoke 4, and A behind 2. End the second set with weaver D behind spoke 3, and C behind 1.

So far we've talked only of structure, and that

3.9 Chasing weave: Randing worked over an even number of spokes with two weavers

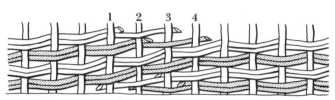

3.10 Double chasing weave

3.11 Double chasing weave: Showing staggered ends at beginning and end

3.12 Chasing weave, worked with one flat and one round weaver

will be our primary interest in this chapter. But you can increase the possibilities by varying your materials in each of these weaves. For example, illustration 3.12 shows an interesting variation of chasing weave woven with one flat weaver and one round weaver.

French Randing

French randing produces a dramatic pattern, which can be particularly interesting when worked with flat reed or a combination of round and flat reed (3.13). It's also a good way to use scraps, because you use a lot of weavers at once and each one can be fairly short.

There is one weaver for each spoke in the basket. Each weaver starts behind the spoke to the *left* of the previous weaver's starting point. As usual, each weaver weaves from left to right as you move it over and under the spokes. Weavers are added to the left; weaving proceeds to the right.

Insert the first weaver between any two spokes. Weave to the right in front of one spoke, behind the next, and to the outside (3.14). You'll notice that the weaver angles upward to the right. Insert the second weaver behind the spoke to the left of the spoke where the first weaver started. Weave the same three-spoke pattern you used for the first weaver: in front, behind, and out. Mark these first two weavers with twist-ties.

Continue to add new weavers, inserting each one behind the spoke to the left of the previous weaver's starting spoke, until you complete the round. The openings for the final two weavers may be tricky to see. Lift the marked weavers in order to open these spaces for the last two weavers (3.15). Check the inside of your basket to make sure there is a weaver leaning against each spoke. Your first row is complete, and you have added as many weavers as you have spokes.

Begin the second row with the marked weaver on the right, weaving in front, behind, and out. Continue as before, working with each weaver in sequence and always taking up the weaver to the left of the one just worked. Weave each one in front, behind, and out (3.16).

To finish the round, lift the last two marked weavers. There will be two weavers in the same space. Weave the lower one first, then the one above it.

To make sure there are the same number of rows for each weaver, count the over-strokes on each spoke, or scan the top of the weaving and be sure that a weaver protrudes from between each pair of spokes. Trim the weaver to the right of each spoke as you look at the basket from the outside.

Packing

Packing, also called *filling in,* refers to randing when it is used to raise the line of a particular area of a basket by weaving back and forth instead of around the basket. There are many methods of packing, but only three are shown here: two use a single weaver, the third uses double weavers. For each of these techniques, begin by determining the area to be packed and marking the spokes at each end of it. As you work back and forth, be sure the spokes stay in their correct positions and do not begin to lean toward the center of the packed area.

For packing with one weaver which works *from the outside to the center,* start by placing the

3.13 French randing

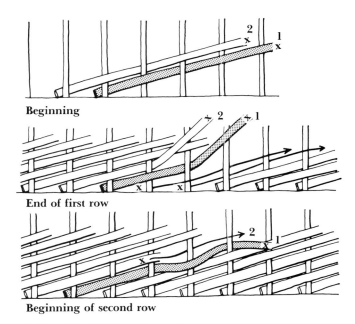

Beginning

End of first row

Beginning of second row

3.14, 3.15, 3.16 French randing

weaver behind the left marked spoke. Rand to the marked spoke at the right, turn the weaver around that spoke, then rand in the opposite direction. Turn the weaver around the spoke to the right of the marked left spoke and weave to the right again. Continue to decrease by turning one spoke sooner in each row until there are only two or three spokes left (3.17).

To begin another area of packing right over the first, take the weaver back to the spoke just beyond the first one and weave the same packing sequence again (3.18).

For packing with one weaver which proceeds *from the center to the outside,* see 3.19. Start at the center, work out to the edges, and then work back to the center again.

Packing can also be done with *double weavers* which are laid in and cut off in each row, instead of being turned around a spoke (3.20 and 3.21). For this laid-in method, designate a single central spoke in the area to be packed, or the packed area will be off-center. Each pair of weavers starts and

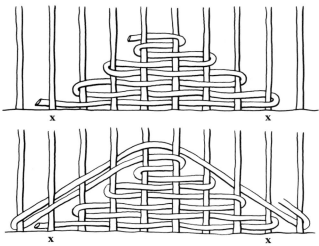

3.17 (above) Packing with a single weaver

3.18 (below) Starting second packing area

3.19 Packing with a single weaver from the center to the edge, then back to the center

3.20 Packing with double laid-in weavers

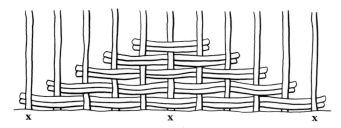

3.21 Double laid-in packing

ends *behind* a spoke, so the cut ends are on the inside of the basket.

JAPANESE WEAVE

Japanese Weave with One or Two Weavers

Japanese weave, also called *rib* or *Chinese randing*, is woven over two spokes and under one (3.22 and 3.23). When worked with a single round reed weaver, the rows pack in closely and create a solid weave which resembles three-rod waling (to be described later). Worked with a flat weaver or with double round reed weavers (and therefore called *double Japanese*), it produces an open weave, because the spokes are exposed.

Japanese weave is easy to work over any number of spokes not divisible by three, because the pattern repeats itself every three spokes. If the number of spokes is divisible by three, plus one, the spiral surface of the basket moves to the left. If the number is divisible by three, minus one, the spiral moves to the right.

If the number of spokes *is* divisible by three, the weave will continue to follow the same path on each round—making vertical "columns" instead of a spiral ridge—unless you adjust the weaver at the beginning of each row. This maneuver takes concentration, so either avoid doing Japanese weave over a number of spokes divisible by three, or weave when you won't be interrupted. To make the adjustment, go under two spokes as you begin a new round before resuming with an over-two stroke. This adjustment moves one spoke to the right on each successive round, so a spiral ridge forms on the inner surface of the basket.

Double Japanese Weave

When you begin double Japanese, using two weavers, stagger the ends as shown in 3.24 so there will be a smooth transition between the rows. To end the weavers behind the spokes where they began, end on a row divisible by three, again staggering the ends to match the beginnings.

Double Double Japanese Weave

Double double Japanese weave (3.25) takes the over-two, under-one pattern of the Japanese weave and adds a second set of weavers. As in chasing weave, this second set follows but never overtakes the first set. It produces a beautiful color design when worked with double sets of weavers in two colors (color photo 20, bottom section). Woven over a number of spokes divisible by three, minus one, the woven spiral moves to the left at the same time that the color spiral appears to move to the right.

To begin, mark any two consecutive spokes with twist-ties. Place the first set of weavers behind spoke 2, staggering the ends as you did for double Japanese. Work Japanese weave to within a few spokes of spoke 1. Place the second set of weavers behind spoke 1, again staggering the ends.

To complete a section of this weave, work a number of rows divisible by three and you will be able to end the weavers behind their corresponding beginning spokes.

PAIRING

Pairing weave, or *twining*, is worked with two weavers over any number of spokes. Pairing is very effective for controlling the shape of a basket, because it locks each spoke in place. This is a transparent weave and makes a good textural contrast to solid weaves. Both weavers are worked at the same time, and as you manipulate them around the spokes they take a twist between each pair of spokes, giving a slant to the weaving (3.26).

Basic Pairing

Mark any two consecutive spokes with twist-ties. Place a weaver behind each of these two spokes (3.27). Bring the left weaver in front of the next spoke to the right, over the right weaver, behind the second spoke and out. The other weaver is now on the left. Repeat this sequence, using the left weaver each time.

Pairing Arrow

A pairing arrow or *chain pairing* consists of two rows—one of regular pairing and one of reverse pairing, which will be described below. Begin by weaving one row of regular pairing. End with the weavers coming from behind spokes Y and Z (3.28).

3.22 Japanese weave with flat reed weaver

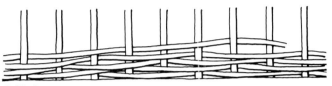

3.23 Japanese weave

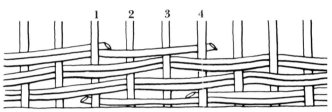

3.24 Double Japanese weave: Showing staggered ends at the beginning and end

3.25 Double double Japanese weave

3.26 Pairing weave

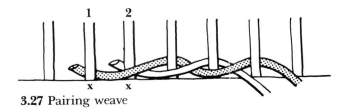

3.27 Pairing weave

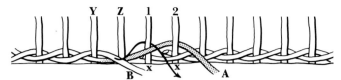

3.28 Pairing arrow: First step of the step-up

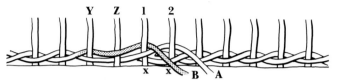

3.29 Pairing arrow: Second step of the step-up

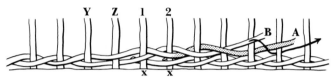

3.30 Pairing arrow: Second row, reverse pairing

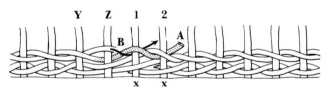

3.31 Pairing arrow: First step of the ending

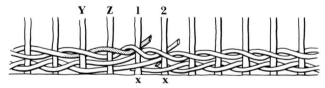

3.32 Pairing arrow: Second step of the ending

3.33 Pairing weave: Reverse pairing worked from the back

The transition between the first and second rows is called a **step-up**. To do this, start by bringing weaver A in front of spoke 1, behind spoke 2, and out (3.28). Complete the step-up by bringing weaver B in front of spoke Z, behind spoke 1, and out (3.29).

The second row is worked in *reverse pairing*.

Reverse Pairing

There are two ways to do reverse pairing, from the front and from the back. From the front, it's easier to visualize how the final pattern is being produced. The from-the-back method may be somewhat easier to work.

To work *from the front,* begin by bringing the left weaver in front of the next spoke, *under* the right weaver, behind the second spoke, and out (3.30). Continue this sequence all the way around, alternating weavers, and end with the weavers coming from behind spokes Y and Z again.

The ending is similar to the step-up, but the weavers must interlace under the top weaver from the beginning of the second round in order to finish in the arrow pattern. Bring weaver A in front of spoke 1 and under the top weaver from the previous row (3.31). Bring weaver B in front of spoke Z and under weaver A, which is on top (3.32). Lay the ends of the weavers flat against the spokes on the inside and trim with a slant cut (3.78).

To work *from the back,* start with the weavers in back of the spokes (3.33). Bring the left weaver (A) over the right weaver, in front of the next spoke, then to the back. Continue this sequence all the way around, always weaving with the left weaver.

Working with a Folded Weaver

Pairing weave can be started with a folded weaver. This trick works well in places where you don't want ends showing, such as over an openwork section or over a section of beads. Soak a flexible weaver, then pinch and fold it almost in half and begin just as you did the regular pairing weave (3.27). (If you fold the weaver exactly in half, both ends will run out at the same time and it will be harder to make neat joins.)

To begin pairing with a folded weaver, start it around spoke 2 (3.34), which will give you the correct spacing for the step-up at the end of the row. Normally two weavers are inserted behind two consecutive spokes, but when you use a folded weaver, the first weaver only goes in front of spoke 2, not behind spoke 1. When you reach the end of the round, think of spoke 1 as having a "ghost" weaver and work a step-up in the normal way.

Continuous Spiraling Pairing Arrows

Continuous spiraling pairing arrows can be worked with two folded weavers. This weave is attractive when worked as a wide band on the side of a basket (3.35) or on a base (3.36).

Start with one weaver folded over a spoke on one side of the basket or base and a second weaver folded over a spoke exactly halfway around the basket or base. Mark both beginning spokes with twist-ties.

Work regular pairing with one set of weavers until you come within a couple of spokes of the other set of weavers. Drop the first set of weavers and with the other set do a row of reverse pairing. On a base, reverse pairing is most easily worked from the back. Each set will chase the other, but must never be allowed to overtake it. Always leave a couple of spokes between the sets.

Be aware that regular pairing slants upward to the right, reverse pairing to the left. Mark the sets so you'll know which is the "regular" pair and which the "reverse." End each set behind its respective beginning spokes.

WALING

Waling requires three (or more) weavers and can be woven over any number of spokes. When you've mastered the idea of three-rod waling, you can try using four, five, or six rods.

Three-Rod Waling

Three-rod waling, also called *triple weave*, is a strong weave, excellent for shaping and controlling the basket because it locks the spokes in place (3.37).

For three-rod waling, mark three consecutive spokes with twist-ties. Insert a weaver behind each of these three spokes (3.38). The weavers move to the right as you work them. Bring the left weaver in front of two spokes, over the right two weavers, behind the next spoke, and out. Repeat this sequence all the way around, using the lefthand weaver each time.

The way you end each row will depend upon whether you are working a wide or a narrow band of waling. When waling is used for the whole basket or for bands several inches wide, allow the

3.34 Pairing weave: Started with folded weaver

3.35 Chain pairing used in a wide band on the side of a basket

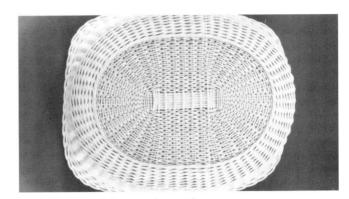

3.36 Chain pairing used on a base

3.37 Three-rod waling

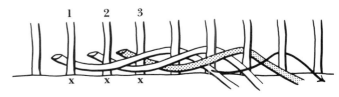

3.38 Three-rod waling

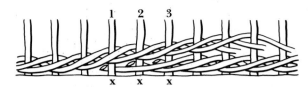

3.39 Spiraling three-rod waling

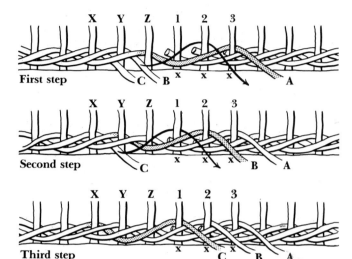

First step

Second step

Third step

3.40 Step-up to complete a round of three-rod waling, for narrow bands or a three-rod arrow

3.41 Three-rod waling: Weaving to the left

3.42 Three-rod arrow

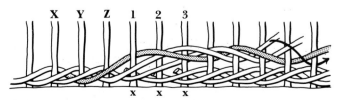

3.43 Three-rod arrow: Second row, reverse waling

waling to spiral (3.39). For narrow bands of waling or for a three-rod arrow, use a step-up at the end of each row so that each row will be complete in itself and won't spiral on top of the preceding row (3.40).

Some of the color patterns I discuss require waling *to the left*. Left-handers may find this version easier, but for color work right-handers will find it worth learning; it gets easier with a little practice.

This is the first technique we've considered where the weavers move to the left as you work them. Begin by marking three consecutive spokes with twist-ties. Spoke 1 is on the right. Insert a weaver to the left of each of these three spokes (3.41). Bring the right weaver in front of two spokes to the left, over the other two weavers, behind the third spoke and out. Continue this sequence, always weaving with the right.

Three-Rod Arrow

A three-rod arrow or *chain wale* consists of two rows: one of regular waling and one of reverse waling (3.42). These instructions will assume that the weaving is moving to the right in both rows.

Weave one row of regular waling and end the row with the weavers coming from behind spokes X, Y, and Z. To do the step-up (3.40), bring weaver A in front of spokes 1 and 2, behind 3, and out. Next, bring weaver B in front of spokes Z and 1, behind 2, and out. Then bring weaver C in front of spokes Y and Z, behind spoke 1, and out.

Reverse waling is used to weave the second row (3.43).

Reverse Waling

Bring the left weaver under the two right weavers instead of over. With your left hand pull the two right weavers straight out toward you so they're completely out of the way. With your right hand bring the left weaver *under* both of the other weavers, behind the next spoke, and out. Repeat this sequence all the way around.

It's important to keep all weavers out to the front—don't let them fall behind or they become hopelessly tangled. If this does happen, unweave until three weavers are coming from behind three consecutive spokes, and begin again.

End the row with the weavers coming from behind spokes X, Y, and Z. To finish the arrow, bring weaver A in front of spokes 1 and 2, then under the top two weavers, and end behind spoke 3 (3.44). There is an easy way to make sure you catch only the top two weavers: insert your awl into the small triangle on the left side of the space between the two spokes. Then bring weaver B in front of spokes Z and 1 and under the top two weavers before ending behind spoke 2 (middle drawing). Bring weaver C in front of spokes Y and Z and under the top two weavers, then end behind spoke 1 (bottom drawing).

Reverse waling from the back is also possible, and you work the weavers over each other, which can be easier (3.45). With the weavers in back, bring the left weaver in front of two spokes, over the right two weavers, and to the back. Repeat this sequence, always working with the left weaver. It's important to keep the weavers to the back at all times.

Three-Rod Arrow Chasing Weave

Three-rod arrow chasing weave is an excellent way to make wide bands of three-rod arrows, or for interesting color designs. It produces a continuous spiral around the basket. Six weavers are used, three for the regular waling row and three for the reverse waling row.

Begin by marking four consecutive spokes with twist-ties. Start the first row by inserting three weavers behind spokes 2, 3, and 4 (3.46). Weave a row of regular waling to within two spokes of spoke 1. Insert three more weavers, to be used for the second row, behind spokes 1, 2, and 3. (Staggering the ends makes a smoother transition for the subsequent rows.) Weave the reverse waling row to within two spokes of the first set of weavers, drop the reverse set, and weave a row of regular waling with the first set.

This weave can be confusing because each row uses a different set of weavers and requires a different technique. You can help yourself keep track by marking the set of weavers used for regular waling with twist-ties. Remember that regular waling slants upward to the right, and reverse waling slants upward to the left.

Finish the band of arrow weaving with a row of reverse waling. The ends of the weavers used for regular waling will finish behind spokes 2, 3, and 4. The ends of the weavers used for reverse waling will finish behind spokes 1, 2, and 3.

Four-Rod and Five-Rod Waling, and the Coil

Waling can be worked with any number of rods as long as the left weaver goes in front of one less spoke than there are weavers. *Four-rod* and *five-rod*

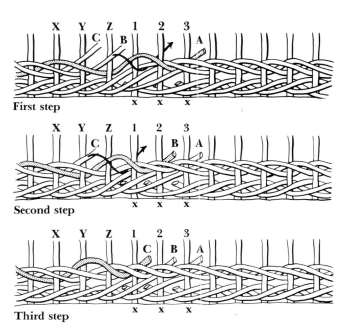

First step

Second step

Third step

3.44 Three-rod arrow: Ending

3.45 Reverse waling worked from the back

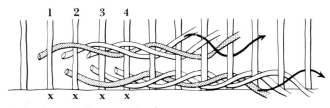

3.46 Three-rod arrow chasing weave

wales are waling weaves worked with four and five weavers, respectively. For example, on a four-rod wale, the left weaver of four goes in front of three spokes to the right, behind the fourth, and out.

A **coil** is a single row of three-rod, four-rod, or five-rod waling worked for just one row; it always ends with a step-up and is sometimes locked. Wales are firm weaves, capable of controlling unruly spokes, and a single row of waling—a coil—can add strength to weak points and help control the shape of the basket. This single row is also very effective as a design element, used either on the base or the sides of a basket.

A coil is also very functional when woven as the first row of the upsett, which is the term for the first few rows of weaving used to "set up" the spokes to form the sides. After the spokes have

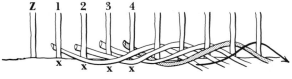

3.47 Four-rod coil

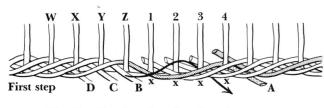

First step

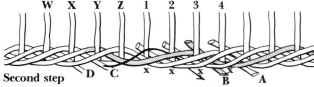

Second step

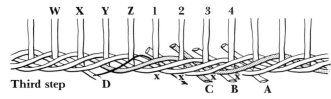

Third step

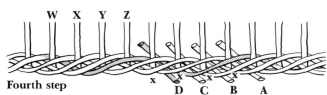

Fourth step

3.48 Four-rod coil: The step-up and lock

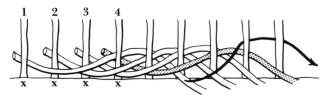

3.49 Two-ply weave

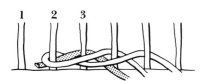

3.50 Beginning three-rod waling with a folded weaver

been pinched to change their direction, this weaving sets them at the correct angle and secures them at the appropriate distance from each other.

A coil woven as the first row of the upsett serves several functions. It keeps the spokes under control, it covers the bend in the spokes, and it forms a "foot" for the basket to sit on. A locked four-rod coil is very similar to a three-rod wale and step-up. If you have done those techniques this will be easy.

To measure the weavers for a four-rod coil used at the upsett, cut each of four weavers to a length which equals the basket circumference plus six inches.

Start by marking four consecutive spokes with twist-ties. Insert a weaver behind each marked spoke (3.47). Bring the left weaver in front of three spokes, over the other three weavers, behind the fourth spoke, and out. Repeat this sequence, working with the left weaver each time. End the row with the weavers coming from behind spokes W, X, Y, and Z (3.48).

To work the step-up (3.48), take weaver A in front of spokes 1, 2, and 3, and behind 4. To lock the weave: pull the beginning end of the weaver A, which is lying against spoke 4, away from the spoke, then thread the working end of weaver A through the space just made, under the coil and to the underside of the base.

Work the step-up and lock the same way with each of the three remaining weavers. In order to push the coil firmly against the side of the base, pull each set of parallel weaver ends tightly in opposite directions. Each locked pair of ends should lie side-by-side as you look at the basket from the side; the ends should not be crossed over one another as you look at the basket from the side. Cut each end on a slant so it lies flush against both the inside and the outside of the basket. (This is the way ends lie in an English join, described on page 31.)

Two-Ply Weave

Two-ply weave is a variation of four-rod waling. It's a double-faced weave used on baskets where both sides show—for example, an old-fashioned flower basket with straight sides and flared ends. It is not an inherently strong weave and shouldn't be used for large areas unless it is reinforced with rows of waling or three-rod arrows.

Begin by marking four consecutive spokes with twist-ties. Insert a weaver behind each of these marked spokes (3.49). Bring the left weaver in front of two spokes, over the right two weavers, behind two spokes and out. Repeat this sequence, always weaving with the left weaver.

Working with a Folded Weaver

Like pairing weave, waling can begin with a folded weaver. When there are three strands, the third element will have a cut end, as usual. This is a good method for beginning waling over a section with beads or fancy weaves, like braid weave or diamond weave (pages 27–28), because there are fewer ends to deal with.

To set this up, soak and pinch a weaver, then fold it in uneven "halves" and place it around spoke 2 (3.50). Place another weaver behind spoke 3. Wale the first two weavers, then thread the beginning of the third weaver (behind spoke 3) into the loop formed by the fold around spoke 2 so it rests behind spoke 2. Continue with regular waling. When weaving a three-rod arrow with a folded weaver, remember the ghost weaver behind spoke 1, and work the step-up in the normal way (see the instructions for pairing arrow started with a folded weaver, on pages 22–23).

BRAID WEAVE

Braid weave is a wonderfully decorative weave used in Oriental baskets (3.51). The Japanese call it *wave weave*. It is a three-strand braid woven horizontally around vertical spokes. The braiding is simple, but working it around the spokes is more complicated. The effect is more pronounced if it is woven with more than a single strand of reed; I suggest double or triple sets of round reed, narrow flat reed, or a combination of round and flat reed. It can be worked over any number of spokes, but if you are going to work just one row of braid weave and want it to come out even, you will need a number of spokes divisible by six.

The basic weaving sequence is like three-rod waling: the left weaver goes in front of two spokes, behind the third, and out. The whole weave is made up of only two types of strokes—the first is like regular waling, the second like reverse waling. The difference between this procedure and true waling is that the left weaver goes over or under only one set of weavers on the right instead of two. You will work the strokes in sets of two: one regular and one reverse.

Begin by marking three consecutive spokes with twist-ties. Insert one weaver (or set of weavers) behind spoke 1 and another behind spoke 2 (3.52). The first two strokes are simply regular three-rod waling strokes. Bring weaver A in front of spokes 2 and 3, over weaver B, behind

3.51 Braid weave

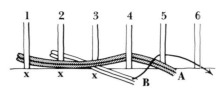

3.52 Braid weave: First and second strokes

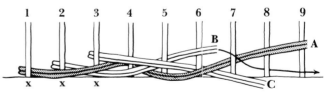

3.53 Braid weave: Adding third pair of weavers; "reverse waling" stroke in progress with weaver B

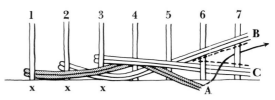

3.54 Braid weave: Splitting two pairs of weavers into a V shape

spoke 4, and out. Then bring weaver B in front of spokes 3 and 4, over weaver A, behind spoke 5, and out.

The third stroke is the reverse waling stroke. Place the third weaver behind spoke 3 on top of the other weavers (3.53). Bring the weaver in front of spokes 4 and 5, under weaver B, then behind spoke 6 and out. Continue this sequence, alternating the regular waling stroke and the reverse waling stroke. (The beginning three strokes of this weave are an anomaly. It starts with two regular wale strokes and one reverse, but the rest of the weave alternates one-and-one.)

If this procedure seems confusing, try another way of looking at it. The result is the same with either method. Take the two weavers on the right and split them so they look like a V lying on its side (3.54). Then take the left weaver, whether top or bottom, and bring it in front of the two spokes to the right and behind the third spoke, which lies in the middle of the V.

Be sure all sets of weavers stay on the outside of the basket. If one of them ends up on the inside, you will lose the pattern. This is most likely to happen when you weave with the top left weaver (the reverse waling stroke). It helps to hold weaver A out toward you as you weave C behind the third spoke and out.

The braid weave is a spiraling weave and doesn't require a step-up between rows. To finish, bring the weavers so they rest behind the three beginning spokes, and trim them neatly. When you weave just one row, overlap the ends to make a neat join (this is possible only if the number of spokes is divisible by six).

End the row with weavers coming from behind spokes X, Y, and Z (3.55). Bring weaver A in front of spokes Y and Z, over weaver C, and behind spoke 1. If you are working with doubled strands, leave the top weaver of set A behind spoke 1 and, following the braid pattern and unthreading the original bottom weaver, bring the ending bottom weaver behind spoke 4 (3.56). Staggering the ends like this will prevent the ending of the braid from looking lumpy.

Next, bring set B from behind spoke Y, in front of spokes Z and 1, over weaver A, then behind spoke 2, again staggering the ends behind spokes 2 and 5 (3.57). Then bring set C from behind spoke Z, in front of spokes 1 and 2, under weaver A, behind spoke 3, staggering the ends behind spokes 3 and 6 (3.58).

For weavers with three strands each, the finishing procedure is shown in 3.59. The top strand will end behind spoke 1, the middle strand behind spoke 4, and the bottom strand behind spoke 7. Unthread the corresponding ends so that only two ends lie behind each spoke.

DIAMOND WEAVE

The diamond weave is another decorative weave found in Oriental baskets. The illustration shows it worked over an even number of spokes, with flat reed as the wide weaver and a flexible #2 or #3 round reed as the thin weaver (3.60). Two or three strands of round reed can be used in place of the flat reed. Each row is woven separately.

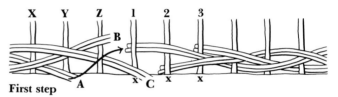

First step

3.55 Braid weave: If you plan to work only one row, end the weavers to the left of the beginning three spokes

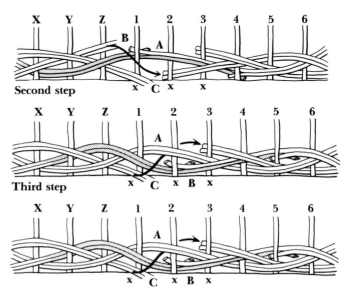

Second step

Third step

3.56, 3.57, 3.58 Braid weave: Ending a single row

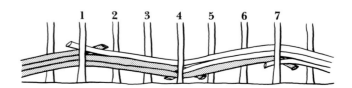

3.59 Braid weave: Ending for triple set of weavers

Diamond weave can also be woven continuously over any number of spokes, even or uneven. Woven over an even number of spokes, the diamonds line up vertically (3.61). Woven over an uneven number of spokes the diamonds alternate (3.62).

I'll start with instructions for weaving a *single row* of diamonds. Mark any spoke as spoke 1, using a twist-tie. Begin by inserting the flat reed behind spoke 1, weaving it in front of 2, behind 3, and out. Insert weaver A behind spoke 2 above the flat reed, and weaver B behind spoke 2 below the flat reed (3.63). Bring weaver A diagonally across spoke 3, and behind spoke 4 under the flat reed (3.64). Weave the flat reed in

3.60 Diamond weave: Alternating design woven with flat reed as the background weaver; each row is woven separately

3.61 Diamond weave: Diamonds lined up vertically; woven continuously over an even number of spokes (basket by Theresa Ohno)

3.62 Diamond weave: Diamonds alternating; woven continuously over an uneven number of spokes (basket by Theresa Ohno)

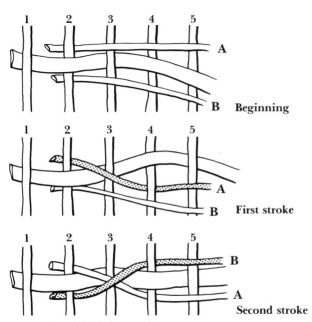

3.63, 3.64, 3.65 Diamond weave

front of spoke 4, behind 5, and out. Bring weaver B diagonally across spoke 3 and the flat reed, behind spoke 4, and out (3.65). Continue this sequence all the way around to spoke 1. End the flat weaver by threading it on top of its beginning and sliding it under spoke 3. Trim the last end to the right of spoke 3.

To continue the weave for a second row *with the diamonds alternating,* insert a new flat reed behind spoke 2, weave in front of 3, behind 4, and out. Bring the narrow weavers diagonally behind spokes 2 and 3, maintaining the same positions of top and bottom elements (3.66).

To continue for a second row *with the diamonds lined up,* insert a new flat reed behind spoke 3, weave in front of 4, behind 5, and out. Bring the round weavers diagonally across the back of spokes 2, 3, and 4 in their corresponding positions as top and bottom elements (3.67).

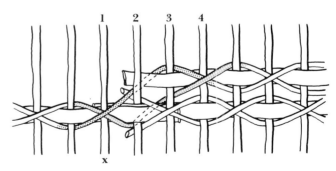

3.66 Diamond weave: Transition between first and second rows for alternating design

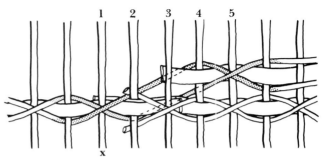

3.67 Diamond weave: Transition between first and second rows for vertically aligned diamonds

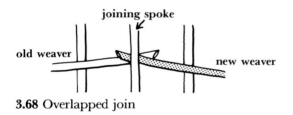

3.68 Overlapped join

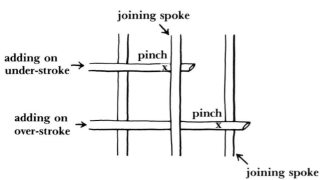

3.69 Hidden join: Cut old weaver to the right of the joining spoke and pinch to the left

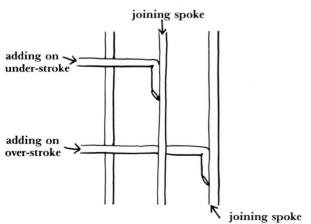

3.70 Hidden join: Pinch and bend old weaver to the left of the joining spoke

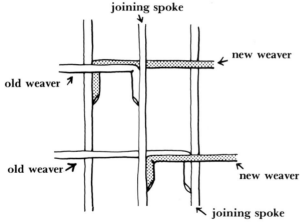

3.71 Hidden join: Add new weaver to the left of the joining spoke

ADDING WEAVERS AND TRIMMING ENDS

Weavers run out, and weavers end. The resulting ends must be neatly secured. There are several ways to add new weavers when the old ones run out, and there are some tricks to trimming off the final ends. Finishing loose ends is like hemming a dress. Do it carefully and the whole project will reflect the extra attention.

Overlapped Join

The easiest and fastest way to add a new weaver is by overlapping. This method can be used with all weaves, and is especially good with transparent weaves like randing and pairing, and in places where there's no room to tuck the ends. The disadvantage is that the ends are completely exposed and are prone to being snagged.

To make the join, simply end the old weaver behind a spoke, then add a new weaver behind the same spoke, crossing it over the top of the old weaver (3.68).

Hidden Join

The hidden join is more time-consuming, but neater. It is best used with waling or two-ply weave, which are solid weaves that completely hide the tucked ends.

End the old weaver either behind or in front of the joining spoke, cutting it to the right of that spoke so that about ¼″ of the weaver shows (3.69). The joining spoke can be on the under-stroke, or it can be on the first spoke of the over-stroke. Pinch the old weaver to the left of the joining spoke (do this accurately so the weaver won't bulge to the outside) and run it down into the weaving on the left side of the joining spoke (3.70). Pinch a new weaver ⅜″ from its end. Insert the bent part into the weaving on the right edge of the spoke just to the left of the joining spoke (3.71). If the old weaver ends on the under-stroke, bring the new weaver behind the joining spoke and out. If the old weaver ends on the over-stroke, bring the new weaver in front of the joining spoke.

In two-ply weave, add the new weaver on the over-stroke. The old weaver will go behind two spokes before being tucked in to the left of the joining spoke. Add the new weaver as shown at the bottom of 3.71.

Combined Join

This method combines the previous two techniques. It is a universal join that can be used on any weave. It works particularly well on transparent weaves, such as randing and pairing, when you want a join that is firmer than overlapping.

End the old weaver behind the joining spoke, cutting it at a slant behind that spoke. Add the new weaver as you did for the hidden join (3.71). Take the new weaver behind the joining spoke, over the short end of the old weaver, and to the outside of the basket (3.72).

English Join

This in-and-out method of adding a new weaver is frequently used in English willow basketry. It can be used with both waling and pairing weaves. It works best when spokes are very close together and is particularly useful for the first one or two joins on a Japanese-weave base (pages 38–39). One of the trimmed ends appears on the outside, so be careful where you use this join; the exposed end may snag things. And if you use this technique for dyed reed, the trimmed ends will be very noticeable.

End the old weaver in front of the joining spoke. Add the new weaver by pulling the end of the old weaver out and sliding the end of the new weaver to the right side of the old one (3.73). They are held in place by bracing against each other. For that reason, neither end has to lie against a spoke.

Joins in Multiple Sets

This method is for adding a new weaver in a set of weavers, if they are all of the same color. When the bottom weaver runs out on either a double or triple set of weavers, add the new weaver on top of the whole set (3.74). When the top weaver runs out, add the new one on the bottom (3.75). When the middle weaver of a set of three runs out, add the new weaver either top or bottom (3.76).

Avoiding Problems in Joining

Adding spokes or handles can create problems with some of these joins. Try to avoid using the hidden join or the combined join where a spoke or handle will be inserted. If this situation is unavoidable, slip the spoke or handle under the

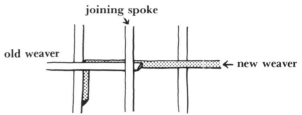

3.72 Combined join: Cut old weaver to the left of the joining spoke, and add new weaver as for hidden join

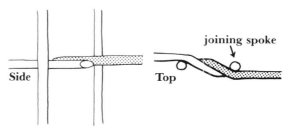

3.73 English join: End old weaver in front of joining spoke, then place the new weaver behind the spoke to the left, behind the old weaver

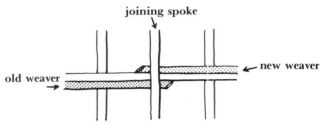

3.74 Joins in multiple sets: New weaver added on top

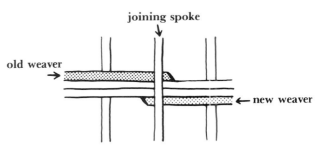

3.75 Joins in multiple sets: New weaver added on bottom

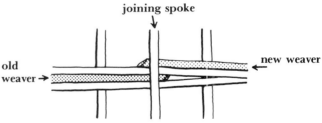

3.76 Joins in multiple sets: Old weaver ending in middle of three weavers; new weaver added on top

spoke being added

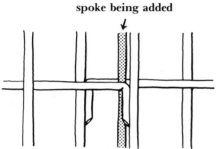

3.77 Inserting spoke under weaver at hidden join

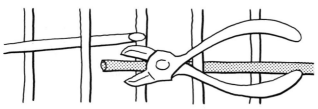

3.78 Position of pliers for trimming weavers on inside of basket

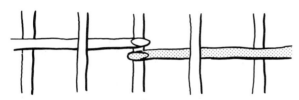

3.79 Trimmed ends inside of basket

joining weaver (3.77). If the handle or spoke pushes the join aside, a bulge will appear on the outside. The join can be soaked and pinched again to reduce the bulge.

Trimming

It is very important to trim the weaver ends correctly. Hold the flat edge of your diagonal cutting pliers on the weaver flat against the basket. Have the point of the pliers facing the short end of the weaver (3.78) and cut the weaver as flush as possible. Be *sure* the end you are trimming lies against a spoke. If it's cut too short it will pop to the outside. Trimmed ends should look like those in illustration 3.79.

It's a good idea to trim as you go. In a very rounded or narrow basket, the ends are almost impossible to trim once the basket is finished.

1 Checkerboard (page 87)

2 Vertical stripes or blocks with pairing weave
(page 87)

3 Horizontal stripes (page 87)

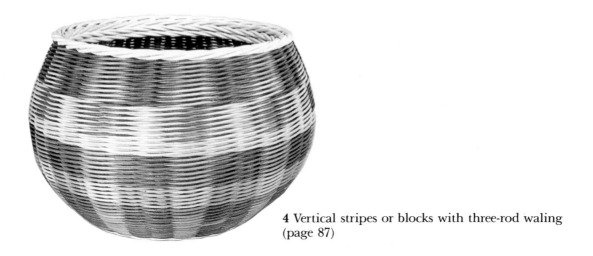

4 Vertical stripes or blocks with three-rod waling (page 87)

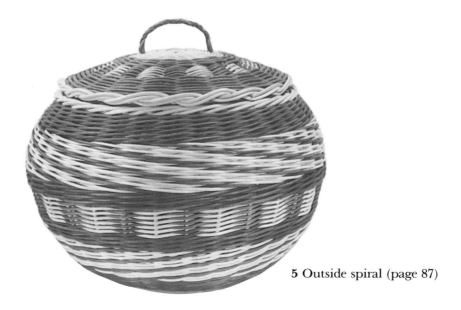

5 Outside spiral (page 87)

6 Inside spiral (page 87)

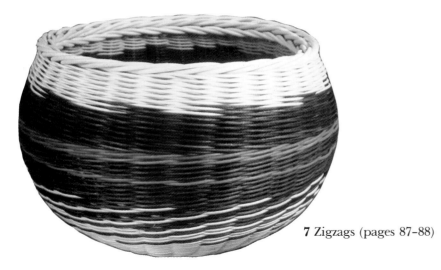

7 Zigzags (pages 87–88)

Inside a Hong Kong rattan-cutting factory.

Rattan being sorted by grade at the factory in Hong Kong. Each division of markers indicates a grade or length.

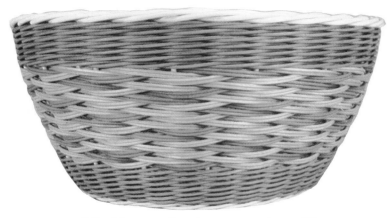

8 Braid weave: Random pattern (page 88)

9 Braid weave: Vertical stripes (page 88)

10 Braid weave: Giant arrows (page 88)

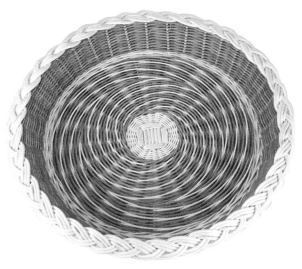

11 Reversing spirals occur when three-rod waling is worked in both directions with three different colors (instructions on page 142)

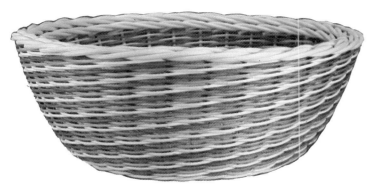

12 Spiraling basket: The design occurs when three-rod waling is worked in three different colors (instructions on page 141)

13 Spiraling arrows are produced with three-rod arrow chasing weave (instructions on page 143)

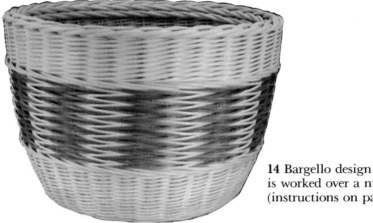

14 Bargello design results when three-rod arrow weave is worked over a number of spokes divisible by three (instructions on page 144)

15 Dart pattern basket, with several patterns developed from three-rod waling (instructions on page 145)

16 Block design basket is also worked with three-rod waling (instructions on page 147)

Flat reed being coiled.

17 Braid weave basket I shows how dramatic arrows can be produced (instructions on page 148)

18 Braid weave basket II displays vertical stripes (instructions on page 149)

19 "Step-up to stripes" is a basket which combines vertical and horizontal stripes, formed with pairing and three-rod waling (instructions on page 146)

20 Sampler basket includes a variety of weave variations (instructions on page 150)

CHAPTER 4
Bases

We covered weaving techniques first, because a passing acquaintance with them is essential before you can begin, but the base, or bottom, is the physical starting point of a basket. While weaving it, you select a number of spokes, join them together, and separate them so they are evenly spaced. The shape of the base determines the shape of the finished basket. We will deal with two fundamental base shapes, round and oval.

A round base is the easiest to make, and therefore is the best choice for a beginner. Oval bases are not difficult to weave and control once you have mastered round bases.

In addition to shape, the other things you want to think about in selecting a base are:

Do you want a base which is open, or one which is solid?

What decorative effect would you like?

In some cases, will the base be strong enough to support a large basket?

Will the base and side spokes on your basket be continuous, or will you work the base on short spokes and then add separate spokes to work the sides?

The relative merits of various bases are outlined under their descriptions. Look over the sample baskets in the step-by-step section to see how some of the bases work in practice, and if you are unsure of yourself, use the samples as models until you become familiar enough with the possibilities to make educated choices.

Before we get into details, there are a few general pieces of information which apply to the making of bases.

- The base spokes are the strongest spokes of the basket, and must be equal to or larger in

size than the side spokes. They must not be smaller.

- Bases can be woven from spokes that are long enough to extend up the sides, or the side spokes can be separate and added later. There are advantages to each, which will be discussed below.

- I prefer to work so that the surface facing upward as the base is woven ends up on the inside of the basket.

- A well-shaped basket requires base spokes that are evenly spaced, like the spokes of a wheel. If the base spokes are incorrectly spaced, the sides of the basket will be distorted.

- Work to keep the base spokes lying in the same plane; you can accomplish this in part by making the weaver do all the bending as it moves around the spokes. You'll need to pay particularly close attention as you begin the base, before the spokes are spread apart. If the weaver doesn't do the bending, the base will have a ridged or corrugated appearance (3.4).

- Soak all materials before you work with them.

The decision about whether to weave the base separately or to begin with spokes which are long enough to extend up the sides is personal. In the English tradition, where willow branches of variable lengths were used, the separate base is more common than in the Japanese tradition, based on the use of bamboo, which can produce very long strands. I like to weave separate bases, for several reasons. First, I don't have to deal with the full spoke length while I am weaving the

4.1 Interwoven base

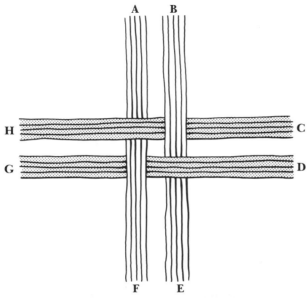

4.2 Interwoven base: Layout of the slath

4.3 Interwoven base: Beginning weaving

base. Second, I find the separate base offers more possibilities for experimentation with size and shape.

If you plan to add a handle to your basket, you may need to plan ahead at the time that you select a base. This is particularly important with oval bases. If you are new to basketmaking, you can simplify your learning by practicing on baskets without handles, or by following one of the patterns in Chapters 9 and 10. When you are ready to consider a handle to a basket of your own design, see page 69 in Chapter 7 before you start weaving.

You will begin a base by cutting a number of spokes and placing them in the arrangement which will become the foundation for your weaving. This initial arrangement of spokes is called the **slath.** There are several different ways to lay out spokes and form the slath. The method you choose will depend on the type of base you intend to weave, and individual directions are given below.

Once you have the slath in order, you will begin to weave. The first rows will be woven around groups of spokes, and will hold the slath in position. On the next set of rows, you will begin to divide the spokes into smaller groups. As you work toward the outside of the base, you will continue to divide the spokes, separating them and altering their relative positions until you achieve the even, wheel-like arrangement mentioned above.

In the following instructions, specific weaving techniques are in italics. Directions for these techniques can be found in the preceding chapter; page numbers are given in the index. Preparations for weaving the sides will be covered in the next chapter.

ROUND BASES

I'll describe four basic round bases, each with variations. The first two (interwoven base and double-cross base) are open bases, usually woven with a single set of spokes forming both base and sides. The second two (over-laid base and split-spoke base) are tightly woven, and therefore stronger. They can also be woven with continuous base and side spokes, but are excellent as bases woven separately from the sides.

OPEN ROUND BASES

Interwoven Base

This base is a simple one, good for beginners. It can be worked with either an uneven or an even number of spokes. If it is woven with randing, you will need an uneven number of spokes, and if it is woven with chasing weave or pairing weave you can proceed with an even number.

Laying out and securing the slath. Begin by soaking the spokes well, so they lie straight. Then the slath will be much easier to lay out. If the groups of spokes tend to fly apart, hold them together with clothespins until they are secured by the initial rounds of weaving.

Begin with four groups of four spokes each. Lay two groups horizontally on a table. Insert the left vertical group under the upper horizontal group and over the lower horizontal group. Insert the right vertical group over the upper horizontal group and under the lower horizontal group (4.1, 4.2). Push the groups together so there is a small square hole in the center. Make sure the crossing point occurs at the midpoint of each group of spokes and that all the spokes are lying flat.

Keep the base flat as you weave it. For the first row, this will be easiest if you work on the table. Once the groups of spokes have been secured, you can hold the work in your hands to continue weaving.

Take a long, flexible weaver and place it under the group of spokes marked A (4.3). Weave in a clockwise direction over the next group of four spokes, under the next, and so on around. Weave four rows this way, keeping the strands of the weaver close together.

At the beginning of the fifth row, the pattern changes so the weaver will alternate: it now needs to go under the groups it passed over before, and over those it went under. To accomplish the transition, start the fifth row by bringing the weaver under both groups A and B (4.3), then over C, and under D. At this point, the new pattern has been established, and the second row begins with the weaver going over group A. Complete four rows of this pattern.

After the eighth round has been completed, each group of four is split into pairs. At the beginning of the ninth row, bring the weaver up between the two sets of two spokes in group B (4.4). As you weave around this row, you will split all the groups into pairs, but this is also the point at which you need to decide whether you will work the base with an even or uneven number of spokes.

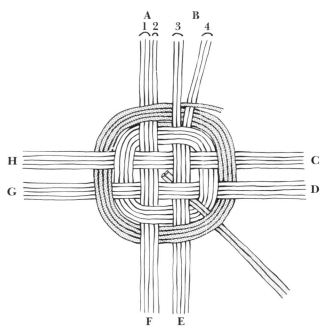

4.4 Interwoven base: Separating spokes into pairs, and adding the odd pair of spokes

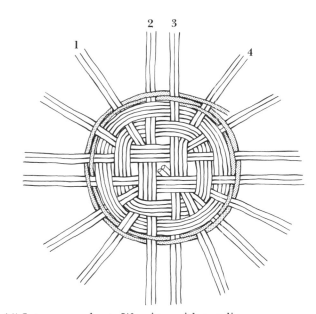

4.5 Interwoven base: Weaving with randing

Proceeding with an uneven number of spokes. So far, the slath has been secured with *randing*, the basic over-and-under weaving pattern. With an even number of spokes, randing always goes over and under the same spokes, unless the pattern is broken, as it was in the fifth row. Then it shifts to the alternate sequence, still going over and under the same spokes in every row until the pattern is broken again.

With an uneven number of spokes, it is possible to continue weaving the base with uninterrupted randing. The uneven number can be established either by cutting out or by adding one set of spokes. In the example, an extra set has been added in the corner diagonally across from the beginning (4.4). To secure the new set, thread it under the four outside rows, over the four inside rows, then down under the slath just enough to hold it in place. Now when you weave, the rows will automatically alternate (4.5).

Proceeding with an even number of spokes. If you want to maintain the even number of spokes, you can weave the base with either *chasing weave* (3.9) or *pairing weave* (3.27). For chasing weave, add the second weaver behind the pair of spokes to the left of the original weaver (spoke 2, 4.4). For pairing weave, add the second weaver behind the pair of spokes to the right of the original weaver (spoke 4, 4.4).

Continuing to weave the pairs. Whether you use an uneven or even number of pairs, weaving the first two rows of "over one pair, under one pair" can be difficult because the pairs of spokes are still close together. Try weaving these two rows with the base on the table, so you can use all available fingers to spread the spokes apart and to push the rows close together. Separate the spokes carefully so they spread evenly, like the spokes of a wheel. If you have added an extra pair of spokes, be especially careful not to pull on it, because it can easily pop out.

Variations on the interwoven base. I've described this base as being made with doubled spokes up the sides. This is necessary when the base is worked with spokes and weavers the same size; doubling the spokes strengthens them, so the framework is not so easily distorted by the movement of the weaver. If you work with spokes and weavers of the same size and *don't* double the spokes, you will find it is almost impossible to make a smooth-sided basket.

If the individual spokes are a size or two larger than the weavers, the doubled spokes can be separated into singles.

The base can also be expanded by interlacing additional groups of four, both horizontally and vertically, to make an attractive openwork design (4.6).

Double-Cross Base

This base is a more decorative variation of the interwoven base (4.7), and the difference is established in the way the slath is laid out.

4.6 Expanded interwoven base (basket woven by Theresa Ohno)

4.7 Double-cross base: Groups of six spokes separated into pairs

Laying out and securing the slath. You will need four groups of six spokes each. Soak the spokes so they will lie straight and flat. If the groups tend to spring apart, use clothespins to keep them together.

Cross two of the groups at right angles at their center points, making an X pattern. Place them on the table in this formation.

Cross the two other groups in the same way and place them on top of the first set, so the new groups of spokes fall between the arms of the first X (4.8).

Keep the base flat as you weave it. Again, this is easier if you work the first row on a table. Once the spokes are secured, you can hold the base in your hands while you weave.

Place a long weaver on top of group A and, working close to the center in a clockwise direction, weave under group B, over C, under D, etc.

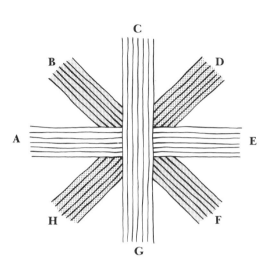

4.8 Double-cross base: Layout of the slath

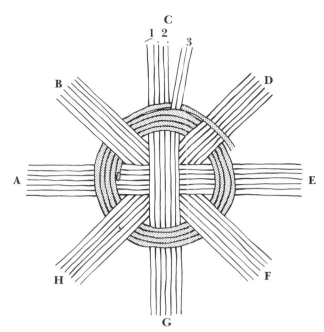

4.9 Double-cross base: Beginning to weave

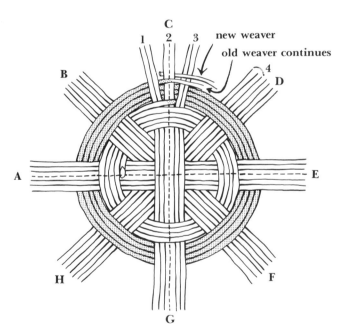

4.10 Double-cross base: Beginning to separate spokes into pairs with pairing weave

4.11 Double-cross base: First row completed with pairing weave

(Left-handers may find it easier to work counter-clockwise.) Weave four rounds in the same way, keeping the rows close together (4.9).

At the beginning of the fifth row, the pattern changes slightly so that the weaver will alternate, and will go under the groups it has previously gone over, and over those it went under. Start the fifth round by taking the weaver over pairs 1 and 2 of the spokes in group C and under pair 3. This shifts the pattern. Then take the weaver over group D, under E, etc. (4.9). On the next three

rounds, the weaver works with the six spokes of group C as a unit, as before, going under the entire group.

At the end of the eighth round, the groups are split into pairs and you change to *pairing weave*. As you complete that round, bring the weaver up to the top between pairs 1 and 2 of group C (4.10). Add the second weaver between pairs 2 and 3 of group C and begin to use pairing weave. The completed first row of pairing weave is shown in illustration 4.11.

Variations on the double-cross base. You can vary the numbers and arrangement of spokes. The illustrated base has groups of six spokes (4.7), but groups of four can be used for a smaller basket.

The groups of spokes can be separated in different ways. If you work with groups of six, you can separate them into twos, as described here, or into threes (4.12), or into singles. With groups of four, you can choose between twos (4.13) and singles (4.14, 4.15). Your choice will depend on the strength of the spokes in relation to that of the weavers and/or to the size of the basket.

Alternate methods for weaving this base include *three-rod wale* (3.38) and *chasing weave* (3.9). For three-rod wale, add the second weaver between pairs 2 and 3 and the third weaver between pairs 3 and 4 (4.10). For chasing weave, add the second weaver behind the pair to the left of pair 1 in group B (4.10).

TIGHTLY WOVEN ROUND BASES

This type of base is strong and solid. It's intended for baskets which will be capable of supporting significant amounts of weight. Before going to the specific details of the over-laid and split-spoke bases, we need to consider a technique called doming or crowning, and to discuss the fine points of producing a smooth base.

Doming or **crowning** refers to shaping the base so that it looks an upside-down saucer. This process makes the basket sit better, increases its strength, and causes the weight of a load (say, apples) to be distributed as evenly as possible within the basket.

Having worked the simpler open bases, you will be ready to add doming to your list of skills. Begin to shape the dome after an inch of weaving has been worked to secure the slath; continue to shape it gently throughout the weaving of the base. When you have completed a domed base, its center will be raised one half to three quarters of an inch above the ends of the base spokes. Because of this shaping, the basket will sit on the outer edge of its base, instead of wobbling on the slath.

Always work with your left hand on top of the base, pushing the spokes downward with a slight but consistent pressure as you weave (4.16). The dome can get away from you very quickly and end up like a mountain instead of a saucer. Practice will tell you just how much pressure to apply. Some people find that working over a knee is a good way to form the dome.

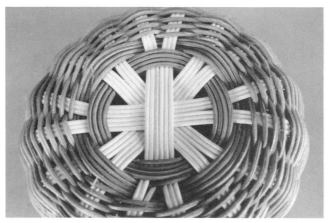

4.12 Double-cross base: Groups of six spokes separated into threes

4.13 Double-cross base: Spokes separated into pairs with pairing weave

If the base is domed too much you can try to flatten it. First be sure the base is wet. Then place it on a table, convex side up, and push on it firmly with the palm of your hand. It may flatten out nicely with a creak and a groan, but if the spokes begin to twist into a spiral, there is no hope for it. The base has to be woven again from the beginning. In this case it's better to start over with new materials; used materials seem to have the wrong shape programmed into them.

Although the variations sections include other possibilities, I prefer to use *Japanese weave* (3.23) for a tightly woven base; it gives a **smooth surface** by covering up the spokes. If Japanese weave is used to work the base, the number of spokes should not be divisible by three, or each row of the weave will follow the same path as the previous row, and the rows will not alternate.

Be aware that when you have secured the

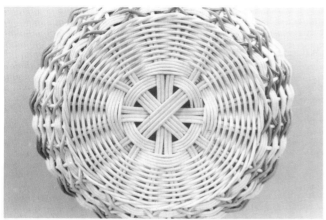

4.14 Double-cross base: Spokes separated into singles with chasing weave (basket woven by Theresa Ohno)

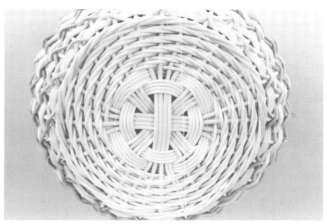

4.15 Double-cross base: Spokes separated into singles with over-two, under-two (basket woven by Theresa Ohno)

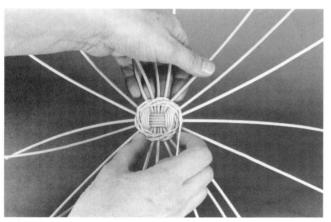

4.16 To dome the base, hold your left hand on top of the base (shown on an over-laid base)

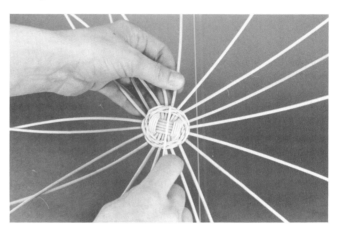

4.17 For a smooth base, make the rows of weaving close together by pulling the weaver down across the center after each stroke (shown on an over-laid base)

slath and begun to weave the base, Japanese weave will look jumbled for about eight rows. At that point the weaving will take on a recognizable pattern and the spokes should be splayed out evenly like spokes of a wheel.

The secret of a nice smooth base is to keep the rows of weaving close together by pulling the weaver down across the center as you make each over-two, then each under-one, stroke (4.17). Remember, the weaver does all the bending. With your left hand, hold the spokes straight as you weave around them so they don't spring up (on the under-one stroke) or crumple under (on the over-two stroke) when you pull the weaver across the center. Don't weave over two and under one and *then* try to pull the weaver tight. The rows won't compact and the spokes will shift to different levels. You can stop pulling down on the weaver after weaving enough rows that the diam-

eter has increased two inches and the spokes have spread apart enough that you can just lay the weaver in place.

Another secret to a nice-looking base is to separate the spokes as soon as possible, to prevent the weaving from building up in the middle of each set of spokes. The weaving will take on a square shape if the spokes aren't separated soon enough.

There are several ways to add weavers neatly on a base worked in Japanese weave. At the beginning of the weaving, when the spokes are very close together, either overlap the ends or use *English join*. As you work farther from the center, use either *hidden join* or *combined join* to make smooth joins. These joining methods are described and illustrated in Chapter 3.

4.18 Over-laid base: Layout of the slath

4.19 Over-laid base: Tying the slath

4.20 Over-laid base: Separating the spokes with Japanese weave

Over-Laid Base

This is a simple, tightly woven base for baskets with continuous base and side spokes. I find the split-spoke base, which has a smoother slath, to be a more satisfactory closed base for times when I want to make the base separately and to add side spokes.

Laying out and securing the slath. For a five-over-five base, make two groups of five spokes each. Lay one group horizontally, then lay the other group vertically on top of it, matching the centers (4.18). Hold the spokes in the upper left corner with your left hand. Then place the end of a long, flexible #2 weaver behind the horizontal group and hold it tight (4.19). Bring the weaver over the top group of five, under the bottom group, and so on around. After you have woven several rows, trim the starting end close to the basket.

The first row must be tight, but not so tight that the spokes bunch up. If the cross isn't wound tightly from the first row, it's harder to spread the spokes when you begin Japanese weave. And if the weaving is too loose, the spokes will tend to pull out or crawl on top of each other. Follow this pattern for four rows, keeping the rows close together.

Separating the spokes. When you have completed four rows, begin Japanese weave at the top group of five spokes by bringing the weaver first over two spokes, then under one spoke (4.20, 3.23). Continue with Japanese weave until the base reaches required size, gently doming or crowning the base as you weave (see page 38).

Variations on the over-laid base. An over-laid base can be made with as few as two-over-two spokes, for a miniature basket, or as many as seven-over-seven—or more—for a large basket. It can also be made with unequal numbers of spokes in each group. Combinations can include two-over-three, or three-over-four, and so on, depending on the desired size of the base. Finer size increments for the diameter of the base can be achieved this way.

If you intend to make an over-laid base with side spokes included, you will need to keep in mind that a limited number of spokes can be bound together smoothly. The number of spokes in the sides of the basket and the distance between them affects the strength of the finished basket. I design baskets with spokes that are light enough to be easy to manipulate, and I use a lot of them, closely spaced, to ensure sturdiness. If you begin an over-laid base with too many spokes, they will bunch together and make the slath lumpy.

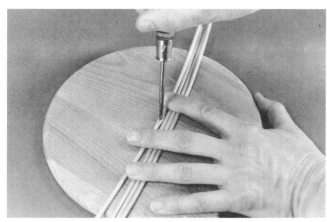

4.21 Split-spoke base: Run an awl through the center of the spokes to split them

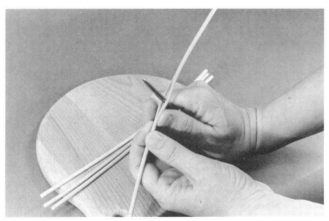

4.22 Split-spoke base: Make the holes large enough to thread the other spokes through

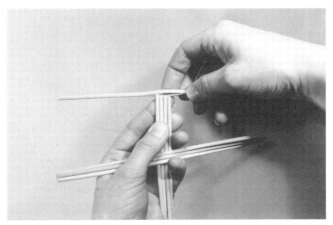

4.23 Split-spoke base: Thread the other spokes through the split spokes

Although I prefer to work this base in Japanese weave, other choices that can be used include *chasing weave* (3.9), *pairing weave* (3.27), or *three-rod arrow weave* (3.46). You may want to experiment with three-rod arrow weave on the sides of a basket before applying it to the flat plane of a base.

Split-Spoke Base

The split-spoke base is the smoothest and the most finished of the round bases. It can be used either for a basket with a separate base or for a basket with continuous base and side spokes. It's my favorite choice for a basket with a separate base, and I will describe that arrangement here. The split-spoke technique for assembling the slath is also the fundamental method used for oval bases.

Laying out and securing the slath. To make a four-through-four base, cut eight spokes each eight inches long. Soak and then manipulate them so they are absolutely straight. Place four of the spokes on a work surface, such as a cutting board. Run an awl through the center of each spoke, right through to the board (4.21); work slowly to protect your hands. Carefully wiggle the awl back and forth to make a hole large enough to accommodate the other group of four spokes (4.22). Reed that has been well soaked will hold together better; dry reed splits too easily.

Hold the other four base spokes together and thread the split ones onto them one by one (4.23, 4.24). Center the spokes and position them at right angles to each other.

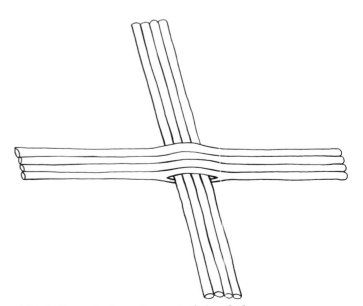

4.24 Split-spoke base: Layout of the slath

Take a long, flexible #2 weaver and with roundnose pliers pinch a fold in it twenty inches from one end. Fold the weaver at the pinch point, then place the fold around the set of spokes with the holes (arm A, 4.26), keeping the short end of the weaver to the back.

Four rows of *reverse pairing weave* are used to tie the slath. The front and back weavers will cross between the arms of the slath. The crosses formed by the weavers must line up at a 45-degree angle between the arms (see dotted line, 4.26).

You'll be weaving in a clockwise direction while turning the base counterclockwise. Begin with arm A upward (4.25). Hold the back weaver out of the way and bring the long, top weaver down behind B. Then bring the short back weaver up on top of B (4.26). Next, turn the cross counterclockwise so B is upward, hold the back weaver out of the way, and bring the top weaver

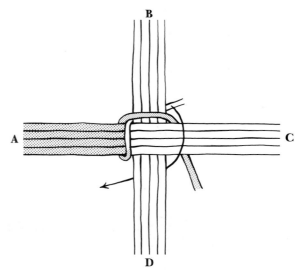

4.27 Split-spoke base: Tying the slath, second position

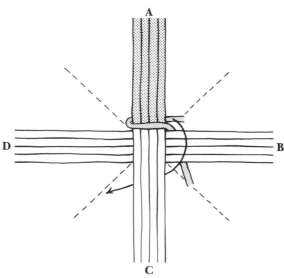

4.25 Split-spoke base: Place the folded weaver over arm A, with the short end of the weaver to the back

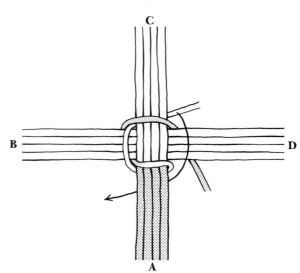

4.28 Split-spoke base: Tying the slath, third position

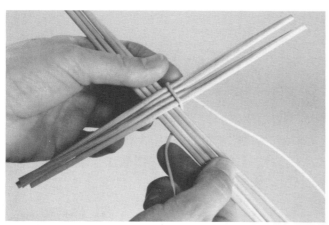

4.26 Split-spoke base: Tying the slath, first position

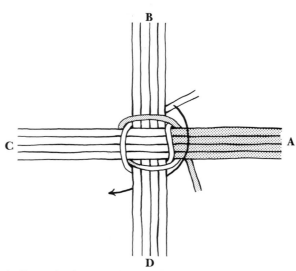

4.29 Split-spoke base: Tying the slath, fourth position

down behind C. Bring the back weaver up on top of C (4.27). Continue this sequence of bringing the top weaver down and the back weaver up at each corner, turning the cross counterclockwise so that the corner being worked is always at the right (4.28, 4.29).

Complete four rows of the reverse pairing, ending with the short weaver behind A. The long weaver will pass over the end of the short weaver and hold it in place. Weave a row or two before trimming the short end.

Separating the spokes. Use the long weaver to continue weaving. Separate the spokes with *Japanese weave*—over two and under one (3.23, 4.30, 4.31). Using gentle hand pressure to shape the basket's dome (page 38), continue working Japanese weave until the base is the desired diameter (4.32).

Variations on the split-spoke base. When a split-spoke base is used for a basket with continuous base and side spokes, it is worked the same as the over-laid base and requires the same techniques. When it is used for a separate base, a range of basket sizes can be made from a limited number of base spoke combinations. By varying the size and length of the base spokes on either a four-through-four or a five-through-five base, baskets can be made from ten to twenty inches in diameter.

Other weaving patterns which you may want to use include *pairing, chaining,* and *three-rod wale.*

Tips for Well-Rounded Bases

To make a symmetrical base, the spokes must radiate evenly from the center in straight lines, and all the spokes must be the same distance apart at the outer edge. There is a visual trick which will help you achieve this goal. It works for any round base which has an even number of spokes, which means you can use it for everything except the interwoven base with an added set of spokes.

As you weave, think of a right-angle cross superimposed over the slath, following the lines of the center spokes. On a double-cross base with groups of six, the center line will be the middle pairs on the top layer of spokes (4.10). On a four-through-four split-spoke base, the superimposed cross will fall in a space, not on a spoke (see dotted line in 4.31). If a spoke moves into that space during the weaving it will affect the symmetry. On a five-through-five base, the center line will be the center spoke of each group of five (4.20).

4.30 Split-spoke base: Begin to separate the spokes with the long weaver, using Japanese weave

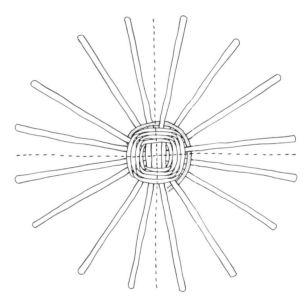

4.31 Split-spoke base: Separating the spokes with Japanese weave

4.32 Split-spoke base: The upper side of the completed base, showing the dome

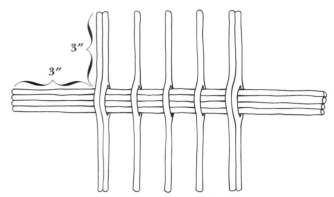

4.33 Basic oval base: Layout of the slath

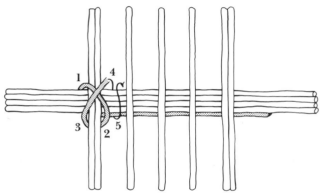

4.34 Basic oval base: Tying the first cross and winding the spine

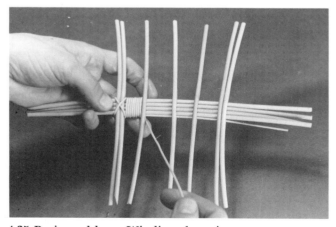

4.35 Basic oval base: Winding the spine

OVAL BASES

Think of an oval base as a circle cut in half, with the halves spread apart. The space between the halves is filled with a series of parallel spokes, while the end spokes radiate from the slath like those of a round base.

The structure of the oval base is similar to that of the split-spoke round base. The slath consists of a specific number of short spokes split and threaded onto a spine of three to-five long spokes. As the slath is tied, the spine is wrapped with a flexible weaver. When a consistent number of wraps is placed between each set of shorter spokes, those spokes are simultaneously spaced and secured.

A word of caution: Never use *pairing weave* as the only weave on an oval base because the twist in the weave will warp the base. *Chain pairing* can be used because each row of regular pairing is countered by reverse pairing.

Basic Oval Base

Laying out and securing the slath. Split the short spokes in the middle according to the method used for the split-spoke base, and thread them onto the long spokes (4.33). A pair of short spokes should be placed at each end of the long spokes, a short distance in. See Chapter 9 for information on figuring exact measurements.

To begin tying the slath, thread a flexible #2 weaver through all the split short spokes so that it lies against the long spokes (4.34). Bring the weaver under the slath to point 1, diagonally across to 2, under the double spokes to 3, diagonally across to 4, then behind the slath to 5. To begin winding the spine, bring the weaver behind from upper right to lower right.

Wind the weaver around the spine between the spokes eight times (or enough wraps to measure the space needed between spokes), then push the next short spoke snug against the last wrap (4.35). Bring the weaver diagonally from upper left to lower right behind that spoke and wind another eight times. Continue wrapping and tightening in the spokes this way until you reach the other set of double spokes. Bring the weaver under the double spokes to point 1, diagonally across to 2, under the double spokes to 3, and diagonally across to 4 (4.36). Finish by bringing the weaver under the double spoke to point 5.

Add a second weaver at point 6 (4.36) and work two rows of *pairing weave* without separating any of the groups of spokes (4.37). If you try to separate the end spokes too soon and don't get the rows of weaving close enough together, a "dog bone" effect can result: the ends develop nobs while the weaving along the sides sticks to the spine, causing the base to look like a dog's bone.

Separating the spokes. When you have finished two rows of pairing, cut off the weaver which ends behind the spine and with the other weaver begin to separate the spokes, using *Japanese weave* (4.38, 4.39). Continue Japanese weave until the base is the desired diameter. Dome the base according to the instructions (4.40 and page 38).

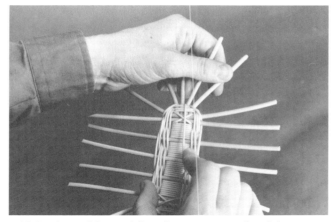

4.39 Basic oval base: After the two rows of pairing weave, begin to separate the spokes with Japanese weave

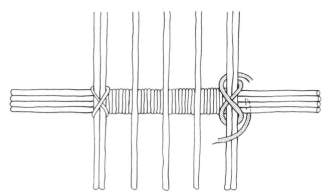

4.36 Basic oval base: Tying the second cross, and adding the second weaver for pairing weave

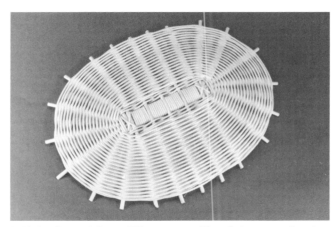

4.40 Basic oval base: The upper side of the completed oval base, showing the dome

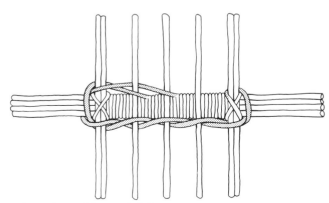

4.37 Basic oval base: Pairing weave

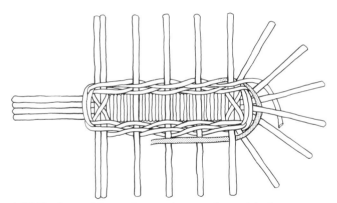

4.38 Basic oval base: Separating spokes with Japanese weave

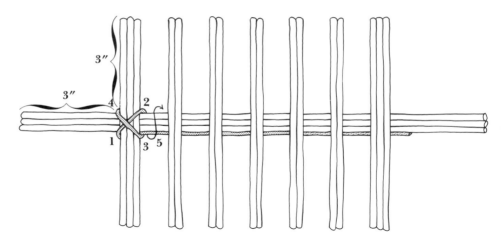

4.41 Large oval base: Tying the first cross and winding the spine

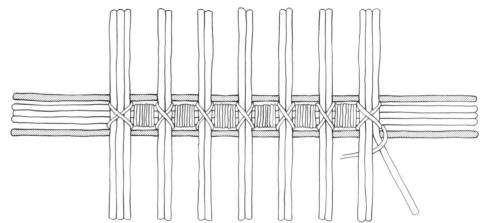

4.42 Large oval base: Adding the supporters

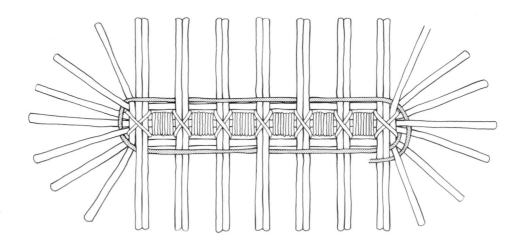

4.43 Large oval base: Separating spokes with Japanese weave

Large Oval Base

Larger baskets need stronger bases. This version of the oval base is inherently stronger because of supporters added along the spine, and because of the doubled short spokes. In addition, the technique used for initially binding the short and long spokes together incorporates a cross at each intersection.

Laying out and securing the slath. Split the short spokes and thread them onto three long spokes. See Chapter 9 for help in determining the exact number of spokes and their measurements. Set up the two groups of three spokes several inches in from each end and space the other pairs at equal intervals between them (4.41).

Thread a long, flexible #3 weaver through the holes of all the short spokes so it lies against the long spokes. Bring the weaver diagonally across the group of three from 1 to 2, under the spine to 3, diagonally across the front to 4, then diagonally across the back to 5 (4.41). (This starting technique can also be used on the basic oval, and the crosses at the intersections can either be used or eliminated. However, this start *must* be used in order to get the weaver going in the right direction to make crosses.)

Wind the spine eight times (or the number of wraps needed to obtain a specific measurement between the short spokes) and bind the next set of double spokes with the same cross. Continue this sequence along the spine.

Adding supporters. Run the other two long spokes through the holes in the short spokes on each side of the spine (4.42). Pointing the ends of the spokes and opening up the holes with an awl will make this job less frustrating. It may be easier to pull the extra spokes through with needlenose pliers.

Separating the spokes. There is less tendency for the dog bone effect to develop with this base, so *Japanese weave* can be used to separate the spokes right away without first working two rows of *pairing weave* (4.43). Dome the base as for the basic oval base. Doming will be more difficult because the spokes are heavier and are doubled, but be persistent (4.44).

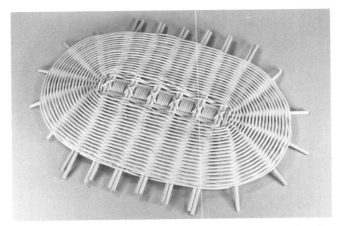

4.44 Large oval base: The upper side of the completed large oval base, showing the dome

CHAPTER 5
Preparing to Weave the Sides

5.1 Bi-spoking: Open up a space alongside a base spoke with an awl

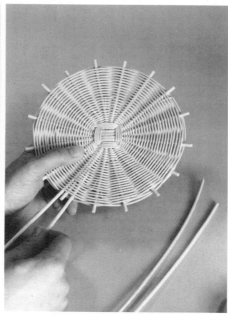

5.2 Bi-spoking: Run the side spoke in as close to the slath as possible

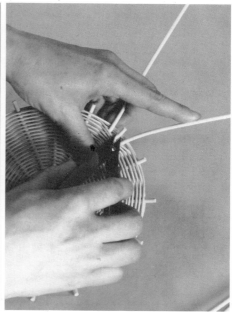

5.3 Bi-spoking: Trim the base spokes so they are below the level of the weaving

ADDING SPOKES

Continuous Base and Side Spokes

If the side spokes are a continuation of the base spokes, the spokes need only be pinched and bent upward before you begin weaving up the sides. For an example of this process, see the sample basket on page 99.

Spokes can be added to make a large basket. They can be inserted along only one side of the existing base/side spoke, for a medium-size basket, or on both sides, for a large basket. Add the new spokes a few rows before you expect to begin the sides. Weave several rows to separate all the spokes and space them equally, then pinch and bend all the spokes.

Separately Woven Base

If the base has been woven separately, additional spokes need to be inserted into it to form the

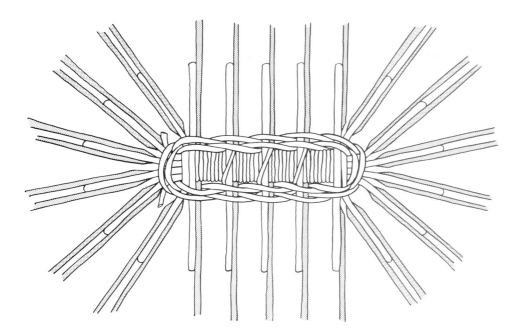

5.4 Bi-spoking: Basic oval base (for clarity, only the first two rows of weaving are shown, although bi-spoking is done a few rows before you expect to begin the sides)

framework for the sides. This is called **bi-spoking** or *staking up.*

Round bases. On a separate round base, two side spokes are generally inserted for each base spoke, one on each side. To determine the basic number of side spokes, multiply the number of base spokes by four.

The actual number of side spokes can vary and depends on whether the design requires an even or uneven number, or whether a specific number is needed to achieve a particular color design. Make sure that any additions or deletions are evenly spaced around the base. Don't add or delete in just one area. If the design requires more than the basic number of spokes, place each extra alongside another bi-spoke, in the same space. If the design requires fewer spokes than the basic number, insert side spokes on just one side of the appropriate number of base spokes.

To bi-spoke, turn the base over so the concave side is facing you. The spokes on the underside of the base are more exposed than those on the upper side, and it's easier to see where you're inserting the side spokes.

Cut one end of each side spoke on a slant for easier insertion. With your awl, open up a space next to one of the base spokes, being careful to go under any joining weaver that may be there (5.1, 3.77). Run the side spoke in as far as it will go, preferably right up to the slath (5.2). Add another spoke in the same way on the other side of the same base spoke.

Be careful not to lose the dome when you are bi-spoking. It is easy to flatten the base if you're not careful. If you hold the base in your hand

when adding the side spokes instead of working on a table, there is less chance of flattening it.

Each base spoke can be trimmed before the next spoke is added, or they can all be cut after the entire base has been bi-spoked (5.3). After trimming, the base spokes should end below the level of the weaving. Any portion of a base spoke which protrudes will cause a gap in the weaving between the base and the sides.

Oval bases. Separate oval bases are bi-spoked differently. Each of the long end spokes requires two side spokes, while each of the short spokes requires only one side spoke (5.4). On a larger oval base, the center end spoke can be split to allow insertion of an extra side spoke (5.5).

The number of side spokes can vary with the design of the basket. On an oval base, spokes are added or deleted only at the ends, not on the short spokes along the side of the base. A basket with straight sides needs fewer side spokes inserted on the ends than does one with rounded sides; see Chapter 9 for complete information on these design variations.

SEPARATING THE SIDE SPOKES

After a separate base has been bi-spoked, the spokes are rather close together. If you work a *three-rod arrow* before pinching and turning the spokes upward, the spokes will be evenly separated and the sides will be easier to weave (3.38, 3.40–3.44).

Work the three-rod arrow from the inside of the base, or with the upper or convex side of the base facing upward (5.6, 5.7). Weave the rows close together and separate the spokes evenly as you weave. The second row of the arrow is likely to be loose, so be sure to pull each weaver tight as you work.

To trim the weavers on the completed arrow, turn the base over and carefully lay each end down onto its corresponding spoke. Trim the ends close, on a slant, so they lie flat (5.8, 3.79). Trying to hide the ends on an arrow makes it lumpy and distorts the weaving.

THE UPSETT

Upsett is the term used to describe the point at which the side spokes are pinched and bent upward. More specifically it refers to the first few rows woven on the outside of the basket to set the spokes and hold them in position. If you did not separate the spokes with a *three-rod arrow,* as mentioned above, they form V patterns in the first few rows of the upsett. These first few rows are most important, because they determine the shape of the whole basket. Correctly done, these rows make the whole basket easier to weave.

5.6 Three-rod arrow: The first step of the step-up

5.7 Three-rod arrow: Ending

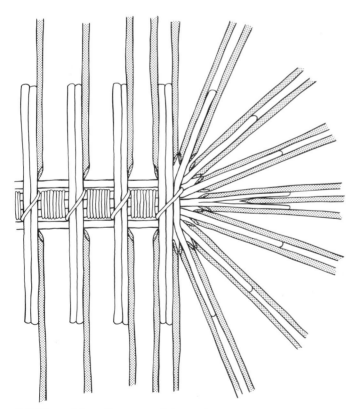

5.5 Bi-spoking: Large oval base (for clarity, only the slath and spokes are shown; the central long spoke has been split for symmetrical spoking)

5.8 Three-rod arrow: The trimmed ends of the arrow on the underside

The spokes must be soaked well and pinched before the upsett can be started. Turn the base over so the concave side is facing upward. Hold the roundnose pliers parallel to the base (5.9) and pinch each spoke firmly (5.10). Remove the pliers; slowly and carefully push the spokes away with your hand (5.11). Pushing slowly and using your hand to apply the pressure allows the spokes to bend with a minimum of cracking. You can *feel* a spoke beginning to crack. Soak it and pinch again to prevent a bad crack. If the crack extends through more than half of the spoke's diameter, replace the spoke. The basket should look like illustration 5.12 when pinching and bending are complete.

The first row of the upsett is a *four-rod coil* worked in reed one or two sizes larger than that used to weave the sides. The coil consists of one row which is finished with a step-up and a lock (5.13, 3.47–3.48). Trim the ends flush with the coil. The basket rests entirely on this coil because of the domed base. Several rows of *three-rod waling* traditionally complete the upsett.

5.11 Upsett: Push the side spokes slowly and carefully away from you

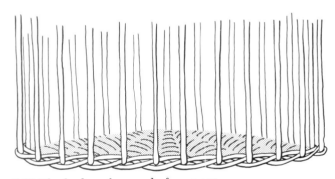

5.12 Pinched spokes ready for upsett

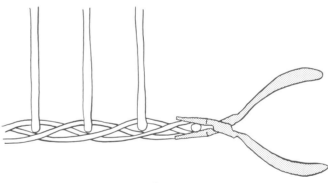

5.9 Pinching side spokes for upsett

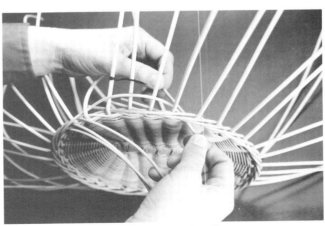

5.13 Upsett: Locking the four-rod coil

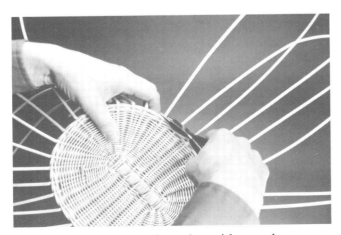

5.10 Upsett: Pinch the side spokes with roundnose pliers

CHAPTER 6
Borders

The sides of a traditional basket are quite straight-forward. Select the weave or weaves you will use, add color patterns if you choose, and gently but firmly maintain a pleasing shape. But once you have woven the sides, how do you neatly deal with the ends of the spokes? You weave them together to create a finished rim, called a border, at the top of the basket or at the outer edge of a lid.

A variety of border patterns are possible, and the particular design must be chosen carefully, keeping in mind the shape and function of the basket as a whole. The border can be unobtrusive, quietly following the lines of the weaving, or it can serve as the focal point of the basket. It can be purely decorative, or it can contribute substantially to the basket's strength. As a general principle, trac borders add height, rolled borders are very tight and compact, and braids stick out both inside and outside of the basket.

Borders can be woven with spokes used singly, in pairs, or in threes. The specific instructions will give details on a variety of designs.

Obviously, a certain length of unwoven spoke will be required to weave each border. You will have to plan ahead to have enough open spoke available for the border you envision, or you will need to select a border which can be woven with the length of spoke you have available.

The amount of spoke required is determined by measuring the distance between two spokes at the top of the basket, and multiplying that amount by a number which is given in the instructions for each border. For example, the basic single-spoke trac border requires open spokes which are four times as long as the distance between any two spokes at the top of the weaving.

However, you need to cut spokes at the beginning of your basket which will be long enough to complete the border of your choice. And you can't physically measure the distance between the spokes at the top until the basket is finished. What you can do is estimate the desired finished top circumference of the basket, and divide that by the number of spokes you plan to use. This will give you the distance between spokes at the basket's top.

A few general guidelines will help you plan and weave graceful borders.

- A border is much easier to weave when the spokes don't shift as you work. If you use waling or pairing as the final weave on the basket before starting the border, the spokes will be locked in place.
- Before you begin the border, be sure the basket is even in height all the way around. Put the basket on a level surface and stand a ruler beside it. Turn the basket, checking the height of the weaving on all sides. Tap down the high spots with the side of your hand.
- Soak the spokes very well before working any border. Three or four minutes in hot water will give spokes the flexibility needed for weaving a good tight border. Only the spokes need to be immersed in the water, so your dishpan may be large enough. If not, try a deep sink or bathtub.
- Spokes for the border should be of equal flexibility. If their flexibility varies greatly, the border will be uneven. The soft spokes will cause lumps, and the stiff ones won't conform to the proper curves.
- Markers are a great help in keeping your

place at the beginning of each row of a border. A hairpin-shaped marker is particularly useful, because it won't fall out. Both ends of one marker are used to mark two consecutive places, thereby forming a hairpin shape.

The spokes for most borders have to be pinched before you begin to form the rim, to prevent them from bending the basket out of shape or causing it to lean to the right. Pinching allows these spokes to be bent at right angles while the spokes in the body of the basket remain straight. (Trac borders and the Japanese braid border are the exceptions to this rule, although spokes for single-spoke trac borders can be pinched if you choose.)

Despite your best efforts, you may break a spoke occasionally as you pinch and bend it. If a spoke cracks halfway through, you can replace it. Cut off the cracked spoke flush with the weaving. Cut another spoke the length of the old one plus two to three inches. Make a long, slantwise cut at the end of the new spoke and run it down along the old one, following its left side as you look at the basket from the outside. The added spoke will cover the cut end of the old one when it's bent to work the border. (Lefties who are reversing the diagrams as suggested on page 7 and are bending the spokes to the left will insert the replacement spoke to the right of the old one.)

After you have completed a border, you can trim the ends of the spokes nearly flush with the final row of the border. Make certain that each remaining end is long enough to be securely braced against the final spoke in its weaving sequence.

TRAC BORDERS

The trac, or running, border is simple to work, and creates a decorative edge which adds height to a basket. Variations of the trac border can be woven with single, double, or triple spokes. The basic trac border is described as being worked with double spokes, and the instructions for the variations give spoke lengths for working with both single and double spokes.

When you work a trac border, each spoke or set of spokes is turned down in sequence, and completes its entire movement before the next spoke is worked. Trac borders have a tendency to pull the spokes of the basket to the right, making the basket look like it's leaning. Take care to keep the spokes straight while working the border.

The spokes in this border are turned down in a smooth curve rather than being bent at right angles, so they need not be pinched, although you may choose to pinch the spokes on a single-spoke trac border. The smooth curve of the turndown must be generous enough to allow subsequent spokes to be woven into it as the border is completed. The longer the weaving pattern of the border, the higher the first loop must be to accommodate the last pairs of spokes. The more complicated, larger variations of trac borders require longer spokes and a larger first loop.

If the spokes are not going to be pinched, the height of the border can be guessed, then adjusted when the border is completed. If you choose to pinch the spokes for a single-spoke trac border, you will need to determine the height of the finished border before pinching the spokes, so the border won't be cramped.

To predict the height, you can weave the border pattern across a portion of the basket with "false spokes," or short pieces of scrap reed in the correct size. Before measuring, be sure you have worked the entire pattern over at least one upright spoke. Measure the height at that spoke, remove the false spokes, pinch at the measured height, and weave the border.

Basic Trac Border

For the trac border illustrated, which is worked in pairs, the length of the spokes above the weaving should measure six times the distance between any two spokes at the top of the weaving (6.1).

Working from left to right, bring the first pair of spokes behind the second pair, in front of the third pair, then to the inside behind the fourth pair (6.2). Make the first loop about half an inch above the weaving so there will be adequate space for the final two pairs of spokes to be interlaced.

Continue this sequence—*behind, in front, and in*—all the way around, until you come to the last two pairs. Bring the next-to-last pair behind the last standing pair, in front of the first loop, and to the inside (6.3). Bring the last pair under the first loop, to the outside, in front of the next pair, and to the inside, following the arrow in illustration 6.3. Be sure each end is braced against a spoke before trimming it.

There are many variations of this border. The following list gives just a few of them.

Trac Border Variation 1

The pattern for this variation is *behind one, in front of two, and in* (6.4). For double spokes, the length of the spokes needed for the border is seven

6.1 Basic trac border: Behind one, in front of one, and in

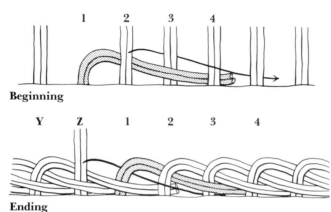

Beginning

Ending

6.2, 6.3 Basic trac border worked with double spokes

times the distance between any two spokes at the top of the basket; for single spokes, it is five times the distance.

Trac Border Variation 2

The pattern for this variation is *behind one, in front of two, behind one, in front of one, and in* (6.5). For double spokes, the length needed is ten times the distance between any two spokes at the top of the basket; for single spokes, it is seven times the distance.

Trac Border Variation 3

The pattern for this variation is *in front of two, behind two, in front of two, and in* (6.6). For double spokes, the length needed is nine times the distance between any two spokes at the top of the basket; for single spokes, it is six times the distance.

Trac Border Variation 4

The pattern for this variation is *behind one, in front of two, behind one, in front of two, and in*

6.4 Trac border variation 1: Behind one, in front of two, and in

6.5 Trac border variation 2: Behind one, in front of two, behind one, in front of one, and in

6.6 Trac border variation 3: In front of two, behind two, in front of two, and in

6.7 Trac border variation 4: Behind one, in front of two, behind one, in front of two, and in

(6.7). For double spokes, the length needed is twelve times the distance between any two spokes at the top of the basket; for single spokes, it is eight times the distance.

ROLLED BORDERS

This kind of border is compact, strong, attractive, and easy to weave. There are many different ways to work rolled borders; the best sequence to use depends upon the size of the spokes and the distance between them. Once you study the variations given here, you will be able to invent rolled border patterns of your own.

Although rolled borders can be woven with doubled spokes, most of the instructions here describe single-spoke versions. One distinctive double-spoke rolled border, described below, is the Japanese braid border.

My favorite rolled border is the four-row version I call the basic rolled border. This can also be worked as a two-row or three-row border, by stopping at the appropriate point in the instructions and trimming. The two-row version is listed as Variation 1, and the three-row version is Variation 2. Beginners may find that these variations offer a good introduction to rolled borders, and are slightly easier to work than the basic four-row sequence. However, don't delay your discovery of the full four-row border too long!

Basic Rolled Border

This four-row rolled border is a good standard one that can be used on many styles of baskets (6.8). Because I like it so well, many of the basket patterns in Chapters 9 and 10 include this border.

The spokes for this border must measure fourteen times the distance between any two spokes at the top of the basket. Soak the spokes very well and pinch them close to the weaving, holding the roundnose pliers perpendicular to the basket (6.9). Remove the pliers; then, with your fingers, bend each spoke slowly and carefully to the right.

Row 1: Behind one and out (6.10). Working to the right, take each spoke in turn behind the next spoke and out (6.11). Continue this sequence all the way around. To end, lift up the first loop and bring the last standing spoke through it from the inside to the outside (6.12, 6.13).

Row 2: In front of two and in (6.14). Place a hairpin marker in the spaces to the right of any two consecutive spokes, as shown in illustration 6.15. Bring each spoke in turn in front of the two spokes to the right, over the two spokes that are

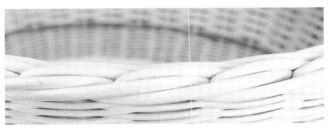

Outside

Top

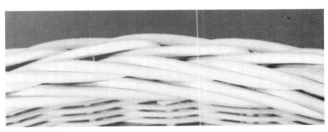

Inside

6.8 Basic four-row rolled border

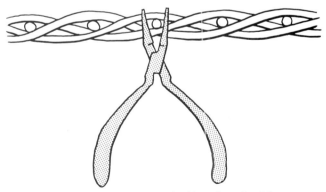

6.9 Rolled border: Position of pliers for pinching spokes

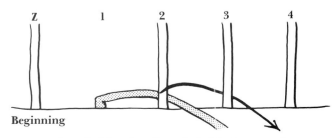

6.10 Basic rolled border: Row 1, behind one and out

sticking out to the front, then to the inside going under the loop formed by the first row (6.15). Continue this sequence—*in front of two and in*—all the way around until there are two unworked spokes left. To end, pull the first two spokes out a couple of inches. Then hold them down and insert the last two spokes, following the spaces indicated by the hairpin marker (6.16, 6.17). Pull the loosened spokes tight. To make sure the rest of the spokes are tight, hold the border with both hands, fingers inside, and push your thumbs firmly against the outside of the border all the way around.

Row 2: In front of two and in

Row 2: In front of two and in

Row 2 ending

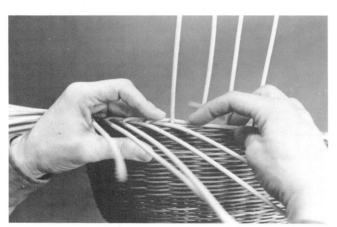

Row 1: Behind one and out

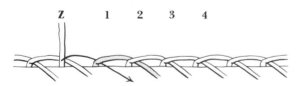

Row 1 ending

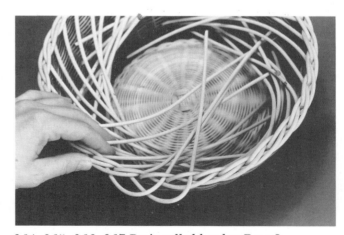

6.14, 6.15, 6.16, 6.17 Basic rolled border: Row 2

Row 1 ending
6.11, 6.12, 6.13 Basic rolled border: Row 1

Row 3: Over two and down. This row is worked on the inside of the basket and doesn't interlace with any of the other rows. If necessary, soak the spokes again. Work from the side closest to you as you look down into the basket. Place a hairpin marker to the right of each of any two consecutive spokes (6.18). Pick up the next spoke to the right and hold all three out straight, pointing toward the center of the basket. Bring the first spoke over the second and third, then down under the fourth spoke. Lay the first spoke in so it just touches the underside of the fourth spoke. Don't pull it straight down into the basket or back toward the left—a permanent lump will result. In illustration 6.19, the first and second spokes have been worked in this pattern, and the path which the third spoke will take is indicated with an arrow.

This inside row must be kept right against the side of the basket. You can do this by pulling the ends of the working spokes up above the level of the border while working the over-two-and-down stroke (6.20). Hold the spoke just worked against the side of the basket with the middle finger of your left hand as you pick up the next spoke to work it.

Continue the sequence of *over two and down* all the way around, until there are two unworked spokes left. The next-to-last spoke goes into the space of the first marker, and the last spoke into the space of the second marker (6.21).

Row 4: Over two and down. Work the fourth row as you did the third, positioning it right under the third row close against the side of the basket. Trim the spokes with a slant cut, so that half an inch of each spoke is visible under the fourth row. To make it easier to trim, pick up the ends of the spokes with an awl (6.22).

Row 3: Over two and down

Row 3 ending

6.20, 6.21 Basic rolled border: Row 3

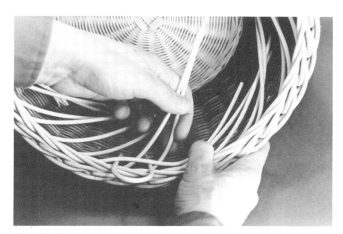

Row 3: Placing the hairpin marker

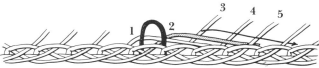

Row 3: Over two and down

6.18, 6.19 Basic rolled border: Row 3

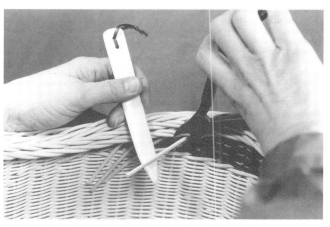

6.22 Basic rolled border: Trimming the spokes

Inside

6.23 Rolled border variation 5: A four-rod coil has been worked just before the border, which makes it look like a double-row border

Rolled Border Variation 1

This consists of the first two rows of the basic rolled border. The length of the spokes should be six times the distance between any two spokes at the top of the weaving.

> *Row 1: Behind one and out.*
> *Row 2: In front of two and in.*

Rolled Border Variation 2

This consists of the first three rows of the basic rolled border. The length of the spokes should be ten times the distance between any two spokes at the top of the weaving.

> *Row 1: Behind one and out.*
> *Row 2: In front of two and in.*
> *Row 3: Over two and down.*

Rolled Border Variation 3

This is a two-row border, similar to the first two rows of the basic border (Variation 1), except that in the first row each spoke goes behind *two* spokes and out. The length of the spokes should be ten times the distance between any two spokes at the top of the weaving.

> *Row 1: Behind two and out.*
> *Row 2: In front of two and in.*

Rolled Border Variation 4

This three-row variation builds on the ideas in Variations 2 and 3. The length of the spokes should be ten times the distance between any two spokes at the top of the weaving.

> *Row 1: Behind two and out.*
> *Row 2: In front of three and in.*
> *Row 3: Over two and down.*

Rolled Border Variation 5

This is a four-row version of Variation 4. The length of the spokes should be fourteen times the distance between any two spokes at the top of the weaving. See illustration 6.23.

> *Row 1: Behind two and out.*
> *Row 2: In front of three and in.*
> *Row 3: Over two and down.*
> *Row 4: Over two and down.*

Rolled Border Variation 6

All of the previous variations have begun the first row with the working spoke going behind one or two other spokes. This three-row variation takes the working spoke in front of two spokes (6.24). The length of the spokes should be twelve times the distance between any two spokes at the top of the weaving.

> *Row 1: In front of two and in.*
> *Row 2: Over two and down.*
> *Row 3: Over two and down.*

Rolled Border Variation 7

This is like Variation 6, but in the first row the working spoke goes in front of three spokes. The length of the spokes should be fourteen times the distance between any two spokes at the top of the weaving.

Row 1: In front of three and in.
Row 2: Over two and down.
Row 3: Over two and down.

Japanese Braid Border

This variation of the rolled border creates a braided top edge, and is popular in Japanese basketry (6.25). It can be worked in either two or three rows, with the same sequence as the two- or three-row versions of the basic rolled border (Variation 1 or 2). However, the spokes are not pinched, to preserve the curve of the braid.

The length of the spokes above the weaving is seven times the distance between any two spokes at the top of the weaving. Soak the spokes well, but do not pinch them.

Row 1: Behind one and out. Working to the right, take each pair of spokes in turn behind the next pair and out (6.26). Continue this sequence all the way around until one pair of unworked spokes remains. To end, lift the first loop and bring the last standing pair of spokes through it from the inside to the outside (6.27).

Row 2: In front of two and in. Place a hairpin marker in the space to the right of any two consecutive pairs of spokes. Bring each pair of spokes in turn in front of two pairs to the right, over the two pairs that are sticking out to the front, then to the inside, going under the loop formed by the first row (6.28). Continue this sequence all the way around until two unworked pairs remain.

To end, pull out the first two pairs of spokes about two inches to make it easier to see where the last two pairs will go. The next-to-last pair goes in the space of the first marker, the last pair in the space of the second marker (6.29). Pull the loosened spokes tight. Make sure the rest of the spokes are tight by running your thumbs along the outside border as you did for the rolled border.

The border can be finished here and the ends trimmed on the inside, or a third row can be added.

Row 3: Over two and down. This row is worked on the inside of the basket and doesn't interlace with any of the other rows. Work from the side closest to you as you look down into the basket. Place a hairpin marker to the right of each of any two consecutive pairs of spokes (6.30).

Bring the first pair of spokes over the second and third, then down under the fourth pair (6.30). Continue this sequence—*over two and down*—all the way around until there are two unworked

Outside

Top

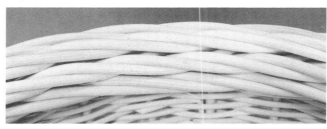

Inside

6.24 Rolled border variation 6

6.25 Japanese braid border

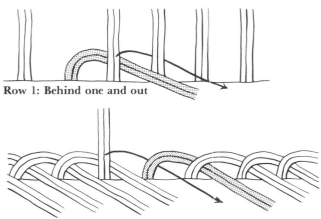

Row 1: Behind one and out

Row 1 ending

6.26, 6.27 Japanese braid border: Row 1

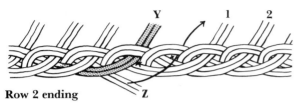

Row 2: In front of two and in

Row 2 ending

6.28, 6.29 Japanese braid border: Row 2

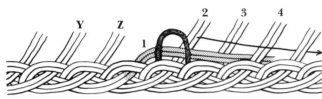

Row 3: Over two and down

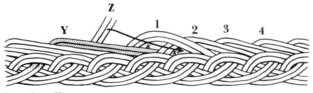

Row 3 ending

6.30, 6.31 Japanese braid border: Row 3

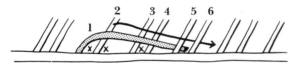

Row 3 variation: Over three and down (single spokes)

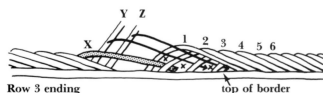

Row 3 ending   **top of border**

6.32, 6.33 Japanese braid border: Row 3 variation

pairs left. The next-to-last pair goes in the space of the first marker, and the last pair goes in the space of the second marker (6.31).

Trim each pair of spokes on a slant so about one-half inch shows under the third row.

Row 3 variation: Over three and down. This alternate sequence for row 3, worked with single spokes, produces a very smooth finish. Separate the pairs into singles. Place markers to the right of any three consecutive spokes (marked X in 6.32). Bring the first spoke over the next three to the right, and down under the fourth spoke (6.32). Work this sequence (*over three and down*) all the way around, until there are three unworked spokes left.

To end, insert the third-to-last spoke in the space of the first marker, the next-to-last in the space of the second marker, and the last in the space of the third marker (the final two spaces are marked X in 6.33).

ARROW BORDER

This border combines a trac and a rolled border to create an arrow design (6.34). By following the sequence of the four-row basic rolled border but substituting a trac pattern for the first row, you get the arrow. The spokes are pinched to make the border more compact, so the arrow will be well defined.

For this single-spoke border, the length of the spokes above the weaving measures fourteen times the distance between any two spokes at the top of the weaving.

Soak the spokes well. Hold the roundnose pliers perpendicular to the basket and pinch the spokes one-quarter inch above the weaving. (For clarity, the pinch point is shown farther from the weaving in the illustrations.)

Row 1: In front of two, behind two, and out. This is the trac portion of the border. The sequence is not exactly like any of the variations listed above.

Place two hairpin markers to the right of any four consecutive spokes (6.35). Bring spoke 1 in front of spokes 2 and 3, behind spokes 4 and 5, then to the outside. Continue this sequence all the way around, working each spoke in turn in front of two spokes, behind two spokes, and out.

To end row 1, thread the last four spokes through the beginning spokes in the same sequence (6.36). Bring spoke W in front of spokes X and Y, behind spokes Z and 1, then to the outside under the one loop between spokes 1 and 2. Bring spoke X in front of spokes Y and Z, behind spokes 1 and 2, then to the outside under both loops between spokes 2 and 3. Bring spoke Y in front of spokes Z and 1, inside under the one loop formed by spoke 1, behind spokes 2 and 3, then to the outside under all the loops between spokes 3 and 4. Bring spoke Z in front of spokes 1 and 2, inside under the two loops between spokes 2 and 3, behind spokes 3 and 4, then to the outside under all the loops between spokes 4 and 5.

Rows 2 through 4 are identical to rows 2 through 4 of the basic rolled border.

Row 2: In front of two and in. Follow the instructions for row 2 of the basic rolled border (6.37, 6.38; see also 6.15, 6.16).

Rows 3 and 4: Over two and down. Follow the instructions for rwo 3 of the rolled border (6.19, 6.21).

Outside

Inside

6.34 Arrow border

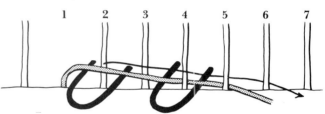

6.35 Arrow border: Row 1, in front of two, behind two, and out

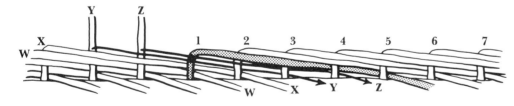

6.36 Arrow border: Row 1 ending

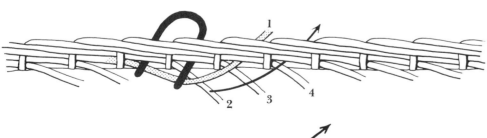

6.37 Arrow border: Row 2, in front of two and in

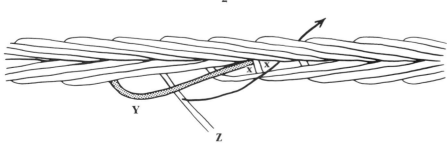

6.38 Arrow border: Row 2 ending

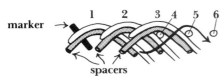

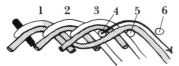

Placement of markers and first spacer

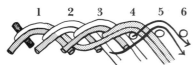

Laid-down spoke 1 behind spoke 5

Standing spoke 4 behind spoke 5

6.39, 6.40, 6.41 Three-rod plain border: Starting and weaving

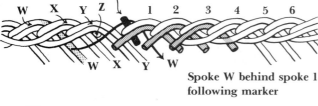

Spoke W behind spoke 1 following marker

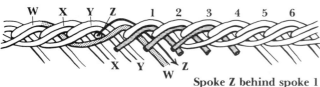

Spoke Z behind spoke 1

Spoke X replaces first spacer

6.42, 6.43, 6.44 Three-rod plain border: Ending

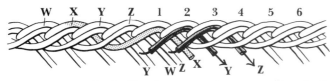

Spoke Y replaces second spacer, and spoke Z replaces third spacer

Spokes trimmed on outside

6.45, 6.46 Three-rod plain border: Ending continued

THREE-ROD PLAIN BORDER AND FOLLOW-ON TRACS

Another useful border is the three-rod plain, or commercial, border. It's used extensively in the basketry trade because of its strength and neat appearance. Although it is more difficult to work than the rolled borders, it offers more design possibilities because it can be used alone or combined with trac sequences (called "follow-on tracs").

A more descriptive name for this border is the *three-rod behind-one border,* named for the actual number of turn-downs. Other variations include the *three-rod behind-two border,* the *four-rod behind-one border,* and the *four-rod behind-two border.* The illustrated three-rod plain border is a good basic version of this type.

For a small basket the basic three-rod plain border by itself is fine, but a larger basket needs a thicker border. This is where the follow-on trac sequences come in handy. Each follow-on trac has its own distinctive character; this makes the three-rod plain border and its follow-on variations an extremely versatile set of finishes.

Basic Three-Rod Plain Border

The basic border, worked in one row with single spokes, requires spokes measuring seven times the distance between any two spokes at the top of the basket. If you plan to continue with rows of follow-on trac, for each row add the length of four times the distance between any two spokes. Add another inch or two overall for ease of handling and basic fudge factor. Soak the spokes well and pinch as for the rolled border (6.9).

You will need one marker and three spacers, to hold open the spaces into which the last three spokes will be threaded to complete the border. Take reed the same size as the border spokes and cut four pieces four inches long.

Starting the pattern. Place the marker to the right of spoke 1 (6.39). Lay down spoke 1 over the marker, behind spoke 2, and out. Place the first spacer between spokes 1 and 2, so it lies parallel to spoke 1 as you're looking at it from the top; see the illustration. Lay down spoke 2 behind spoke 3 and bring it out. Place the second spacer parallel to spoke 2, between laid-down spoke 2 and standing spoke 3. Lay down spoke 3 behind spoke 4 and bring it out. Place the third spacer parallel to spoke 3, between laid-down spoke 3 and standing spoke 4.

There are now three pairs of laid-down spokes; each of these first pairs consists of one laid-down spoke and one spacer. The spacer will be replaced by an actual spoke as the first round is completed. Subsequent pairs will be composed of two spokes.

Only the right spoke of each pair will be used in the three-rod plain border. The left spoke will be used later for the follow-on trac.

The weaving sequence. Bring laid-down spoke 1 in front of 3 and 4, behind 5, and out (6.40). Lay down standing spoke 4 behind 5 and bring it out, parallel to spoke 1.

Bring laid-down spoke 2 in front of 4 and 5, behind 6, and out (6.41). Lay down standing spoke 5 behind 6 and bring it out, parallel to spoke 2.

Continue this sequence all the way around, each time bringing the right spoke of the left laid-down pair in front of two spokes, behind the second standing spoke (which is actually the third spoke), and out; then lay down the left standing spoke parallel with it, to make a pair. At the end of the row, one standing spoke will remain (6.42).

Ending the pattern. Bring laid-down spoke W behind spoke 1 and out, removing the marker. Lay down standing spoke Z parallel with W (6.43).

Bring laid-down spoke X in front of spokes Z and 1, replacing the first spacer (6.44). Be sure to follow the path of the spacer *exactly*. Replace the second spacer with laid-down spoke Y, and the third spacer with laid-down spoke Z (6.45).

Check to see that the border has even tension all the way around before trimming the spokes or weaving a follow-on trac. Push each outside loop with your thumbs, as you did for the rolled border, to tighten all the loops.

For a small basket, the spokes can be trimmed flush on the outside of the basket (6.46).

Follow-On Trac 1

This one-row trac produces an arrow design on the outside of the basket (6.47). The sequence is *under two and in*. Bring one of the outside spokes under the two spokes to its right, and to the inside in the space under the second spoke (6.48). Continue this sequence all the way around, lifting the loops of the first two spokes to open the spaces for insertion of the last two. Trim the spokes on the inside of the basket, making sure each is braced against an upright spoke before it is cut.

Outside

Top

Inside

6.47 Three-rod plain border with follow-on trac 1

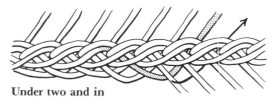
Under two and in

6.48 Three-rod plain border with follow-on trac 1

Top

6.49 Three-rod plain border with follow-on trac 2

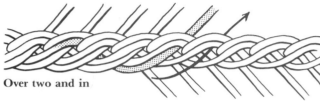

Over two and in

6.50 Three-rod plain border with follow-on trac 2

Outside

Top

Inside

6.51 Three-rod plain border with follow-on trac 3

Follow-On Trac 2

This one-row trac increases the top width of the border (6.49). The sequence is *over two and in*. Bring one of the outside spokes over two spokes and in (6.50). The space into which it will go is tight and must first be opened with an awl. Trim the end of the spoke on the diagonal to make insertion easier.

You can trim the spokes on the inside at this point, or weave an extra row of *over two and down* (6.19) to make the border stronger and to hide the ends more effectively.

Follow-On Trac 3

This pattern consists of two or three rows of a rolled border woven on the outside of the basket (6.51). At least two rows are needed to make this border effective. A single row is too skimpy. This border can be confusing, so work it carefully, step by step, and do it when you won't be interrupted.

Row 1: Over two and down. Place a hairpin marker to the right of any two consecutive spokes (6.52). On the outside of the basket, bring the first spoke over the second and third spokes, and down under the fourth spoke. Repeat the *over two and down* sequence all the way around.

Weave the last two spokes in turn into the marked spaces, with the next-to-last spoke in the space of the first marker, and the last spoke in the space of the second marker (6.53).

Row 2: Over two and down. Still on the outside of the basket, start a second row of *over two and down* right below the first, keeping it against the basket and directly under the previous row. Use the hairpin marker again, to make the ending easier.

A third row of the same sequence is optional. Make sure the border is right against the side of the basket before you trim the spokes. The trimmed ends should lie flush against the bottom line of the outside border.

BRAIDED BORDER

The braided border makes a firm, attractive rim on a basket (6.54). Of the borders presented here, it is the most difficult to work, but it is so attractive that it's worth the effort required to learn it. The braid can be worked so that it is at a right angle to the basket, producing a very wide border. Or it can be made to slant downward along the outside of the basket at about a 45-degree angle, by pushing the spokes into that position while working the border.

The basic braided border described here is known as a *two-rod three-stroke braid,* or a *three-pair plait.* It is a good basic representative of this type of border; once you understand it, you can experiment with the other possibilities. *Two-rod* means that two spokes are used. *Three-stroke* means there are three moves requiring spacers before the strokes of the regular pattern begin. Other commonly used variations include the *two-rod four-stroke braid,* the *two-rod five-stroke braid,* and the *three-rod three-stroke braid.*

The spokes needed for the two-rod, three-stroke braided border should measure eleven times the distance between any two spokes at the top of the basket.

Soak the spokes well. Pinch them close to the weaving with roundnose pliers, holding the pliers at a 45-degree angle to the basket (6.55). Bend each spoke carefully to check that it won't crack while you are working the border.

From reed the same size as the spokes, cut a six-inch marker and three twelve-inch spacers, to be used alongside the first three spokes. For one version of the border finish (and the one that I prefer), the spacers will remain as an integral part of the border; therefore you should cut them from the same quality reed as you use for the border.

Starting the pattern. Place one end of the six-inch marker between any two spokes (6.56) and label the lefthand spoke as spoke 1. Bend spoke 1 over the marker and down, slanting to the right at a 45-degree angle. Place a twelve-inch spacer on the right side of spoke 1, leaving three inches of the spacer projecting to the inside.

Bring the other end of the marker over the end of spoke 1, then between standing spokes 2 and 3 (6.57). Bend spoke 2 down over the marker, and place another twelve-inch spacer on the right side of spoke 2, with three inches projecting to the inside.

Bring spoke 1 and its spacer down over spoke 2 and its spacer in a loose curve, then inside between standing spokes 3 and 4 (6.58). Bend spoke 3 down over spoke 1 and place the last twelve-inch spacer on the right side of spoke 3, with three inches projecting to the inside.

Bring spoke 2 and its spacer over spoke 3 and its spacer in a loose curve the same size as the first one, then to the inside between standing spokes 4 and 5 (6.59). There are now two pairs on the inside, each composed of a spoke and a spacer.

The weaving sequence. Bend spoke 4 down over the pair at its base (spoke 2 and its spacer), and bring the pair just to its left on the inside of the basket (spoke 1 and its spacer) out along the

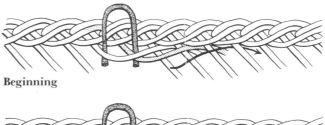

Beginning

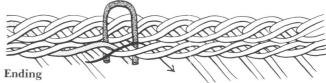

Ending

6.52, 6.53 Three-rod plain border with follow-on trac 3, over two and down on outside

6.54 Braided border

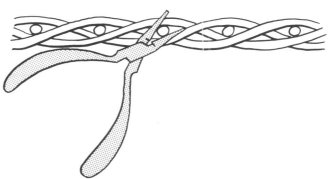

6.55 Braided border: Position of pliers for pinching spokes

right side of laid-down spoke 4 (6.60). This makes the first group of three on the outside.

Bring the next pair of outside spokes on the left (spoke 3 and its spacer) over the group of three, then to the inside between standing spokes 5 and 6 (6.61).

Bend spoke 5 down over the two (spoke 3 and its spacer), and bring the left inside pair out along the right side of spoke 5 (6.62). There are now two groups of three on the outside.

The sequence proceeds in this manner, but as the weaving progresses and you are dealing with groups of three on the outside, only the two left spokes in each group will move to the inside. The right spoke of every outside group of three will be left out each time.

Continue this sequence, *outside left pair in, left standing spoke down, left inside pair out beside the spoke,* around the basket. Another way to remember the pattern is *two spokes in and three spokes out.*

Ending the pattern. When you reach the beginning, you will have just one pair of spokes on the inside and two groups of three on the outside (6.63). All three groups must be inside before you can proceed.

Bring the left pair over the right group of three and thread it through to the inside, following the path of the first marker. Bring the last outside pair inside, following the path of the second marker exactly. Now all three pairs are on the inside.

There are two ways to finish the braid. The first is to remove each spacer and thread the right spoke of each inside pair through in its place. To finish off the remaining spokes inside, bring each in turn over one spoke to the right and down in that space.

The second method, which is illustrated, is much easier and there's less chance of breaking a spoke or distorting the border. Lift the left inside pair and thread the three-inch inside end of the left spacer into the space to the right of that pair, then to the outside under the border (6.64). Secure the ends of the other two spacers the same way.

Next, take the right spoke of the pair to the right of the first spacer and thread it on top of the spacer, and then under the border to the outside (6.65). Work the righthand spoke of each of the other two pairs in the same way.

Cut the remaining inside spokes close to the border. Turn the basket over and trim the outside ends on a slant, so that none protrudes beyond the edge of the border.

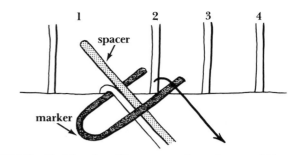

6.56 Braided border: Placement of markers and first spacer

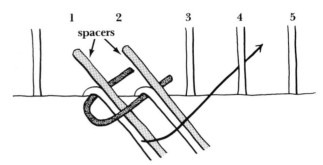

6.57 Braided border: Placement of second spacer

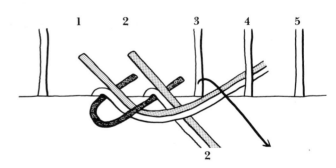

6.58 Braided border: Making first loop

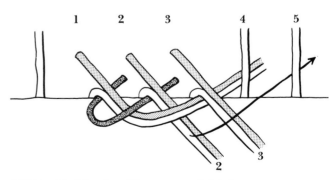

6.59 Braided border: Placement of third spacer

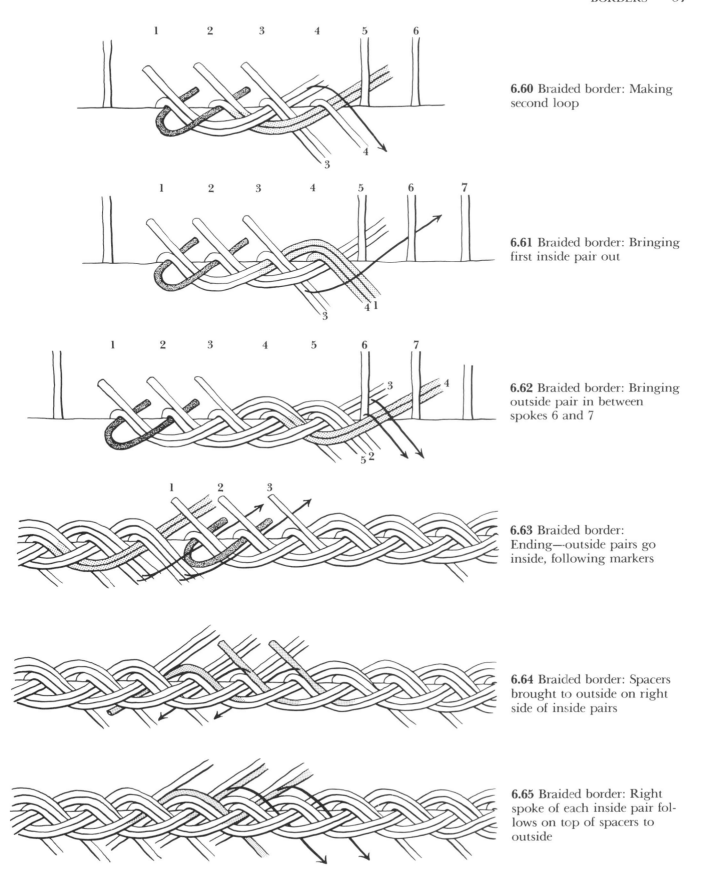

6.60 Braided border: Making second loop

6.61 Braided border: Bringing first inside pair out

6.62 Braided border: Bringing outside pair in between spokes 6 and 7

6.63 Braided border: Ending—outside pairs go inside, following markers

6.64 Braided border: Spacers brought to outside on right side of inside pairs

6.65 Braided border: Right spoke of each inside pair follows on top of spacers to outside

CHAPTER 7
Handles

Handles are added after the basket has been woven and the border has been added. A handle consists of a core of heavy reed which is inserted into the basket, then wrapped with a finer weaving material to fasten it to the basket. There are two basic ways to tie the handle to the basket, both of which turn out also to be decorative.

Your choice of a handle design must be compatible with the design of the basket. There are three fundamental types used in this book: **overhead, side,** and **double overhead.** The handle or handles must also be in proportion to the basket. You don't want a thin, wispy handle on a large basket, or a thick handle on a small, delicate one. The handle must be strong enough to carry the weight which is likely to be placed in the basket, but neither so thick that it looks bulky nor so thin that it looks flimsy.

Beyond selecting the basic type of handle, you need to determine its placement, its height, and its weight (which is determined by your choice of reed sizes). Keep in mind both the shape of the basket and its function as you read through the possibilities and make your decisions.

INITIAL DECISIONS ABOUT HANDLES

Your first decision relates to the **type** of handle or handles you want: overhead, side, or double overhead. In some cases, you will need to decide which kind of handle you will make before you begin the base.

Take a look at your basket, in reality or in your imagination. Compare it to the examples in this book and elsewhere, paying close attention to the basket's function and shape, before you make your final decision.

The **placement** of the handle is critical to the symmetry of the basket, and the number, length, and location of the base spokes can either help or hinder your efforts. There are several guidelines for handle placement, all of which relate to the construction of the base.

- Position the ends of the handle so they line up with the original crossing of the base spokes. If the handle ends do not relate to the basket's initial symmetry, the handle may appear slightly askew as you look down into the basket (7.1).

- It is easiest to place handles well on baskets made with an even number of spokes. In this case, the ends of the handle can be positioned exactly opposite each other. If you need to put a handle on a basket with an odd number of spokes, the handle will always be slightly off-center. In this case, find the best possible location that you can, knowing that if you place the ends of the handle "opposite" each other, there will be an odd number of spokes separating the handle ends on one half of the basket, and an even number separating them on the other half.

- Oval bases require particularly close planning for handles; the side spokes must be in the right positions for the kind of handle desired (7.2). A central *short* spoke is required for handles that go from side to side, for example, a single overhead handle or double handles that straddle a central spoke. A central *long* spoke is required for the same kinds of handles that go from end to end. No central spoke is needed for double overhead handles that are inserted alongside two adjacent spokes, or which straddle two spokes.

Handle **height** is the measurement of how far the handle extends above the basket. As a minimum, a handle needs only to be high enough to slip a hand into (for side handles) or an arm under (for overhead handles). For side handles, this can be between three and four inches above the basket's top edge, and for overhead handles this can be as little as six or seven inches above the edge. Beyond these lower limits, your choice of handle height depends upon individual taste and the use and appearance of the basket.

Many people have an easier time estimating the size for side handles, and find figuring an appropriate length for an overhead handle to be trickier. There are two rule-of-thumb measurement techniques which will give you a starting point for thinking about how long an overhead handle should be. Each gives an approximate length for the exposed part of the handle.

Measure the basket from one rim down across the bottom to the other rim, or measure half the circumference at the top of the basket. These will give you ballpark figures for handle length. If the basket is deep and narrow, the length of the exposed handle will fall somewhere between the two measurements.

Whether you are making overhead or side handles, the total **length of the core** which you cut for each handle will include not only the exposed section of the handle, but also the ends which will be inserted into the basket. A strong handle will need to be inserted well down into the basket's sides, extending along a side spoke to a point as near to the base as possible.

To determine the total length of a handle's core, begin with the exposed length, which you have determined. Measure the side of the basket from an inch above the base to the border, double that figure (because the handle has two ends), and add the resulting number to the length planned for the exposed handle.

HANDLE BASICS

You know the design you will use, and the length of each handle core. Now you need to know what size reed to use and how to prepare it. There are two general rules for determining the size of reed in a handle core, one for overhead handles and one for side handles.

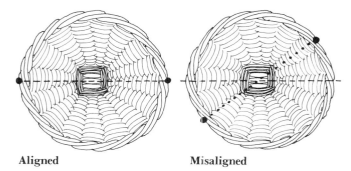

Aligned   **Misaligned**

7.1 Align the handle core with the original direction of the slath

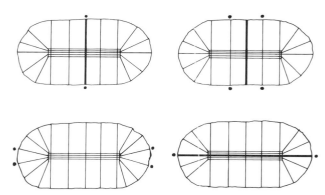

7.2 On an oval base, the number and arrangement of spokes will determine where you can place handles

Size of Reed to Use

For overhead handles, the core reed should usually be double the size of the spokes. For example, if you make a basket with #4 spokes, use #8 reed for the handles; if you use #5 spokes, select #10 for the handle.

For side handles, there is a straightforward guideline, but it may be easier to use a chart. For spokes between sizes #4 and #7 (the range which I consider useful), each size increase in the basket spokes corresponds to a handle increase of two sizes. For example:

Side Spokes	Handle Core
#4	#6
#5	#8
#6	#10
#7	#12

Preparing the Handle Core

For both types of handles, the core piece of reed is fairly sturdy, and once you have cut it you need to shape it. This involves forming the handle core into the curve the finished handle will take, and tapering the ends, so they can be inserted into the basket.

Shaping the handle core. You can form the handle's curve either off the basket or on it. In either case, soak the reed, then taper the ends of the handle core as described below.

To form the handle off the basket, bend the reed around your knee or use your thumbs on the inside of the curve to give it the shape you want (7.3). Tie a string around the ends to hold the shape, and let the handle dry. When it is dry, remove the string and insert the handle into the basket.

To form the handle on the basket, use the tapering and insertion instructions below to join the well-soaked handle core to the basket. Shape the handle core to the desired curve with your hands. Tie a string around the handle core near

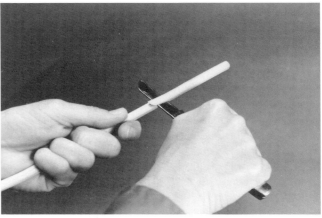

7.4 Tapering: Carve away half the diameter with a knife

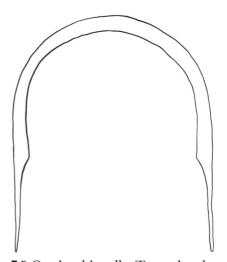

7.5 Overhead handle: Tapered ends

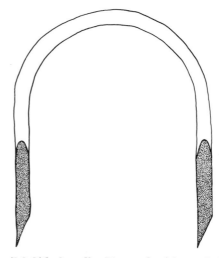

7.6 Side handle: Tapered with angled cut

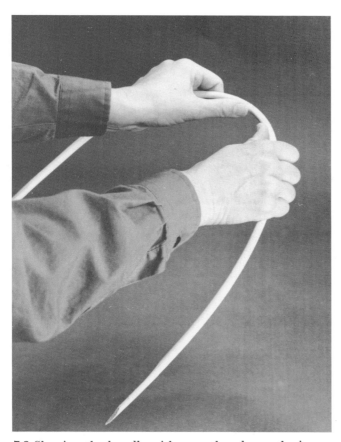

7.3 Shaping the handle with your thumbs on the inside of the curve

the border, so the handle will conform to the basket instead of causing the basket's sides to spring out, and let it dry.

Tapering and angling the ends. For overhead handles, taper the ends by shaving away half the diameter of the reed with a knife. Start carving about three inches from each end; the actual length of the taper will depend to some extent on the overall height of the basket's sides. Both ends will be tapered on the same side of the reed, on the inside curve of the handle core (7.4, 7.5).

For side handles, taper the ends on one side of the reed as shown in illustration 7.6. With a knife, shave off half the diameter of the reed about three inches from each end (again, the exact amount depends on the basket), on the side of the handle core which will face the inside of the basket.

Next, for both types of handles, hold the handle core with the tapered side of each end facing you and make an angled cut with your diagonal cutting pliers (7.7, 7.8). This will give you a narrowed point which will slide down the spoke when you insert the handle core into the basket.

Inserting the handle core. Some basketmakers prefer to use spacers during the weaving of the sides, to leave openings into which the ends of the handles will be inserted. They find it easier to get the handle ends in place without disturbing the pattern of the border.

I prefer to make handle openings carefully with an awl. The spacers leave a larger hole than I want, and I find that with careful tapering I can securely insert the handle ends without misaligning the border.

To make an opening, locate the spoke next to which the handle will be located. You will open a space to the left of the bend the spoke makes in the border as you look at the basket from the top (7.9). Run a large awl down into this space alongside the spoke, then wiggle the awl a little to make the space larger. (This may cause one of the border spokes to loop out. After the handle has been inserted, simply push it in with your thumbs to eliminate the bulge.) Take out the awl and run the tapered end of the handle down into the basket in the opened space.

ATTACHING THE HANDLE TO THE BASKET

The handle is now a part of the basket, but it must be permanently attached in a way that will support the weight the basket may contain. This is accomplished by wrapping a finer weaving material around the handle core and under the

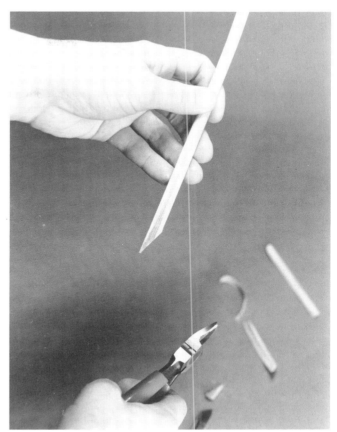

7.7 Tapering: Make an angled cut with diagonal cutting pliers

7.8 Overhead handle: Angled cut on tapered end

7.9 With an awl, open up a space to the left of the bend in the border spoke

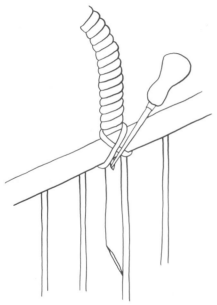

7.10 Pegging: Opening up a space with an awl

border. There are two common ways of doing this. **Roped** handles are secured by winding the handle core with reed of about the same weight as has been used to weave the basket's sides. **Wrapped** handles are wound with a flat material, like cane, flat reed, or flat oval reed.

The roped handle is more secure, because the weaver is brought under the border many times. The wrapped handle has only a decorative cross-pattern going under the border, so the core for a wrapped handle must be further fastened by pegging it.

Pegging the Handle Core

Pegging the handle core in place will keep it from sliding out of the basket. Start by soaking the ends of the handles where they go into the basket.

For each handle end which you plan to peg, you will taper to a point one small piece of #5 reed—this is the peg itself. You can cut its end at an angle with diagonal cutting pliers, or use a knife to make the point. At each end of the handle, insert an awl under the border and make a hole in the handle core at an oblique angle (7.10, 7.11). Run one of the small tapered pieces of reed through each hole so it extends a short distance into the basket. Trim the pegs flush with the surface of the weaving, both inside and out (7.12). The spring action of the handle core will hold the pegs in place, but if you want to secure them further, put a dab of glue on the pegs and let them dry.

ROPED HANDLES

The winding of a roped handle resembles the smooth twist of a rope. This handle is the strongest of all, because the weaver wraps tightly around

7.11 Pegging: Run the awl at an oblique angle into the handle reed, underneath the border

7.12 Pegging: The pegs in place

the handle core and is passed repeatedly under the border to fasten the handle securely.

The illustrations for the roped overhead handle show the weaver going under the border; those for the roped side handle show the weaver going under the final band of waling. These methods of securing the handle are interchangeable. Use the one which you think will look best on your basket, no matter which type of handle you are constructing. The figures also show the several strands being worked only in the space between the handle and the spoke to its left, but the wraps can be divided equally between the left and right sides of the core.

For a roped handle, the weaver should be the same size as those used in weaving the sides of the basket. Choose your longest and most pliable weavers to wind rope handles, so there will be as few joins as possible. Joins are made on either end of the handle, never in the middle, and the technique for making joins is explained on pages 77–78.

Japanese Handle

The Japanese handle is an easy version of the roped handle. It forms a decorative cross pattern, yet it can be done rapidly. It is very strong, because of the angle of the wraps which go under the border. These instructions call for the use of a single weaver; you can vary the Japanese handle by using two or three weavers together (7.13).

Soak a pliable weaver twice the length of the handle plus six inches. Loop it (don't pinch it) at its halfway point. With an awl, open a space on each side of the handle, under the border, and bring the ends of the weaver out, one on each side of the handle. Position the loop at the back of the handle (7.14) so that an equal length of the weaver sticks out on each side.

Wind the right weaver around the handle core, spacing the wraps evenly about one inch apart. End the weaver on the other side by bringing it over the border on the outside, then inside under the border to the right of the handle. Secure and hide the end of the weaver by bringing it to the outside just below the border, behind the next spoke to the right, in front of the next spoke, and in (see 7.16).

Cross the left weaver over the first wrap of the right weaver, being sure that the points where the weavers cross each other are centered both on the top and under the handle. Continue to wrap the left weaver over the right weaver until you reach the other side of the basket (7.15). Secure

7.13 Japanese handle wrapped with double weavers

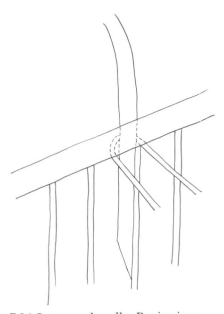

7.14 Japanese handle: Beginning

and hide the end of the left weaver as you did the end of the right one (7.16).

Roped Overhead Handle

For this handle one weaver is secured and wrapped from one end of the handle to the other, with the wraps spaced evenly and an inch or two apart on the first pass across the handle core. When the weaver returns, it follows the previously established pattern, instead of crossing it as on the Japanese handle. And at each end, the weaver is taken under either the border or the final band of waling; in either case, the result is a very firm connection between the handle and the sides of the basket (7.17).

The sample handle is about fourteen inches long and requires seven wraps of the weaver in each pass. The distance between wraps is about two inches; shorter handles will require fewer wraps.

Establishing the pattern. Start by running several inches of a long, pliable weaver under the border from the inside to the outside at point A (7.18). Weave this short end over the spoke to the left of the handle, then to the inside at B to hold it (7.19). With the long end, wrap the weaver around the handle seven times, following the arrows in illustration 7.18 and spacing the wraps evenly.

The first and seventh wraps are close to the border. The fourth wrap passes over the top center of the handle. Space the other four wraps evenly,

two between wraps one and four and the other two between wraps four and seven.

Depending on the length of your handle, you may work with either an uneven or an even number of wraps. With an uneven number, the middle wrap will always be on top of the center of the handle. With an even number, the middle wrap will be under the center of the handle.

Continuing to wrap. At the other end of the handle, run the weaver to the outside of the border, then under the border from *outside* to *inside* in the space to the left of the handle (7.20, 7.21). (The weaver is worked from *inside* to *outside* only at the very beginning or when a new weaver is added.) Keep the first round which goes under the border tightly against the spoke to the left of

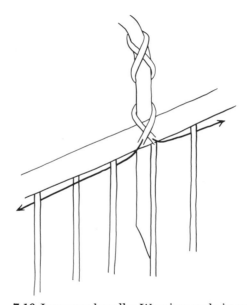

7.16 Japanese handle: Weaving ends in under border

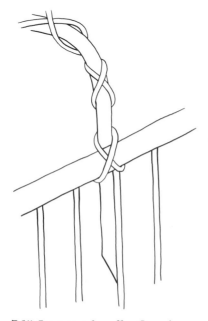

7.15 Japanese handle: Crossing weavers over handle

7.17 Roped handle: Wrappings worked underneath the border on a single overhead handle

the handle, because subsequent rounds will fill in the space to the right of this first wrap.

Next, bring the weaver from inside the basket up over the outside of the handle, keeping it close to the first wrapping, and wrap it back to the other side (7.20). At the other end of the handle bring the weaver from outside to inside under the border, to the right of the other wrap.

Continue winding the handle this way until there are no empty spaces; the weavers should not, however, lie on top of each other. As the weavers pass under the border, keep them to the right of the rounds already there.

The under side of the handle will fill in sooner than the upper side, and slight gaps may appear on the upper side. Wind until the under side is closely wrapped, with none of the weavers overlapping. If necessary, adjust the top weavers so the wraps are even.

It's very important to keep the last round on the right as it goes under the border to the inside. If it crosses to the left, the connection between handle and basket won't look smooth and even.

If the space under the border between the handle and the spoke to its left is too small to accommodate all the rounds, make half the securing rounds to the right of the handle (7.22). Usually there will be three or four rounds on each side, depending on the size of the weaver and the diameter of the handle.

Trimming the ends. All the ends are secured and trimmed after the handle has been completely

7.19 Roped handle: Weave the short end to the left to hold it

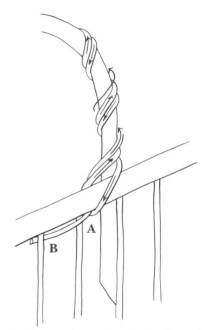

7.20 Roped handle: Beginning of third wrapping

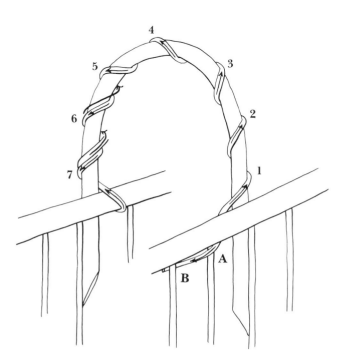

7.18 Roped handle: Beginning of overhead roped handle

7.21 Roped handle: Run the weaver from the outside to the inside, underneath the border

wrapped. At each end of the handle, bring all the ends out to the right of the handle under the border, in front of the next spoke to the right, then to the inside. Pull the weavers tight; they should be positioned securely against spokes and then trimmed. Do this at each end of the handle.

Binding. A binding around the base of the wrapped handle makes a neat finish (7.17). For the binder, soak a very pliable weaver of the same size as the weaver on the handle. Run it about two inches down into the basket along the right side of the handle (7.23). Make sure the rounds at the base of the handle are neat and in order as you bring the binder around the back of the handle at a point about three-quarters of an inch above the border. Wrap the binder tightly from left to right seven times.

Hold the binding tight as you place the handle on the edge of a table (7.24). Push your awl carefully through the handle above the binding (7.25). Try not to split the wraps on the other side of the handle as the awl pokes through. Wiggle the awl to open up a good space. Take the awl out, then quickly run the end of the binder through the hole (7.23). Pull the binding tight and cut off the end of the binder flush with the handle. The spring action of the handle reed will hold the end of the binder in place.

Roped Side Handles

Establishing the pattern. To begin roping a side handle (7.26), insert the soaked weaver under the border to the left side of the left end of the handle (7.27). To secure the end of the weaver, bring it from behind the handle and out at point A, in front of the next spoke to the right, then to the inside at point B. Take the long end over the border and begin to wrap behind the handle, following the arrows in illustration 7.27.

Wrap five times, placing the third wrap at the center of the handle on the upper side. Bring the fifth wrap in front of the border at the right end of the handle, and run the end to the inside under the border to the right of the handle. Place this round as far to the right as possible in that space, because subsequent rounds will fill the space between the first round and the handle.

Continuing to wrap. Bring the weaver from under the border to the front of the handle, following the arrows in illustration 7.28. Keep this round tight against the first one. Wrap across, following the path of the first wrapping.

On the left end of the handle, bring the weaver outside the border to the left of the first round. Run it under the border, and diagonally across the back of the handle (7.28). Wrap the third row to the right end of the handle, following the arrows for the third round.

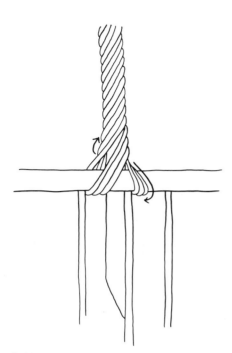

7.22 Roped handle: Wraps on both sides of handle

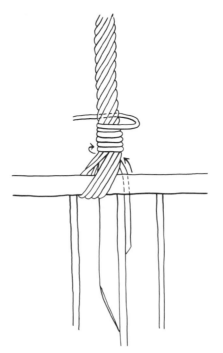

7.23 Roped handle binding

On the right end of the handle, bring the weaver to the left of the first round, diagonally across the front of the border, and under the border to the inside, keeping the weaver against the handle as it emerges on the inside of the basket.

Continue winding this way until the handle is completely covered. As with the previous roped handle, the under side will fill in faster than the upper side. Stop winding when the under side is completely covered. Adjust the top if necessary to make the wraps even, and secure and trim the ends.

Adding a New Weaver on a Roped Handle

To add a new weaver on an *overhead roped handle,* end the old one on the inside, under the border at one end of the handle. Leave at least a four-inch tail. At the same end of the handle,

7.26 Roped side handles: The weavers of the roped handle inserted under the waling

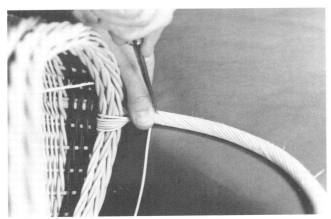

7.24 Roped handle binding: Brace the side of the handle against the edge of the table when you run the awl through the handle

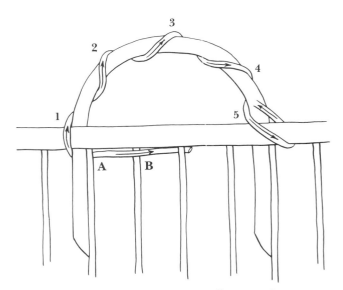

7.27 Roped side handle: First row, five rounds

7.25 Roped handle binding: Run the end of the binder through the hole

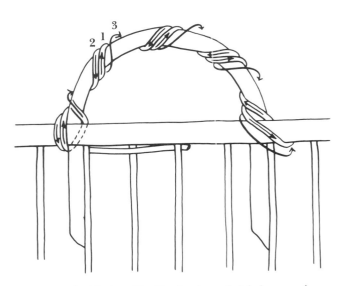

7.28 Roped side handle: Beginning of third wrapping

bring the end of the new weaver from the inside of the basket to the outside under the border, keeping it to the right of the old weaver (7.29). Weave the short end of the new weaver in front of the next spoke to the left, then inside to hold it.

To add a new weaver on a *side handle,* insert it to the left of the wrapping, moving from the inside to the outside. Weave the short end of the new weaver to the left, in front of the first spoke, and then in (7.30).

On both types of handles, continue wrapping as before, using the long end of the new weaver. Leave the ends of the old weavers inside until the handles are completely wrapped, then secure and hide the tails. Do this by holding all the ends together. Weave them out to the right side of the handle, over the next spoke, and then in.

WRAPPED HANDLES

Wrapped handles allow the basketmaker great potential for embellishment, because of the variety of decorative techniques that can be used. This handle consists of a core which is wrapped with a narrow, flat weaving element, such as cane or very flexible narrow flat or flat oval reed. Wrapped handles need to be pegged (page 72) for strength.

The basic wrapping element finishes the handle, but extra pieces of cane, reed, or other fibers, called *leaders,* can be added for decoration. Leaders lie on the surface of the handle. The wrapping cane travels over and under the leader or leaders in any of a number of sequences which produce different patterns.

The larger the basket, the larger the cane you use for wrapping should be. Common cane (3½ mm) is usually the largest size used for a wrapped handle. Wrapping uses a lot of cane, so you will need to learn to join additional pieces. This information is on pages 80–81.

The Basic Wrap

The basic wrap can be used for both overhead and side handles.

Starting the cane. With the handle in place, run the soaked wrapping cane under the border to the left of the handle at point 1 (on some baskets, it may look better to run the end under several rows of weaving) (7.31). Hold a two-inch end against the back of the handle.

Take the long end diagonally across the front to point 2, around the back of the handle to point 3, then diagonally across the front again to the right of the handle to point 4. Run it back inside the basket and bring it diagonally across

the back to point 5 to begin wrapping the handle horizontally.

Wrapping the handle. You can wrap the handle without adding pattern, or you can begin to work a design incorporating one or more leaders after you have completed several rows of plain wrapping.

One very simple pattern requires only one leader. Tuck its end under the initial rows of wrapping and lay it flat against the top of the

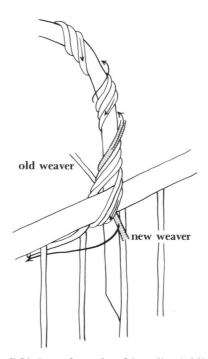

7.29 Roped overhead handle: Adding a new weaver

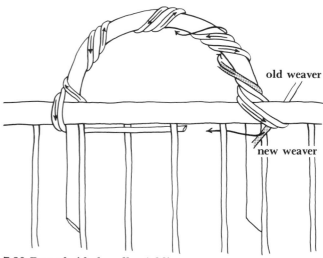

7.30 Roped side handle: Adding a new weaver

handle. Begin wrapping over and under the leader in any kind of pattern that you like; the illustration shows two wraps over, two wraps under (7.32). Directions for a number of different patterns are given at the end of this chapter.

Ending the cane. To finish the wrapping, bring the cane from the right side of the handle at point 1 diagonally across the front to point 2 (7.33). Insert it under the border or band of weaving at point 2, and bring it vertically up behind

the border to the left of the handle at point 3. Run the cane diagonally across the front to the right of the handle, then to the inside at point 4.

To secure and hide the end, run it across under the vertical wrap behind the border, fold it back on itself, and slip it down under several rows of weaving in the basket (7.34). Pull it tight and trim it.

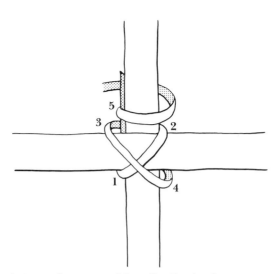

7.31 Basic wrapped handle: Beginning

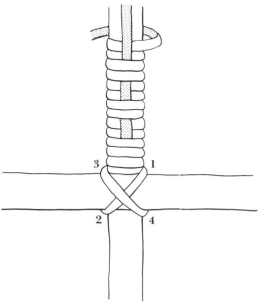

7.32 Basic wrapped handle: Adding a leader to make the design

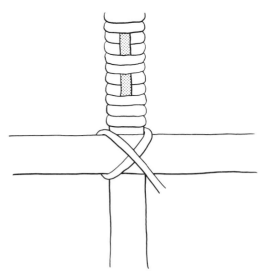

7.33 Basic wrapped handle: Finishing the wrapped handle

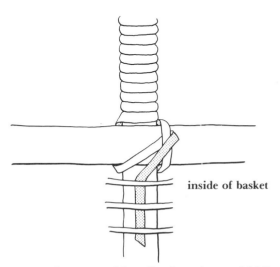

7.34 Basic wrapped handle: Securing and hiding the end

Wrapped Double Handle

A nice variation which is possible with the wrapped construction is a double overhead handle. This consists of two parallel overhead handles, with their ends positioned a slight distance apart. They are wrapped separately where they join the basket, but are bound together by the wrapping at the center top.

For a double handle, wrap both ends of one of the handles with the basic wrap (7.31) from the border up to the point where the two handles will join, usually between four and six inches above the border. Secure the end of the wrapper by running it through a hole made with an awl into the handle reed just above the wrapping (7.35). Pull the wrapping tight and leave about two inches of cane protruding from the other side of the hole. The protruding end will be trimmed when the two handles are wrapped together.

Wrap one end of the second handle with the basic wrap from the border to a level even with the wrappings on the first handle. Hold the two handle cores together; continue with the second handle's cane and wrap them together until you reach the point where they will separate.

With the same cane, continue to wrap down the other end of the second handle to the border (7.35). Secure the cane as usual for a wrapped handle.

7.35 Wrapped double handles: Run an awl through the handle reed above the wrapping

Adding New Cane on a Wrapped Handle

Make all joins on the inside or under side of the handle. Try not to join a new piece at the center top of a handle; the join is lumpy enough to be felt when you carry the basket.

Two methods of joining are used on handles: the mitered join and the twisted join. The mitered join is not as strong; it is appropriate for use when wrapping a single handle. The more secure twisted join is essential when two or more handles are being wrapped together.

Mitered join. This is also called a *butted join*. The ends of two pieces of cane are simply folded to form matching diagonals and then placed against each other. The ends are secured inside the wrappings (7.36).

To make this join, leave a ten-inch end on the old piece of cane. Place a new piece of cane on the inside of the handle reed with its shiny side against the handle. Wrap the old piece around the end of the new cane for several rows to hold it in place. Turn the end of the old cane at a 45-degree angle so the shiny side is against

the handle, and running toward the unwrapped portion. Pinch it with flatnose pliers to make it lie flat. Turn the new cane at a 45-degree angle so the fold lies against the fold on the old cane. Pinch it, then continue wrapping the handle with the new cane, covering the old end.

Twisted join. The twisted join varies only slightly from the mitered join, but it is more secure, because the two pieces of cane are wrapped around each other at the joining point. As on the mitered join, the ends of both new and old canes are secured within the wrappings.

Begin as you did for the mitered join: start the join when you have ten inches of the old cane left, lay in the new cane with the shiny side against the handle core, and wrap the new cane's end with the old cane.

The difference comes when you are ready to secure the end of the old cane and switch to wrapping with the new cane. Twist the two pieces around each other before you lay the old cane's shiny side against the handle (7.37). Then continue your wrapping with the new cane.

Pinch or lightly hammer the join smooth.

Run the end of the wrapper through the hole to hold it

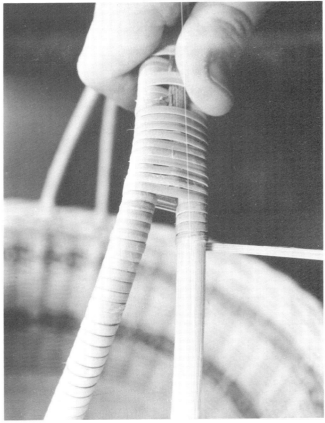

Wrapping down the end of the second handle after the double section

Decorating the Handles

In addition to the simple pattern described above, wrapped handles lend themselves to more elaborate decoration. Leaders can be any flat or round fibrous material that appeals to you: colored reed, natural cane, or items from farther afield.

While you can decorate single or double wrapped handles, the section at the top of a doubled handle, where the two handles are wrapped together, offers a broad and appealing surface to embellish. Wrap several plain rows before and after you add a leader or leaders, to set off the design.

Simple over-and-under design. This appears in illustration 7.32. Wrap the cane under the leader twice and over twice. You can also wrap over once, under once, and this can become the foundation for the diagonal and herringbone patterns described below.

Twill design. This is a more complicated design, woven with three leaders in a four-row pattern (7.38). Repeat these four rows as many times as you like for the design.

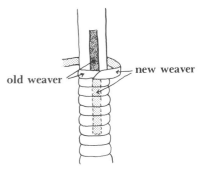

7.36 Mitered join

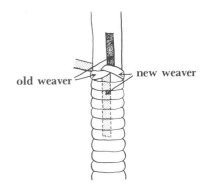

7.37 Twisted join

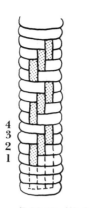

7.38 Twill design

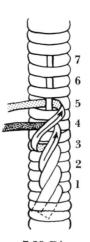

7.39 Diagonal design: In progress

7.40 Diagonal design: Completed

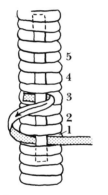

7.41 Herringbone design: Beginning

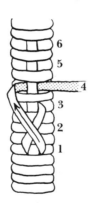

7.42 Herringbone design: Looping the cane up

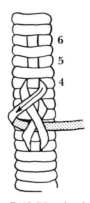

7.43 Herringbone design: Looping the cane back

7.44 Herringbone design: Completed

Row 1: Under one, over two.
Row 2: Under two, over one.
Row 3: Over one, under two.
Row 4: Over two, under one.

The next two designs, the diagonal and the herringbone, are woven over the leaders after the handles have been completed. For each design, complete the handle with a simple *over one, under one* pattern, using either a flat or a round leader.

Diagonal design. At the point where the leader has been woven in, slip two long pieces of soaked cane under the plain wrapped section. Place them side by side, shiny side out. Take the right cane from right to left, turn it so the underside is up, and insert it under the leader in space 1. Take the left cane the same way under the leader in space 2 (7.39).

At the end of each pair of strokes, both canes will protrude to the left. From this point on, take the lower cane, turn it so the right side faces upward on top of the leader, and insert it under the leader two spaces away, underside up, from right to left. Repeat until you reach the other end of the handle.

Finish the pattern by running the two ends under the plain wrap at the other end, side by side (7.40).

Herringbone design. Insert one end of a long, soaked piece of cane into space 3, underside up, from right to left. Put it under the leader just far enough to hold it in place. Loop it around so the shiny side is upward over the leader, then bring the end down to space 1 and insert it from left to right with the underside facing upward. Pull it snug (7.41). (After pulling the cane snug, you may have to readjust the leader to keep it in the center of the handle.)

Loop the cane up to space 4, shiny side up, and insert the cane from left to right, underside up (7.42). Pull it snug. Loop back to space 2 (7.43).

Continue this sequence of going up three spaces and down two, always looping the cane with the shiny side up and inserting it from left to right with the underside facing up.

To end, run the cane from left to right into the third space from the end (7.44). Trim the cane close to the leader. A dab of glue to secure the end is optional.

CHAPTER 8
Color

You don't need to know about color in order to make beautiful baskets. Even when the materials are undyed, there's plenty of interest in the natural colors, the shaping, and the textures. At the same time, color in basketry can add new dimensions both to your finished baskets and to the pleasure of making them.

Color can add depth and excitement to your basket designs. Because people respond differently to various colors, you can use color to create moods and feelings that range from the serene and subdued to the dramatic and electric. Once you are familiar with the basic weaves and structures, working them in color will also expand your understanding of exactly how they function.

If you do want to play with color in your baskets, you don't need to wait until you have mastered the craft. Obtain some colored reed, keep an open mind, and use this chapter as a resource.

Dyed reed is available from some suppliers, and simply buying an assortment of colors is a good way to get started, but you may want to dye your own materials. So this chapter will first discuss dyes and the dyeing process, and then will offer techniques and formulas for many different designs. If you would like help in using color in baskets, the patterns in Chapter 10 give you the chance to practice all your weaving skills—this time in color.

DYEING THE REED

There are two major categories of dyes: natural and synthetic. Natural dyes were the only kind available until 1856, when an Englishman,

William Henry Perkin, produced the first synthetic dye. Since then nearly 2000 kinds of dyes have been developed, most of them for industrial use. Each synthetic dye has been formulated for use on a particular type of fiber.

The major failing in many dyes, not only those suitable for home use, is that they are not completely lightfast. This means that over time, and with exposure to light, the colors will change. Direct sunlight causes the most loss. The colors usually don't fade to "ugly" tones—in fact, the changes can be pleasing—but they will often be less clear and bright. Therefore, the degree of lightfastness is an important part of the description of various dyestuffs. You may find yourself making a choice between ease of application and the color's durability.

The other matter of primary importance is how safe a particular dyestuff is to use. Be sure to read the information on safety, below.

Types of Dyes

The dyes listed here work on reed, are packaged for home use, and give good results. They will provide you with a broad palette, and may be sufficient for all of your basketmaking. If you want more information on both natural and synthetic dyes, I have listed several good books in the bibliography.[1]

---

[1] Although it's not marketed as a dye, Kool-Aid® can also be used to color reed. It's readily available and easy to use, although for dyeing large quantities household or fiber-reactive dyes are more economical. The actual dyestuff in the formula is

Natural dyes create beautiful, earthy tones, but the colors are not always lightfast. The dye-stuff itself is generally safe to use, but the mordants, which are chemicals that make the dye bond to the fiber, can be very toxic.

Because they are easier to obtain, use, and predict, my discussion will concentrate on synthetic dyes, although you may want to explore the use of natural dyes on your own. Of the many classes of synthetic dyes, I find two to be generally useful for basketry materials: household or union dyes, and fiber-reactive dyes.

Household dyes like Rit,® Tintex,® and Cushing® are multipurpose dyes compounded from several types of synthetic dyes. When you immerse your fiber, the appropriate dyes are absorbed and the rest stay in the liquid. Household dyes are inexpensive and easy to use, and they come in a wonderful range of colors. Their disadvantage is that they're not lightfast. The special basketry dyes which have recently been formulated fall into this group.

Fiber-reactive dyes actually bond to the fiber molecule to make a lightfast color. They are formulated specifically for cellulose fibers, or those derived from plants (as opposed to protein fibers, like wool, from animal sources). Consequently, they work on reed. The dyeing process is more involved than that for household dyes, but is certainly manageable.

Safety

There are precautions that should be taken when you use dyes. Please read all instructions carefully. Once you have established equipment and habits, dyeing can be safe and easy. But pay attention to these guidelines:

- Keep dyes and chemicals out of the reach of children. All dyes are toxic, some to a greater degree than others. Label all containers clearly as to contents, and use "poison" or "Mr. Yuk" labels.
- Don't dye in your kitchen. Set up your

workplace in a well-ventilated, draft-free area, such as a garage or laundry room.
- Never use dye equipment for anything else, particularly food preparation.
- Wear a mask when mixing powdered dyes. Prolonged exposure to dye powder, particularly that of fiber-reactive dyes, can lead to respiratory problems.
- Avoid breathing steam from the dyepot.
- Wear rubber gloves to prevent skin contact with the dye.
- Use enamel or stainless steel pots, or plastic pans. Never use galvanized or aluminum pots, because they will react with the dyes. If nicks occur in the surface of an enameled pot and the metal underneath is exposed, patch it with an enamel repair kit or Bondo® (a car body filler). Otherwise the exposed metal will affect the dye, or the pot will rust through at that point. (Bondo is very toxic; follow the safety precautions on the label.)
- Wear old clothes for dyeing, and wash them separately because spots of dye can transfer to other clothes.
- An old stove is ideal for heating dye, but an electric hot plate or propane stove is an excellent alternative. Hot plates usually have short cords so you may need an extension cord. Be sure to use the heavy duty kind; a regular household extension cord will overheat.
- Place the hot plate on a hard, flat surface. Don't put newspapers under it, because they can catch fire.
- Use stainless steel or plastic spoons and glass cups for measuring and mixing chemicals.
- For mixing and stirring, use large stainless steel or plastic spoons. Wooden spoons or dowel rods absorb dye, which can redissolve in another dyepot. They work well if you can keep the colors separated—or if you like surprises.
- Household dyes can be saved for later use if the color hasn't been exhausted. Plastic gallon containers are good for this purpose, although the dye will eat through them eventually.
- Use a plastic funnel to transfer dye from the dyepot to a container.
- Pour dye through a strainer before you reuse it. Dye tends to grow mold or gunky chunks when kept for any length of time. Unless they are removed, these things will glue themselves to the reed. When reusing dye, always test one piece of reed to see what

usually used on protein fibers, but it is also impossible to get out of rugs and Formica counter tops. Why not reed? Kids get a kick out of Kool-Aid dyeing, and the process is so fast and easy adults may want to play, too. Just dissolve unsweetened Kool-Aid in warm water and let the reed soak for about 30 minutes. The depth of color will depend on the number of packages used; I use one package for about 2 ounces of #2 reed. Rinse the reed, and it's ready to use.

will happen; that way you won't ruin a batch of reed.

• Have plenty of old rags and towels handy for cleanup. It's important to keep your work surfaces clean.

Dyeing with Household Dyes

Fill the dyepot with enough water to cover the reed—between one and two gallons, depending on the size of the pot. Dissolve a package of powdered dye in the water and heat to a simmer.

If you are dyeing by the pound, loosen all the large ties on the coil. Leave in place the small tie which holds all the strands together at the end. (Recently, coils of reed have come without that tie. If it's missing, put one on to keep the reed from tangling.) The dye will penetrate better if you soak the reed in warm water for five minutes before you put it in the dyepot.

Put the soaked reed into the simmering dyepot. If you want the color to be even, turn the reed frequently. Dyeing times can range from one to twenty minutes, depending on the depth of color you want and the type of dye you are using. The "basket" dyes take really quickly, while Rit and Cushing are slower. If you need to add more dye, remove the reed from the dyepot, stir in the additional dye to dissolve it completely, then put the reed back in.

The color will be lighter when the reed is dry. When the reed is slightly darker than you want it to be in the end, take it out. Standard procedure at this point is to rinse the reed until the water runs clear, but I find that if the reed dries overnight without rinsing, the dye penetrates better and less dye comes off when it is rinsed later.

Dyeing with Fiber-Reactive Dyes

Small packages of fiber-reactive dye, with the "fixer" chemicals included, can be purchased at some craft and yarn shops. They come with instructions and can be used in a manner similar to that described for the household dyes.

The same type of dye is also available in bulk, and its use is suggested for the serious dyer. Soaking and dyeing a batch of reed requires two hours, plus rinsing time (but you can do other things while the reed is in the dyebath).

These dyes are a one-shot deal—the dye can't be saved—and they have a short shelf-life. So mix only what you'll need and use the solution within two or three days. The type I use is Procion MX.

In addition to the dye itself, you will need Calgon® water softener, uniodized salt, and soda ash (washing soda). The water softener neutralizes the chemicals which make water hard. The salt makes the dye penetrate the reed—the more salt you use, the darker the color will be. Soda ash causes the dye to bond to the reed. The most reliable way to obtain this chemical is to buy soda ash from a dye supplier. You can find it also at the grocery store, called Arm & Hammer Washing Soda Booster,™ but do *not* buy Arm & Hammer Super Washing Soda,™ which contains bleach and other chemicals that prevent the dye from bonding.

For a medium shade, use 2 to 3 gallons of hot tap water (or enough to cover a pound of reed), 1 tablespoon of dye, ¾ to 1 cup of salt, 1¼ tablespoons of Calgon per gallon of water, and 3 tablespoons of soda ash. Lighter shades require less dye and less salt; for darker shades, use more dye and more salt. Experimenting will help you come up with exact measurements. It is very important to keep accurate records of the different dyebaths and samples of dyed reed if you want to be able to repeat colors.

1. Mix the dye with a small amount of hot tap water to make a paste. Add more water gradually, to make the solution liquid.

2. Stir this liquid dye into the hot tap water in the dyepot, and add the water softener and salt. Stir to dissolve completely.

3. Loosen all the ties on the coil of reed and soak it for 30 minutes in clean, warm water.

4. Put the reed into the dyepot and weight it down with a stone or brick, so it is completely covered. Leave it for 30 minutes.

5. Remove the reed and add the soda ash to the dyepot. Stir to dissolve it completely. Put the reed back in for an hour, stirring frequently to prevent streaks.

6. Remove the reed and rinse it until the water runs clear.

COLOR DESIGNS

One easy way to introduce color into your baskets is to change the color of the weaver or weavers for a particular section. The description of horizontal stripes, below, works on this principle, but you can discover other applications in the sample baskets. For example, if you are working three-rod arrow against a background of pairing weave, you can use colored weavers for the arrow.

When two or more weavers are involved, the possibilities multiply because you can produce more complex color patterns by using weavers of several different colors at once. Many of the color designs described in this section "just happen" when you select a particular weave and work it with colored weavers. Often the number of spokes over which you are working affects the pattern which develops.

Horizontal Stripes

Work *three-rod waling* (see 3.38) over any number of spokes. If you use a *step-up* at the end of each row (3.40), clear-cut rows will appear, without the normal spiraling effect of waling. This becomes a color pattern of horizontal stripes when you change the color of the weavers; all three weavers in use at a single time will be the same color. The number of rows for each stripe can vary; one application of this idea is shown in the basket in color photo 3.

Vertical Stripes or Blocks

Work either *pairing* (3.27) or *chasing weave* (3.9) over an even number of spokes, with two weavers of contrasting colors. This makes vertical columns of alternating colors; an example appears in color photo 2.

Or you can work *three-rod waling* over a number of spokes divisible by three. Use two or three contrasting colors. The blocks look like those in color photo 4.

Checkerboard

Work either *pairing* or *chasing weave* over an even number of spokes with two weavers of contrasting colors. Weave the desired number of rows with the weavers in one position. End the section at the beginning spokes. Switch the positions of the weavers, then weave the same number of rows with the weavers in this relationship to each other. An example appears in color photo 1.

Outside Spiral

Whenever you work a spiral, one side of the basket will show the design clearly and the other side will look tweedy. An outside spiral appears on the outside of the basket; see color photo 5 for an example. Work *three-rod waling* over a number of spokes divisible by three minus one. Use two or three contrasting colors.

A variation appears in the bottom section of color photo 20. To get this effect, work *double double Japanese* over a number of spokes divisible by three minus one. Begin the first set using the main color behind spoke 1, staggering the ends as in illustration 3.24. Weave one round, ending several spokes to the left of spoke 1. Add a second set of weavers in the contrasting color behind the spoke to the left of spoke 1, again staggering the ends. Chase one set of weavers after the other. At the end of the section of weaving, finish each set at its corresponding beginning spoke.

Inside Spiral

Sometimes you'll work a very open or flat basket and want the spiral to appear on the inside. The outside of the basket will look tweedy, as in the basket in color photo 6. To produce this effect, work *three-rod waling* over a number of spokes divisible by three plus one. Use two or three contrasting colors.

Reversing Spirals

Reversing spirals occur when you work alternating bands of regular waling and three-rod waling worked in the opposite direction. The spirals will be clear on the outside of the basket if you work over a number of spokes divisible by three minus one, and on the inside if you work over a multiple of three plus one.

Work *three-rod waling* in two or three contrasting colors. To reverse the spiral, cut off all three weavers and place them behind the same spokes but going in the opposite direction. Work three-rod waling to the left (3.41). Color photo 11 shows reversing spirals.

Arrows

For vertical arrows, work the *three-rod arrow chasing weave* (3.46) over a number of spokes divisible by three. Weave with six weavers of two or three contrasting colors. An example appears in color photo 14.

A variation, shown in color photo 13, produces spiraling arrows. Work *three-rod arrow chasing weave* over a number of spokes divisible by three minus one. Use six weavers of two or three contrasting colors.

Zigzags

This is an interesting variation of the spiral; see color photo 7 for this pattern. Work *three-rod waling* with two contrasting colors over a number of spokes divisible by three minus one.

Begin weaving to the right with the main color. Then, for three consecutive rows, cut off the main color weaver at spoke 1 and add a contrasting color weaver. Since there will be a number of weavers joining at spoke 1, the overlapped join (3.68) is the best to use. (Note: With this number of spokes, there will be one "short" zigzag spanning two spaces instead of three; it will appear at spokes 1 and 2.)

Darts

Darts are created by making a reverse zigzag over a regular zigzag. The basket in color photo 15 shows this pattern. Work *three-rod waling* to the left (3.41) to make a reverse zigzag. Place a main color weaver behind spoke 1 and two contrasting color weavers behind the two spokes to the left of spoke 1. For the next two consecutive rows, cut off the weaver in the contrasting color and add a weaver in the main color behind spoke 1. Weave to the desired height and end at the three beginning spokes of this reverse wale section, in other words, at spoke 1 and the two spokes to its left.

Braid Weave Variations

There are several designs that can be made with the braid weave (3.52–3.54). You can use either round or flat reed, or a combination of the two.

Vertical stripes (shown in color photo 18) can be produced when you work the *braid weave* over a number of spokes divisible by six. The sets can be made up of two or three weavers each. Use two or three contrasting colors.

For a **random pattern** like the one in color photo 8, work the *braid weave* over a number of spokes divisible by three minus one. The sets can be made up of two or three weavers each. Use two or three contrasting colors.

Giant arrows like those in color photo 10 result when you work the braid weave over an odd number of spokes divisible by three. The sets can be made up of two or three weavers each. Use two or three contrasting colors.

Examples of spoke numbers for various patterns

If the instructions say to use a number of spokes which is divisible by:	*Some examples are:*
three	30, 33, 36
three (uneven number)	27, 33, 39
three plus one	19, 22, 25
three minus one	20, 23, 26
six	30, 36, 42

Patterns and Designing

CHAPTER 9
Baskets to Learn From

BEGINNING BASKETRY

The first six patterns in this chapter are from my beginning classes. They are graded so that you will learn new techniques with each basket, building on what you've already learned with the previous ones. For the first six baskets, close-up photographs clarify details to help you through the transitional points.

The remaining patterns in this chapter and the next are based on techniques learned in this initial series. They also introduce new skills, but by the time you have completed the introductory series of six you should also be able to improvise.

Each basket pattern will specify certain weaves, a type of base, a border, and, where appropriate, a handle. Detailed instructions for the techniques are found in Chapters 3 through 7. It is a good idea to read the introductory material in those chapters before you begin your first project, as well as the section below, "A Good Basket."

A GOOD BASKET

Before you soak and cut reed to start a basket, consider what makes a good basket and the methods for reaching these goals.

A basket should be symmetrical and evenly shaped all the way around, so that it looks good from any angle. To achieve this appearance, the spokes must be kept straight and evenly spaced, and the shaping must be precise.

Shaping is one of the most difficult techniques in basketry. It requires a lot of practice to really understand the process. Shaping is a combination of pushing on the spokes with one hand and pulling the weavers taut with the other. Only

experience will tell you how hard to push and pull to achieve the exact shape you want. To achieve smooth, even weaving, it's very important to keep all materials well soaked while you work.

For right-handers: Since most weaving is done from left to right, the right hand manipulates the weaver while the left hand controls the spokes. The left hand straightens and positions the spokes after each stroke made with the weaver. The left hand also controls the inward and outward movement of the spokes and keeps them in the same plane.

For left-handers: If you reverse the diagrams as suggested on page 7, most weaving will be done from right to left. In this case, the left hand manipulates the weaver while the right hand controls the spokes. The right hand straightens and positions the spokes after each stroke made with the weaver. The right hand also controls the inward and outward movement of the spokes and keeps them in the same plane.

Pushing on the spokes immediately above the weaving and pulling on the weaver to tighten the gap is the only process that will shape the basket (9.1). When shaping a basket, never push on the part that's already been woven—that will most often distort the basket.

You may also experience problems which can be traced to the flexibility of a particular spoke or weaver; with good quality reed, these problems should be minimal, but knowing that they *can* happen may be the ounce of prevention—or simple cure—you need in a particular case.

For example, even one weak spoke in a group will make weaving and shaping difficult, because it won't hold its form. And with any weaving technique which employs two or three weavers at once, like chasing or pairing weave, a difference in flexibility among the weavers can knock the spokes out of line (3.4). A very flexible weaver can stretch, pulling tight against the spoke. If one flexible weaver is used in combination with two stiffer ones, the difference will be noticeable.

The basket should be strong. **Strength** lies in the right combination of spoke sizes, the distance between the spokes, and the size of the weavers. This subject is discussed more fully in Chapter 11, but some aspects of strength warrant attention here.

To maintain the overall strength of the basket, the spokes must not spread too far apart. The farther apart the spokes, the weaker the basket. If the basket gets wider in the middle by design, the spokes have to be brought back in at the top to maintain its strength. If a basket seems weak or wobbly, three-rod arrows (3.40–3.44) worked in a larger reed size or bands of three-rod waling (3.37–3.39) can be used to add stability.

Double side spokes (used in baskets 5 and 12) give strength without bulk, especially on larger baskets. After the upsett, a second spoke, called a *supporter,* is added alongside and to the right of each original spoke. The original spoke and its supporter are worked as one throughout the weaving of the sides. When the top of the basket is reached, these reinforcing spokes can be worked into the border (6.1), or cut off at the top before a single-spoke border is made (see basket 5).

The border is your final chance to add stability to the basket. Braided borders are strongest, plain rod borders and four-row rolled borders are next, and trac borders are least substantial.

Once the border has been worked, the basket can still be subtly shaped. Although the basic form has been set as you have worked, you can soak the basket well and gently refine its balance.

After the basket has been completed, you may want to **finish** it by getting rid of the "hairs" which have worked loose from the reed. There are two ways to do this: you can cut off the hairs with small, pointed cuticle or embroidery scissors, or you can carefully singe them off. Don't pull hairs off reed that has been dyed because it will take the color layer off and leave a white stripe.

Singeing is not a procedure for the weak-hearted (9.2). Although the work takes place on a wet basket, the best sources of flame are a gas stove, or a butane lighter with a long snout (the kind used for lighting barbecues and pilot lights). Matches and candles do the job, but they give off carbon which smudges the basket.

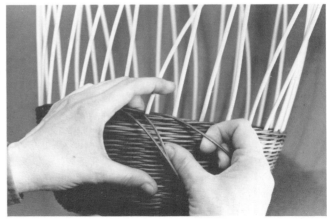

9.1 Shaping the basket by pushing on the spokes above the weaving

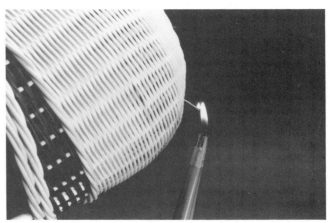

9.2 Singeing the hairs off the basket with a butane lighter

Before you begin to singe the hairs, *wet the basket thoroughly. And keep it wet.* Pass the wet basket quickly back and forth across the flame, turning it to singe all surfaces. Small hairs will spark briefly. Longer, larger hairs should be cut off, because burning them can also burn the surrounding area.

Finishes are unnecessary on rattan. I prefer to leave my baskets without color unfinished. Natural reed is very porous and absorbs dirt readily, but can be washed clean in warm water. Baskets with color can be given a polyurethane finish; I like the satin variety. This coating firms up the basket, brings out the colors and keeps them from fading, and provides some dust-resistance.

THE BASKET PATTERNS

The techniques required for each basket are listed at the beginning of the individual instructions, after a short paragraph which tells you what to expect to learn from that pattern. References to the appropriate illustrations in earlier chapters are included. You may want to mark the relevant pages with Post-It® notes so you can flip back and forth easily as you work. In the directions for each basket, each change of technique is indicated in *italics,* to make the sequence of movements easier to follow. The amount to work in each technique is listed either as a number of rows or as a measurement in inches, depending upon which is easiest to keep track of.

The use of colored reed is introduced in basket 2. All of the color work in this chapter is optional. You can work the baskets in all-natural colors, and they'll be pleasing because of the textural changes. Or you can purchase or dye reed, and follow the suggested color changes. Information on dyeing is found in Chapter 8. For baskets 9 through 24, it is assumed that you are familiar with the following processes, and these references are not repeated with each of those baskets:

Split-spoke base
    round (4.21–4.32)
    oval (4.33–4.44)
Bi-spoking (5.1–5.5)
Pinching spokes for upsett (5.9)
Three-rod arrow (3.42–3.44)
Four-rod coil (3.47–3.48)
Three-rod waling (3.37–3.39)
Step-up (3.40, 3.48, 5.6–5.8)
Pinching spokes for border (6.9)

The **quantities of reed** listed under "Materials" in each pattern are intended to serve as guidelines, rather than absolutes. It's difficult to tell you precisely how much of each material you will need, because even if you follow the pattern exactly your basket will be a unique creation. Weights are indicated so that you can roughly determine how many baskets you can make out of a pound of a certain size of reed, or can evaluate whether you have enough on hand to start a project. In some cases, you'll need to have a larger quantity of reed available than you will use in the basket in order to have enough long pieces to make the spokes.

If you would like to estimate on the basis of how many feet of a given size you need, you can figure equivalents on the following basis:

    #2 reed—approximately 75 feet/ounce
    #3 reed—approximately 50 feet/ounce
    #4 reed—approximately 30 feet/ounce
    #4½ reed—approximately 22 feet/ounce
    #5 reed—approximately 20 feet/ounce
    #6 reed—approximately 10 feet/ounce
    #8 reed—approximately 7 feet/ounce
    #10 reed—approximately 3-5 feet/ounce
    #12 reed—approximately 2 feet/ounce

1 Small Interwoven Base Basket

9.3 Small interwoven base baskets

This charming little basket is easy to complete in a short time. It is woven entirely with #2 reed (an exception to my usual practice of using heavier spokes), and gives you a feel for working with the reed as well as practice in shaping. By using two weaving techniques—randing and slewing—it's possible to have a decorative band on the sides of the basket where the texture changes. As illustration 9.3 shows, this can be emphasized through the optional use of colored weavers.

The base and sides are woven continuously without changing the direction of the weaving, and the spokes are simply pushed in the new direction when it's time to start the sides. This is not the construction method used in later baskets, but is good for an introduction and also appears in basket number 8. As a result, the ends of the base weavers will be on the inside of the basket. Use the overlapping method to join new weavers.

A simple trac border completes the basket.

After finishing this basket, you can continue to work through the initial six baskets, building your skills, or you can take a detour to basket 8, which builds on the techniques required for basket 1 but works them on a larger scale in vine rattan. It will also serve as an introduction to pairing weave and the pairing arrow.

TECHNIQUES
  Interwoven base (4.1–4.5)
  Randing (3.2, 3.5)
  Slewing (3.6)
  Overlapped join (3.68)
  Basic trac border (6.1–6.3)
DIMENSIONS
  Diameter of base: 4″
  Height: 3″ to 3½″

MATERIALS
  #2 reed (1.75 mm): 1¼ ounces
PREPARATION
From #2 reed, cut:
  16 spokes, each 26″ long
  2 spokes, each 13″ long

Base: Weave throughout with #2 reed. Work the *interwoven base,* adding an extra set of spokes to make an uneven number. *Rand* to a diameter of 4″.

Preparing to weave the sides: Holding the underside toward you, push the spokes away from you as you begin to shape the sides.

Sides: Continue *randing* in the same direction. Work to a height of 1″. Mark one spoke with a twist-tie; it can be any spoke. Add a second weaver on top of the first at the marked spoke and work in *slewing* for six rows. Cut off the shorter weaver behind the marked spoke and change to *randing* for ⅜″.

Border: Work the *basic trac border.* Trim off excess spoke ends.

Variations:

1. Dye the spokes another color (see Chapter 8) and use natural weavers, or leave the spokes natural and use dyed weavers (9.3).

2. Use the *double-cross base* (4.8–4.9), separating the groups of spokes into threes (9.4, right; 4.22). Work *pairing weave* (3.27) for the main part and use ¼″ flat reed for the accent. There is an even number of spokes, so each row of flat *randing* is woven separately, overlapping the ends (9.5).

3. Use the *double-cross base* (4.8–4.9), with groups of four spokes instead of six (4.23; 9.4, left). With *pairing weave*, separate the groups of four into pairs. For vertical stripes, work pairing weave with two different colors over an even number of spokes.

4. Use two different colors in the band of *slewing* in the center (9.3, right).

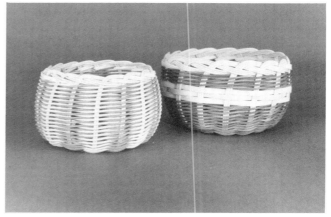

9.4 Double-cross base basket woven with pairing weave over double spokes (left) and triple spokes (right)

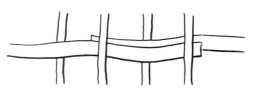

9.5 Overlapping ends with flat reed

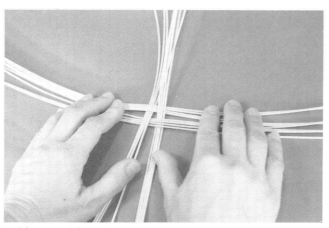

1 After marking the centers of the spokes, set up the base by crossing and interweaving four groups of four spokes each (p. 35).

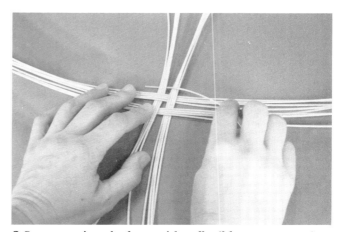

2 Start weaving the base with a flexible weaver, working in a clockwise direction. Go under the first group and over the second.

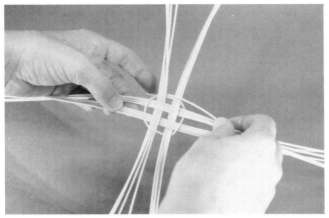

3 At the end of the first round, the weaver will hold the spokes together. Continue this over-and-under pattern (randing) for four identical rows (p. 35).

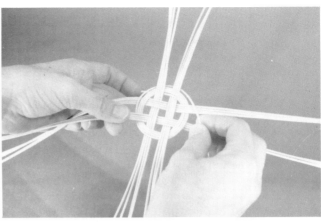

4 To weave the next four rows, you need to alternate the pattern. To make the transition, bring the weaver under both of the first groups.

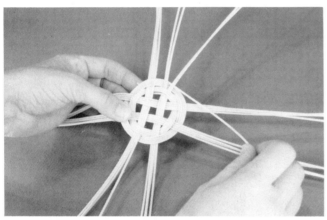

5 After eight rows, split each group of four into pairs, starting with the second group (p. 35). At the same time, add an extra pair of spokes as shown in photo 6.

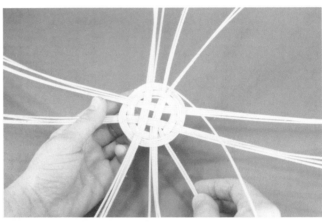

6 Thread the extra pair of spokes under the second set of rows and over the first, working it into the base. Continue to rand; the rows will now alternate without being adjusted as you did before (pp. 35–36).

7 The first row woven on pairs has been completed. Keep the rows of weaving close together as you continue to work. It may be easiest to support the base on a table.

8 Continue to rand, using your index finger to guide the weaver.

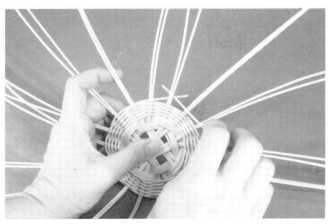

9 When you need to add a new weaver, the overlapped join works well with transparent weaves, like randing. End the old weaver behind a spoke, then add the new weaver behind the same spoke (p. 30). Work another row or two and then trim the join.

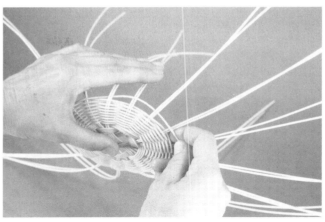

10 When the base reaches a diameter of 4″, begin to shape the sides by pushing the spokes away from you as you weave. Shape the spokes and rand until the sides measure 1″.

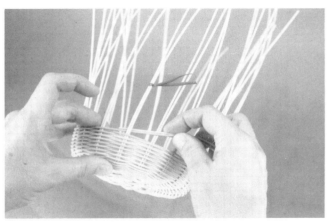

11 Add a second weaver on top of the existing one. Work six rows of slewing (p. 17). Then cut off the second weaver and continue in randing for ⅜″.

12 Start the trac border by weaving a pair of spokes behind, in front, and in (pp. 53–54). Repeat with the other pairs; two have been worked here.

13 Bring the next-to-last pair behind the last standing pair, in front of the first loop, and in.

14 Bring the last pair under the first loop and to the outside.

15 Then bring it in front of the next pair, and in.

16 Trim the spokes on the inside.

2   Plant Basket

9.6 Plant basket

Heavier reed is used for the spokes in this basket. The over-laid base is introduced, and this time the spokes are pinched to make the transition from base to sides. Again there are bands of contrasting textures on the sides; here they are produced by three-rod waling and pairing weave. A sturdy rolled border provides the finish.

TECHNIQUES
    Over-laid base (4.18–4.20)
    Japanese weave (3.23)
    Pairing weave (3.26)
    Three-rod waling (3.37–3.39)
    Overlapped join (3.68)
    Hidden join (3.69–3.71)
    Three-row rolled border (variation 2, 6.10–6.21)
DIMENSIONS
    Diameter of base: 4⅜″
    Height: 4″
    Top diameter: 6¼″

MATERIALS
    #4 reed (2.75 mm): 1 ounce
    #2 reed (1.75 mm): 1¼ ounces
Optional color: Of the above quantities, the following amounts may be dyed, or purchased in colored form.
    #2 reed: 6 to 10 strands
PREPARATION
From #4 reed, cut:
    10 spokes, each 30″ long

Base: Mark the centers of the spokes and arrange the slath. With weavers of natural #2 reed, work the five-over-five *over-laid base*. Work *Japanese weave* to a diameter of 4¼″.

Preparing to weave the sides: Turn the base over and pinch the spokes (5.9).

Upsett: With dyed #2 reed, weave six rows in *three-rod waling*.

Sides: With natural #2 reed, work 2¼″ in *pairing weave*. With dyed #2 reed, work five rows in *three-rod waling*.

Border: Soak and pinch the spokes for the border (6.9). Work a *three-row rolled border* (variation 2).
    Row 1: *Behind one and out.*
    Row 2: *In front of two and in.*
    Row 3: *Over two and down.*
Trim off the excess spoke ends.

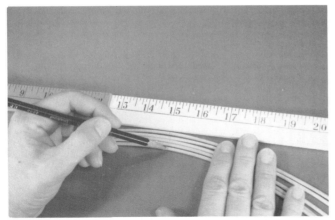

1 Cut ten 30″ spokes, arrange them in two groups of five, and mark the centers of the groups with a pencil (p. 40).

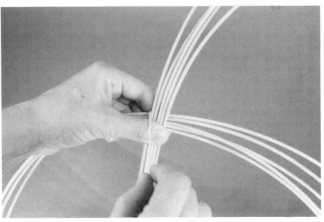

2 Lay the horizontal group of weavers underneath the vertical group, and place a long, flexible weaver in the upper left corner, behind the horizontal group. Bring it over the top group of spokes, under the bottom group, and so forth around.

3 Work four rows, keeping the weaving tight without letting the spokes bunch up. Begin Japanese weave to open up the spokes by bringing the weaver over two spokes in the first group.

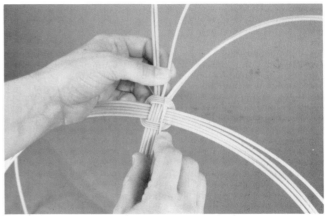

4 Then bring it under one spoke. Continue the over two, under one pattern (pp. 20, 40).

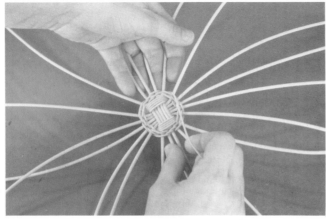

5 To keep the rows close together, pull the weaver down across the center after each stroke, either back or front. This photo shows the first few rows, and the position of the left hand on top.

6 For a hidden join, end the old weaver to the right of the joining spoke, leaving about ¼″ of weaver. The weaver can end either behind or in front of the spoke (p. 30).

7 Pinch the old weaver to the left of the joining spoke and run it down into the weaving on the left side of the joining spoke.

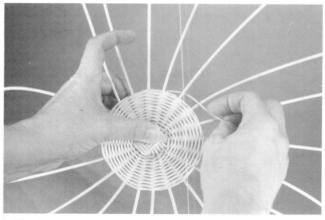

8 Pinch a new weaver ⅜″ from its end. Insert the bent part on the right edge of the spoke just to the left of the joining spoke. Bring the new weaver behind the joining spoke, following the pattern which the old weaver had established.

9 When the base measures 4¼″, turn it over and pinch the spokes (p. 51). Gently bend the spokes up with your fingers. Trim the natural weaver, because you will continue with dyed weavers.

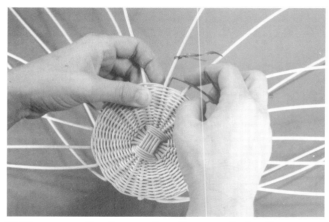

10 To prepare for three-rod waling, mark the first spoke (pp. 23–24). Bend the end of a dyed weaver and insert it on the right side of the first spoke.

11 Bend the ends of two more dyed weavers, and insert them to the right of the next two spokes.

12 Work six rows of three-rod waling with dyed reed (pp. 23–24).

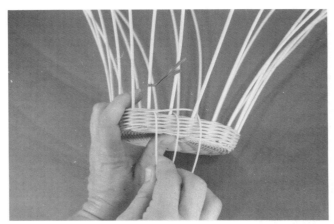

13 When you have completed the six rows, the weavers will come from behind the first three spokes again.

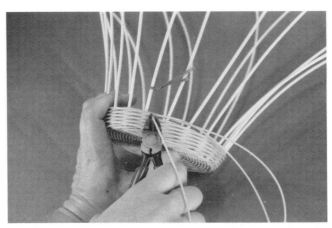

14 If you would like to continue with the colored reed, trim only the weaver which is farthest to the left (as shown). If you are changing to natural reed, secure the ends of the dyed weavers (photo 7) and add two natural weavers.

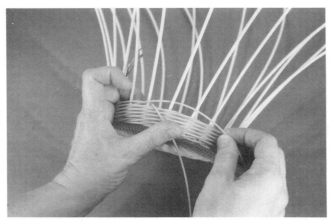

15 Work 2¼″ of pairing weave (p. 21).

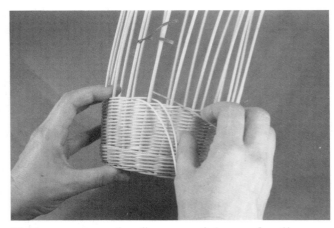

16 Next come another five rows of three-rod waling. The basket shown here has one dyed weaver added to the two natural weavers to produce a spiral design; you could also use three dyed weavers for a solid band.

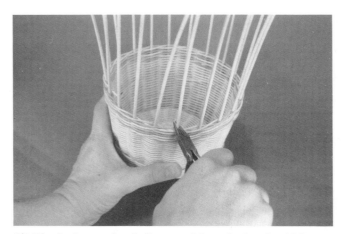

17 Pinch the spokes before working the border (6.9).

18 Bend each spoke slowly and carefully to the right, taking it behind the next spoke and then out. Place a marker to the right of the first spoke.

19 To end the first row, lift up the first loop and bring the last standing spoke through it from the inside to the outside in the marked space. (pp. 55–56).

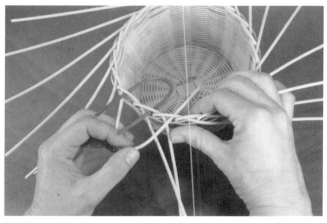

20 Place a hairpin marker in the spaces to the right of any two consecutive spokes. Start the second row by bringing the first spoke in front of two spokes and in (pp. 55–56). Continue until there are two unworked spokes left.

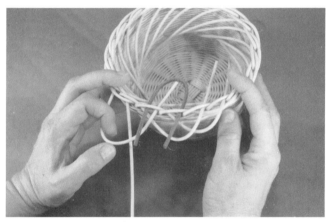

21 To end, pull the first two spokes out a couple of inches. Then hold them down and insert the next-to-last spoke into the space indicated by the first half of the hairpin marker.

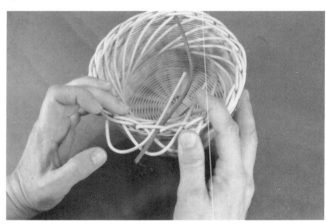

22 Insert the last spoke in the space indicated by the second half of the hairpin marker.

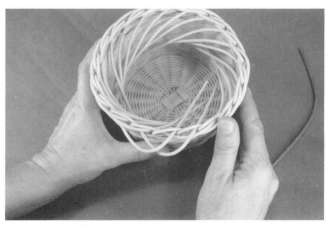

23 Once the final two spokes of row 2 are in place, remove the hairpin marker.

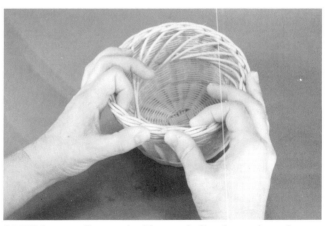

24 With your fingers inside, push firmly against the spokes with your thumbs to tighten the border.

25 To begin row 3, place a hairpin marker to the right of any two spokes (p. 57). Pick up these two spokes and the next spoke to the right; hold all three so they point toward the center of the basket.

26 Bring the first spoke over the second and third, then down under the fourth spoke. Lay it in so it just touches the underside of the fourth spoke.

27 To keep the rows close together, bring the spokes above the level of the border. Continue working over two spokes and down.

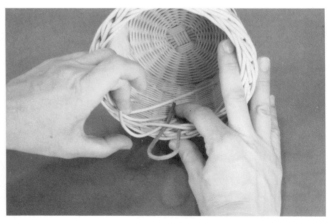

28 When two spokes remain, put the next-to-last spoke in the space of the first marker.

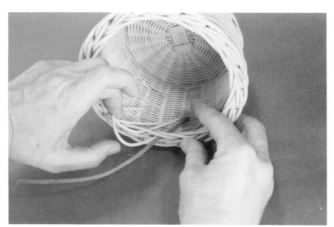

29 Put the last spoke in the space of the second marker.

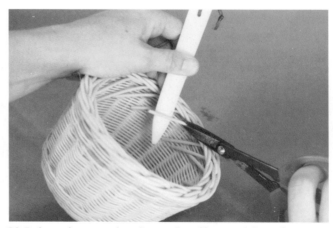

30 It is easiest to trim the spokes if you pick each one up with an awl. Make a slant cut, so that half an inch of each spoke is visible under the third row.

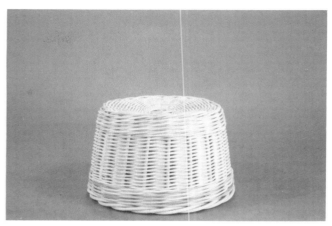

31 Press on the bottom with your thumbs to shape it; if it's stubborn, soak it again.

32 This is the correct shaping of the bottom.

3 Small Child's Basket

A small basket with a two-piece handle, just right for a child, can be made by working minor variations on the plant basket pattern. Again, the basket starts with an over-laid base and finishes with a rolled border. The weaves on the sides are randing (learned in basket 1) and three-rod waling (familiar from basket 2). The unique and easy handle, made from two lengths of reed lightly twisted together and pegged in place, is charming and strong.

9.7 Small child's basket

TECHNIQUES
   Over-laid base (4.18–4.20)
   Randing (3.2)
   Three-rod waling (3.37–3.39)
   Overlapped join (3.68)
   Three-row rolled border (variation 2, 6.10–6.21)
   Simple twisted handle (described here)
   Pegging handle core (7.10–7.12)
DIMENSIONS
   Base: 4⅜″
   Height of basket: 2¾″
   Height with handle: 7½″
   Top diameter: 5½″

MATERIALS
   #4 reed (2.75 mm) for spokes: 1 ounce
   #2 reed (1.75 mm) for weavers: 1 ounce
   ¼″ flat reed for weavers: 7½ feet
   #6 reed (4.50 mm) for handles: 3 feet
Optional color: Of the above quantities, the following amounts may be dyed, or purchased in colored form.
   ¼″ flat reed (all)
PREPARATION
From #4 reed, cut:
   10 spokes, each 23″ long
From #6 reed, cut:
   2 handles, each 16½″ long

Base: Mark the centers of the spokes. With weavers of #2 reed, work the five-over-five *over-laid base,* the same as for the plant basket.

Preparing to weave the sides: Turn the base over and pinch the spokes (5.9).

Upsett: With #2 reed, work six rows in *three-rod waling.*

Sides: With dyed ¼″ flat reed, work five rows in *randing.* Weave each row separately, and overlap and cut the ends (9.5).

With #2 reed, weave five rows in *three-rod waling.*

Border: Soak and pinch the spokes (6.9). Work the same *three-row rolled border* as for the plant basket.

Handle: Taper the ends of the two handles as shown in 7.6. Insert one end of the first handle into the basket alongside a spoke, skip one spoke, and insert one end of the second handle alongside the next spoke. Twist the two handles together four times, then insert the other end of each handle alongside the corresponding spoke on the other side. *Peg the handles* as shown in 7.10–7.12.

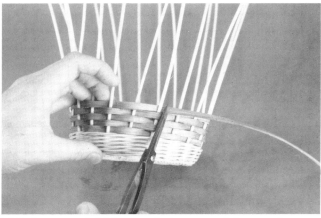

1 Work an overlaid base and six rows of three-rod waling, as on basket 2. Using dyed flat reed, work five rows in randing. Work each row separately and overlap the ends; trim as shown above.

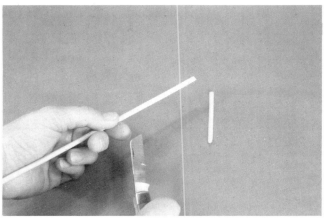

2 Continue with three-rod waling and a three-row rolled border, as on basket 2. Then prepare the ends of the handles by tapering them (p. 70).

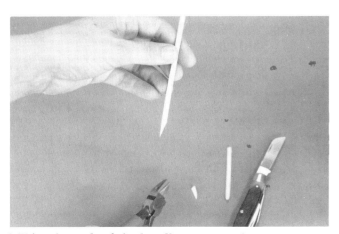

3 Trim the ends of the handles at an angle.

4 For each end of the handles, use an awl to open up a space alongside a spoke.

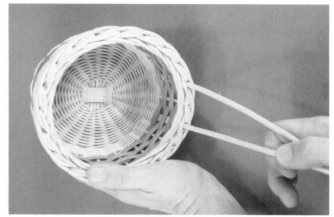

5 Insert one end of each handle into two spaces, with one spoke in between.

6 Twist the handles together three times.

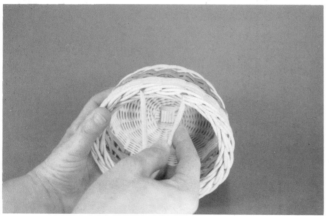

7 Insert the other end of each handle alongside the corresponding spoke on the other side.

8 Prepare to peg the handle ends by running an awl into the core, beneath the border, at an oblique angle (p. 72).

9 Run a small tapered piece of reed into the hole so it extends a short distance into the basket.

10 Trim the peg, both inside and outside. Repeat with the other three handle ends.

4   Fruit Basket

9.8 Fruit basket

This graceful basket introduces the separate base. The split-spoke base is one of my favorites, and you'll see it a lot in later designs. If you feel tentative about splitting the reed, you can substitute the over-laid base until you are ready to accept the worthwhile challenge of this technique.

Bi-spoking, however, is an important skill to master immediately. It plays an important role in many round basket designs, and is essential to the making of oval baskets.

The previous designs have been relatively straight-sided. This basket has a flared shape. While you are learning to control the shape, the bands of texture will feel familiar—they're formed with three-rod waling and Japanese weave. And when you reach the top, the three-row rolled border is the same one you used on baskets 2 and 3.

TECHNIQUES
    Split-spoke base (4.21–4.32)
    Bi-spoking (5.1–5.3)
    Working a flared shape
    Three-rod waling (3.37–3.39)
    Japanese weave (3.23)
    Three-row rolled border (variation 2, 6.10–6.21)
DIMENSIONS
    Diameter of base: 6½″
    Height: 5″
    Top diameter: 11″

MATERIALS
    #5 reed (3.50 mm) for spokes: 4 ounces
    #2 reed (1.75 mm) for weavers: 4 ounces
    ¼″ flat reed for weavers: 1 ounce
Optional color: Of the above quantities, the following amounts may be dyed, or purchased in colored form.
    ¼″ flat reed (all)
PREPARATION
From #5 reed, cut:
    8 base spokes, each 7½″ long
    32 side spokes, each 18″ long

Base: With #2 reed, work the four-through-four *split-spoke base* to a diameter of 6½″.

Preparing to weave the sides: *Bi-spoke* with 32 side spokes, placing one spoke on each side of every base spoke. You can trim the base spokes as you bi-spoke, or after bi-spoking has been completed. Pinch the spokes (5.9).

Upsett: With #2 reed, work 2″ in *three-rod waling.*

Sides: With dyed ¼″ flat reed, work six rows in *Japanese weave.* Taper the beginning end of the flat reed for about 5″. Mark any spoke as spoke 1 with a twist-tie. Begin the Japanese weave at spoke 1. Weave six rows. Taper the final end of the flat reed and finish behind spoke 4. With #2 reed, work 1½″ in *three-rod waling*.

Border: Soak and pinch the spokes for the border. Work the *three-row rolled border* (variation 2).

Row 1: *Behind one and out.*
Row 2: *In front of two and in.*
Row 3: *Over two and down.*

Trim off excess spoke ends.

1 For a split-spoke base (pp. 40–43), mark the centers of the spokes. Then lay four of the spokes on a cutting board and run an awl through the center of each spoke. Work slowly to protect your hands.

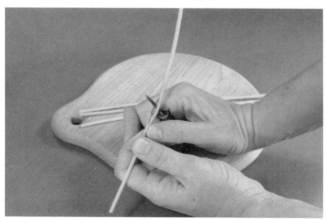

2 Carefully enlarge the hole in each spoke so that the other four spokes can be inserted.

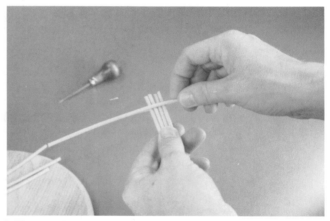

3 Thread the split spokes onto the other four spokes, to form a cross. Make sure the groups of spokes are centered and at right angles to each other.

4 Pinch and fold a flexible weaver 20″ from one end. Then place the fold around the set of spokes with the holes, keeping its short end to the back.

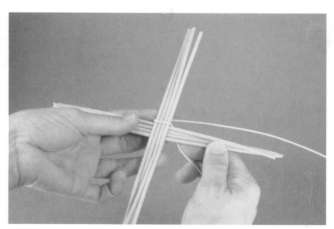

5 Work reverse pairing to tie in the slath (pp. 41–42). Start by taking the top section of the weaver over the split spokes and under the next group.

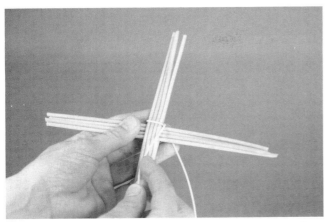

6 Then take the bottom section of the weaver over the second group.

7 After four rows of reverse pairing, separate the spokes with Japanese weave, working over two and under one (p. 42).

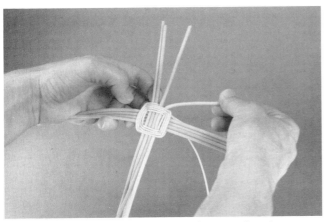

8 Spread the spokes apart firmly; be sure they have been well soaked.

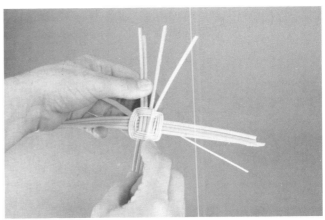

9 To keep the rows close together, pull the weaver down across the slath.

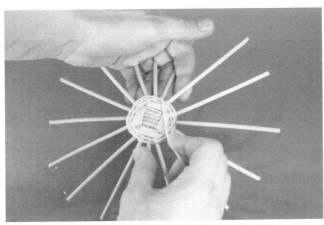

10 Keep your left hand on top, to shape the dome on the base (p. 38).

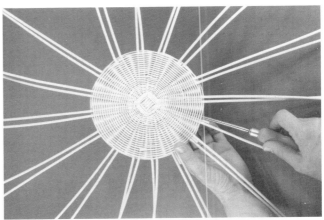

11 When the base measures 6½″ in diameter, use an awl to open spaces on both sides of each spoke. Insert the side spokes, running each one in as far as possible.

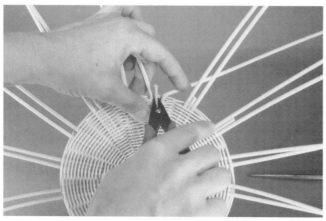

12 Trim the base spokes. Pinch the side spokes. Then work 2″ in three-rod waling, shaping the sides as shown in the photograph on p. 107.

13 Mark any spoke as spoke 1 with a twist tie. Taper the beginning end of a piece of dyed flat reed for about 5″. Starting at spoke 1, work six rows in Japanese weave (over two, under one), continuing to shape the sides.

14 Taper the final end of the flat reed and end behind spoke 4. Work 1½″ of three-rod waling, maintaining the flare of the sides.

15 Pinch the spokes for the border, then bend each pinched spoke to the right, behind one and out.

16 This is the end of row 1 of the rolled border.

17 This is the end of row 2, in front of two and in. Work a third row of over two and down, then trim the spokes.

5 Basket with Japanese Handle

9.9 Basket with Japanese handle

This basket and the sewing basket (pattern 12) use doubled side spokes. For the size of these baskets, a basketmaker would normally choose to use 3.50mm #5 reed for the spokes. However, with doubled spokes we can use lighter reed.

Chasing weave makes its first appearance here, along with the familiar randing and three-rod waling. You'll practice working a step-up on the rows of three-rod waling on either side of the band of flat randing. The three-row rolled border should come easily now, and you can add a Japanese handle to your repertoire.

TECHNIQUES
Split-spoke base (4.21–4.32)
Bi-spoking (5.1–5.3)
Doubled side spokes (page 90)
Chasing weave (3.9)
Three-rod waling (3.37–3.39)
Randing (3.2)
Step-up (3.40)
Three-row rolled border (variation 2, 6.10–6.21)
Japanese handle (7.5, 7.8, 7.13–7.16)

DIMENSIONS
Diameter of base: 7″
Height of basket: 7½″
Height with handle: 14″
Top diameter: 11″

MATERIALS
#4½ reed (3.25 mm) for spokes: 4 ounces
#2 reed (1.75 mm) for weavers: 4 ounces
#3 reed (2.25 mm) for weavers: six 40″ strands
¼″ flat reed for weavers: 12 feet
#10 reed (8.00 mm) for handle: 26″
Optional color: Of the above quantities, the following amounts may be dyed, or purchased in colored form.
¼″ flat reed (all): *orchid*
#2 reed: 2 long strands (for handle) *orchid*
#3 reed: 6 strands *gray*

PREPARATION
From #5 reed, cut:
8 base spokes, each 8″ long
32 side spokes, each 18″ long
32 supporters, each 7″ long

Base: With weavers of #2 reed, work the four-through-four *split-spoke base* to a diameter of 7″. *Bi-spoke* with the 32 side spokes.

Preparing to weave the sides: Turn the base over and pinch the spokes (5.9).

Upsett: With #2 reed, work seven rows in *three-rod waling*. Taper one end of each 7″ supporter at a sharp angle. Run a supporter down into the waling to the right of each spoke until it reaches the edge of the base.

Sides: With #2 reed, work 2¾″ in *chasing weave*. With dyed #3 reed, work two rows in *three-rod waling;* at the end of each row, work a *step-up*. With dyed ¼″ flat reed, work four rows in *randing*. With dyed #3 reed, weave two rows in *three-rod waling*, with a *step-up* at the end of each row. With #2 reed, work ¾″ in *chasing weave*. Instead of cutting off the weavers at the end of this chasing weave section, add a third #2 reed weaver behind the next spoke to the right and begin a section of seven rows in *three-rod waling*.

Border: Soak and pinch the spokes for the border (6.9). Work the *three-row rolled border* (variation 2).
  Row 1: *Behind one and out.*
  Row 2: *In front of two and in.*
  Row 3: *Over two and down.*

Handle: Taper the ends of the handle as in 7.5 and 7.8. Run one end into the basket about 5½″. Insert the other end directly across the basket, sixteen spokes away from the first end. The exposed handle measures 18″. Using two dyed #2 weavers, wrap the Japanese handle as shown in 7.13–7.16.

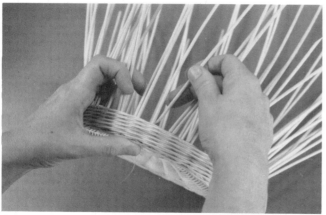

1 Work the base, bi-spoke, pinch the side spokes, and work seven rows of three-rod waling as described above. Taper the supporters, and insert one down into the waling to the right of each spoke until it reaches the edge of the base.

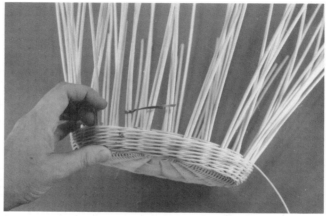

2 Mark a beginning spoke and work in chasing weave (p. 18). This photo shows the first of two weavers in place.

3 Add the second weaver.

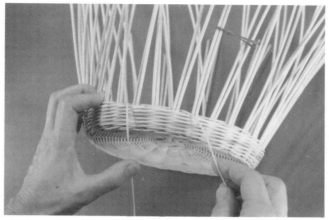

4 When the second weaver is two spokes behind the first weaver, pick up the first weaver and work the next round. Continue until 2¾″ have been worked.

5 Work two rows of three-rod waling, with a step-up at the end of each (pp. 23–24). This is the end of the first row before the step-up.

6 This is the first step of the step-up (see illustration 3.40, p. 24).

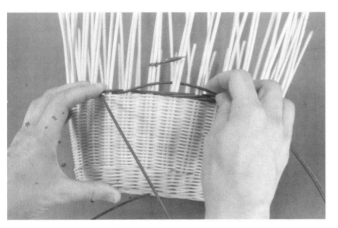

7 This is the second step.

8 This is the third step.

9 This is the end of the second row before the step-up.

10 The second step-up has been completed.

11 Trim all three weavers. Work four rows in randing with flat reed, then, with round reed, two more rows of three-rod waling with a step-up at the end of each row. Work ¾″ in chasing weave, then seven rows in three-rod waling.

12 Soak and pinch the spokes for the border. Cut off the supporters flush with the top of the three-rod wale. Work the border.

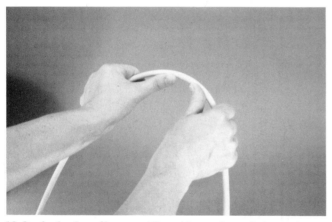

13 Soak the handle core. Taper its ends and shape it.

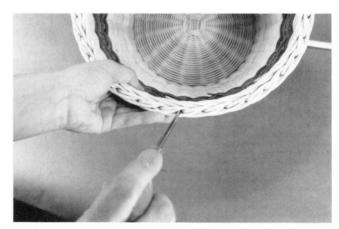

14 With an awl, open spaces alongside spokes for the handle ends. Insert the handle.

15 The border spokes here have been pushed out by the handle.

16 If the spokes on your basket are out of line, use your thumbs to push them back in.

17 Open up a space under the border.

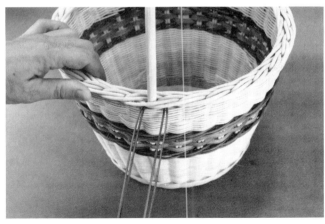

18 Insert the doubled reed for wrapping the handle in the space you just opened (pp. 73–74).

19 Bring the right weaver over the handle to the left and wrap it to the other side. Space the wrappings evenly.

20 End the weaver on the other side of the basket by weaving it in and out below the border.

21 Bring the left weaver over the handle to the right. Cross it over the other weaver. Wrap it to the other side of the basket, crossing the first weaver on each wrap. End the weaver on the other side of the basket, as before.

6 Oval Basket with Handle

9.10 Oval basket with handle

This is a favorite basket among my students. It introduces the oval base and the roped handle, as well as a series of techniques frequently employed to make a smooth transition from base to sides. These include the three-rod arrow (to separate the spokes evenly) and the locked four-rod coil (which gives strength and stability to the base).

The sides are a combination of chasing weave, three-rod arrow, and three-rod waling,

which also secures the spokes before the border is worked. The basic four-row rolled border should be easy after so much experience with the three-row version.

If you'd like to make another oval basket right away, look at basket 9, which employs the same techniques as this basket (there is a slight variation on the handle wrapping) and adds decorative beads.

TECHNIQUES
  Basic oval base (4.33–4.38)
  Bi-spoking (5.1–5.4)
  Three-rod arrow (3.38–3.44)
  Four-rod coil (3.47–3.48)
  Three-rod waling (3.37–3.39)
  Chasing weave (3.9)
  Four-row rolled border (basic, 6.8–6.22)
  Roped handle (7.18–7.22, 7.29)
  Binding (7.23)
DIMENSIONS
  Diameter of base: 9¾″ by 7½″
  Height of basket: 5¾″
  Height with handle: 12″
  Top dimensions: 14″ by 11″

MATERIALS
  #5 reed (3.50 mm) for spokes: 4 ounces
  #2 reed (1.75 mm) for base weavers: 1 ounce
  #3 reed (2.25 mm) for weavers: 5 ounces
  #4 reed (2.75 mm) for four-rod coil and three-rod arrow on side: 1½ ounce
  #10 reed (8.00 mm) for handle: 28″
Optional color: Of the above quantities, the following amounts may be dyed, or purchased in colored form.
  #4 reed: 3 strands, each 2½ yards long
PREPARATION
From #5 reed, cut:
  4 base spokes, each 10″ long
  7 base spokes, each 7″ long
  34 side spokes, each 21″ long

Base: With #2 reed, work the *basic oval base* to a measurement of 8¾″ by 6½″.

Preparing to weave the sides: *Bi-spoke* with 34 side spokes, as shown in 5.4. With #3 reed, work a *three-rod arrow* to separate the side spokes. Work the arrow with the inside of the base facing upward. Turn the base over and pinch the spokes (5.9).

Upsett: With natural #4 reed, work a locked *four-rod coil*. With #3 reed, work six rows in *three-rod waling*.

Sides: With #3 reed, weave 1½″ in *chasing weave*. With dyed #4 reed, work a *three-rod arrow*. With #3 reed, work 1¼″ in *chasing weave*. With #3 reed, weave six rows in *three-rod waling*.

Border: Soak and pinch the spokes for the border (6.9). Work the basic *four-row rolled border*.
Row 1: *Behind one and out.*
Row 2: *In front of two and in.*
Row 3: *Over two and down.*
Row 4: *Over two and down.*

Handle: Taper the ends of the handle as shown in 7.5 and 7.8. To find the places to insert the handle, locate the middle short spoke on the base and follow it up the sides. Run the handle ends down into the basket as close to the base as possible. *Rope the handle* with #3 reed, then add *binding.*

1 Split the short spokes and thread the long spokes through them. Thread a weaver through the holes in the short spokes (pp. 43–44).

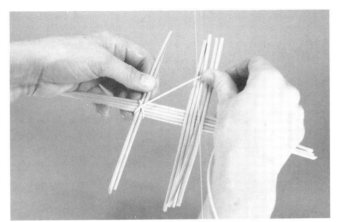

2 Wrap the first cross (p. 44), working over the two short spokes on the end.

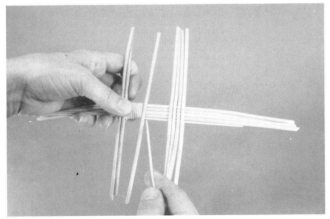

3 After eight wraps around the spine, slide the next short spoke into place. Continue until the last two spokes remain (p. 44).

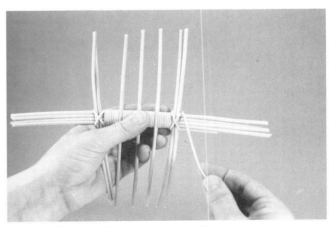

4 Wrap the second cross (pp. 44–45).

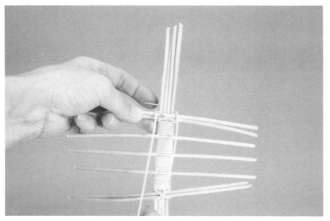

5 Add a second weaver behind the spine.

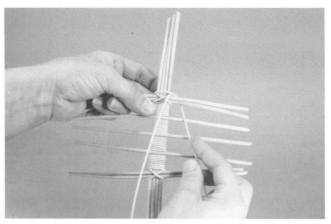

6 Secure the spokes with two rows of pairing weave. This is the start of the first row.

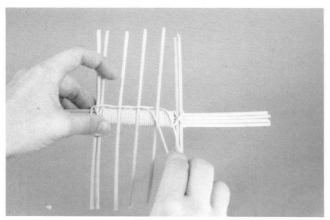

7 This is pairing weave in progress, working down the spine.

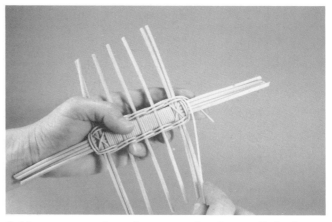

8 After two rows have been completed, cut off the bottom weaver. Begin to separate the spokes, working Japanese weave (over two and under one) with the top weaver (p. 45).

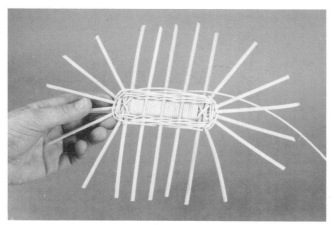

9 Several rows of Japanese weave have been worked. Dome the base as you weave (p. 38).

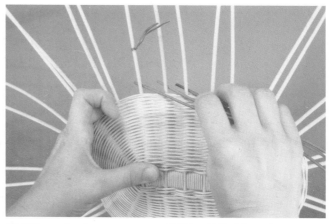

10 When the base measures 8¾″ by 6½″, bi-spoke (p. 49). Then mark the first spoke and start three weavers for a three-rod arrow, with the inside of the base facing up (p. 24). For clarity, the weavers for the three-rod arrow and coil are dark in these photographs.

11 This is the end of the first row of the arrow, before the step-up.

12 The first step of the step-up (see also illustration 3.40, p. 24).

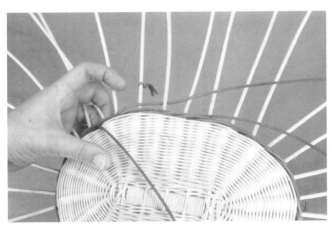

13 The second step of the step-up.

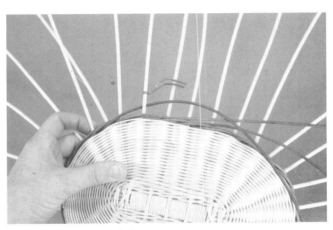

14 The third step of the step-up.

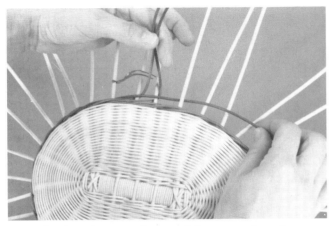

15 Beginning the second row of the arrow (see also illustration 3.43, p. 24).

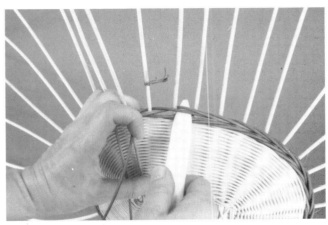

16 To end the arrow, open up a space with an awl (p. 25).

17 For the three steps of the ending, see also illustration 3.44, p. 25. This is the first step.

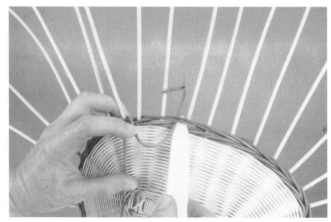

18 This is the second step of the ending.

19 This is the third step of the ending.

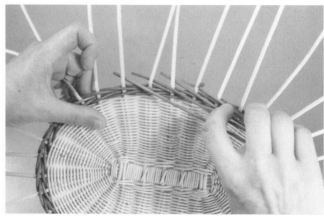

20 Turn the base over and pinch the spokes. Push the spokes away from you. Then add four weavers to work the four-rod coil (pp. 25–26).

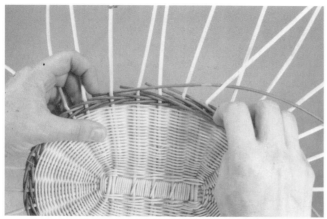

21 To start, the left weaver goes in front of three spokes, over the other three weavers, behind the fourth spoke, and out.

22 This is the end of the four-rod coil, ready for the step-up and lock.

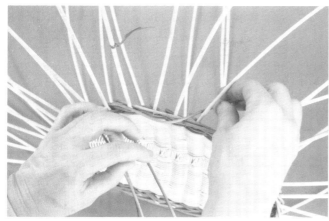

23 For the step-up, the first weaver goes in front of the first three spokes and behind the fourth.

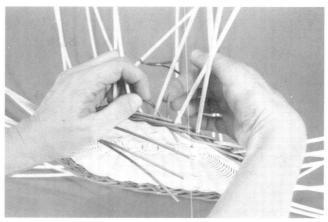

24 To lock the weave, pull the beginning end of the weaver, which is lying against the fourth spoke, away from the spoke and thread the working end of the same weaver through the space. It should lie under the coil and to the underside of the base.

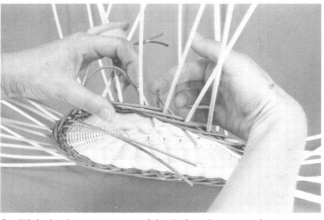

25 This is the step-up and lock for the second weaver.

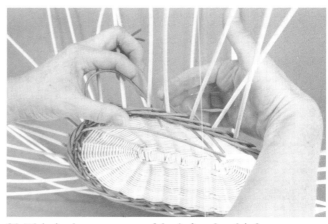

26 This is the step-up and lock for the third weaver.

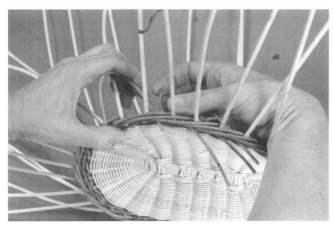

27 This is the step-up and lock for the fourth weaver.

28 Work six rows of three-rod waling, then 1½″ in chasing weave. With dyed reed, work a three-rod arrow (p. 24). The first row of the three-rod arrow is in progress.

29 This is the completed step-up at the end of the first row.

30 The second half of the arrow is worked in reverse waling (p. 24–25).

31 An awl is used to open the spaces for ending the three-rod arrow (pp. 24–25).

32 This is the first step of the ending.

33 This is the second step of the ending.

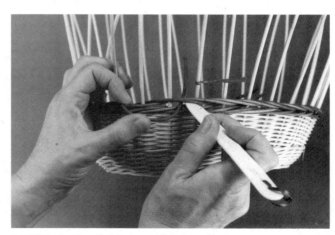

34 This is the third step of the ending.

35 The completed arrow looks like this. With a natural weaver, continue the sides by working 1¼″ in chasing weave and six rows in three-rod waling. Pinch the spokes and work the border.

36 Taper, shape, and insert the handle core. Open a space below the border to insert the weaver for the handle, holding the awl at a steep angle because of the four-row border. To secure the weaver's end, bring it out and over one spoke to the left and in (p. 75).

37 Bring the weaver from the inside and over the top of the handle.

38 The fourth wrap is on the center top of the handle (pp. 74–76).

39 On the other side of the basket, the weaver goes from the outside to the inside.

40 Then bring it from the inside of the basket out on top of the handle.

41 When you need to start a new weaver, leave the end of the old weaver on the inside (pp. 77–78).

42 Add a new weaver by bringing its end to the outside, then over one spoke to the left and in.

43 Secure and hide the ends by weaving them into the basket to the right of the handle. First bring them to the outside.

44 Then guide them to the inside.

45 For the binding (p. 76), run a new weaver down along the right side of the handle.

46 Bring it behind the handle to the left. Then wrap it seven times around the handle.

47 To secure the final end of the binding weaver, place the handle on a table edge and make a hole with an awl (pp. 76–77).

48 Run the end of the weaver through the handle, pull it snug, and then trim it.

7 Basket with Decorative Band and Side Handles

9.11 Basket with decorative band and side handles

All of the major techniques have been introduced, and the remaining baskets in this chapter will add minor variations and refinements to your technique. Notable on this basket are side roped handles (building on the overhead version in basket 6) and a three-rod plain border with two rows of follow-on trac.

TECHNIQUES
    Split-spoke base (4.21–4.32)
    Three-rod arrow (3.42–3.44)
    Four-rod coil (3.47–3.48)
    Three-rod waling (3.37–3.39)
    Chasing weave (3.9)
    Step-up (3.40)
    Three-rod plain border (6.39–6.45)
        with follow-on trac #2 (6.49–6.50)
        and an extra row (6.19)
    Roped side handles (7.6, 7.27–7.28, 7.30)
DIMENSIONS
    Diameter of base: 8″
    Height of basket: 6½″
    Height with handles: 8½″
    Top diameter: 12″

MATERIALS
    #5 reed (3.50 mm) for spokes: 4½ ounces
    #2 reed (1.75 mm) for base weavers: 1 ounce
    #3 reed (2.25 mm) for weavers: 3 ounces
    #4 reed (2.75 mm) for four-rod coil: ½ ounce
    #8 reed (6.00 mm) for handles: 3 feet
Optional color: Of the above quantities, the following amounts may be dyed, or purchased in colored form.
    #3 reed: 6 strands, each 4 feet long, *gray*
    #3 reed: 6 strands, each 12 feet long, *dusty rose*
PREPARATION
From #5 reed, cut:
    8 base spokes, each 8″ long
    32 side spokes, each 22″ long
From #8 reed, cut:
    2 handles, each 18″ long

Base: With weavers of #2 reed, work the four-through-four *split-spoke base* to a diameter of 7″.

Preparing to weave the sides: Bi-spoke with 32 side spokes. With natural #3 reed, work a *three-rod arrow* to separate the side spokes. Turn the base over and pinch the spokes (5.9).

Upsett: With #4 reed, work a locked *four-rod coil.* With natural #3 reed, work seven rows in *three-rod waling.*

Sides: With natural #3 reed, work 1¾″ in *chasing weave.* With gray #3 reed, work one row in *three-rod waling,* with a *step-up* at the end of the row. With dusty rose #3 reed, work five rows in *three-rod waling,* with a *step-up* at the end of each row. With gray #3 reed, work one row in *three-rod waling,* with a *step-up* at the end of the row. With natural #3 reed, work 1″ in *chasing weave.* With natural #3 reed, work seven rows in *three-rod waling.*

Border: Soak and pinch the spokes for the border (6.9). Work a *three-rod plain border* with *follow-on trac #2,* plus one row of *over two and down* on the inside.

Handles: Taper the ends of each handle, as shown in 7.6. Shape each handle core in a curve. Observe the basket, and find two spokes which are opposite each other and centered with relation to the original orientation of the slath. Count two spokes out in each direction from these central

spokes. You will have two sets of marked spokes, with three spokes between the members. Check the position of the second handle by skipping eleven spokes from the position of the first; the twelfth and sixteenth spokes should have been marked.

Insert one end of one handle 5″ into the basket alongside a marked spoke. Skip three spokes and insert the other end alongside the marked fourth spoke. Insert one end of the second handle alongside the twelfth spoke, the other end alongside the sixteenth spoke. The exposed part of each handle should measure 7″. *Rope the handles,* going under the seven rows of waling at the top.

8 Apple Basket

9.12 Apple basket

This bowl-shaped basket is woven with rustic-looking vine rattan. It begins with a double-cross base, which is not specified in any other basket pattern (although it was suggested as a variation for basket 1). The shaping technique for the movement from base to sides is the same subtle pushing that was used on the first basket.

Pairing weave appeared in basket 2, but here it is reintroduced and expanded into a pairing arrow. The two-row trac border is simple to work, although is not exactly like any of the versions in Chapter 6; see 6.2 for the basic idea.

TECHNIQUES
Double-cross base (4.8–4.11)
Pairing arrow (3.27–3.32)
Pairing weave (3.27)
Two-row trac border (described here)
DIMENSIONS
Diameter of base: 7½″
Height: 5″
Top diameter: 11″

MATERIALS
#5 reed (3.50 mm) (smoked) for spokes and weavers: 4½ ounces
smoked vine rattan for weavers: 3½ ounces
PREPARATION
From #5 reed, cut:
24 spokes, each 38″ long

Base: Unless smoked #5 reed is specified, all weavers are smoked vine rattan. Weave a *double-cross base*, separating the spokes with a *pairing arrow*. Work in *pairing weave* to a diameter of 7½″.

Preparing to weave the sides: Continue weaving in the same direction and begin shaping the sides by pushing the spokes away from you as you work.

Sides: Work *pairing weave* for another 2½″. With smoked #5 reed, work a *pairing arrow*. Return to smoked vine rattan and work 1″ in *pairing weave*.

Border: Soak the spokes but do not pinch them. Work a *two-row trac border* with the spokes in pairs.

Row 1: *Behind one pair, in front of one pair, and in.*
Row 2: *Over one pair and down.*

9 Bread Basket with Beads

9.13 Bread basket with beads

The beads on each end give this basket a flowing line, and they're fun to work with. The techniques are very similar to those used on the beginning oval basket with a handle (basket 6).

TECHNIQUES
    The Basics (page 91), plus:
    Three-row rolled border (variation 2, 6.10–6.21)
DIMENSIONS
    Dimensions of base: 9½″ by 7½″
    Height at ends: 3½″
    Top dimensions: 12¾″ by 9¾″

MATERIALS
    #5 reed (3.50 mm) for spokes: 2½ ounces
    #2 reed (1.75 mm) for weavers: 3 ounces
    #3 reed (2.25 mm) for three-rod arrow: ½ ounce
    #4 reed (2.75 mm) for four-rod coil: ½ ounce
    8 beads, 23 mm by 14 mm oval
    4 beads, 18 mm round
PREPARATION
From #5 reed, cut:
    4 base spokes, each 10″ long
    7 base spokes, each 7″ long
    34 side spokes, each 15″ long

Base: With weavers of #2 reed, work the *basic oval base* to a measurement of 8½″ by 6½″.

Preparing to weave the sides: *Bi-spoke* with 34 side spokes. With #3 reed, work a *three-rod arrow* to separate the side spokes. Turn the base over and pinch the spokes.

Upsett: With #4 reed, work a locked *four-rod coil*.

Sides: With #2 reed, work twelve rows in *three-rod waling*. Don't cut off the weavers. Place beads on the six end spokes—four oval beads in the center and the round beads on each side of the oval ones. With #2 reed, weave five rows in *three-rod waling* right over the beads.

Border: Soak and pinch the spokes for the border. Work a *three-row rolled border* (variation 2).
    Row 1: *Behind one and out.*
    Row 2: *In front of two and in.*
    Row 3: *Over two and down.*

10   Oval Basket with Decorative Bands and End Handles

9.14 Oval basket with decorative bands and end handles

Another oval basket, this time dressed up with a band of three-rod arrows, a section worked in a new weave—double chasing—in blue, plus wrapped end handles. This basket introduces both wrapped handles and the use of decorative leaders.

TECHNIQUES
   The Basics (page 91), plus:
   Double chasing weave (3.10–3.11)
   Four-row rolled border (basic, 6.8–6.22)
   Wrapped end handles with decorative leader (7.6, 7.31–7.34)

DIMENSIONS
   Dimensions of base: 9¾″ by 7½″
   Height of basket: 5¾″
   Height with handles: 8″
   Top dimensions: 13½″ by 11″

MATERIALS
   #5 reed (3.50 mm) for spokes: 4½ ounces
   #2 reed (1.75 mm) for weavers: 5 ounces
   #3 reed (2.25 mm) for three-rod arrow separating side spokes: ½ ounce
   #4 reed (2.75 mm) for four-rod coil and band of three-rod arrows on side: 1½ ounces
   #8 reed (6.00 mm) for handles: 3 feet
   narrow medium cane (2.75mm) for wrapping the handle: two long strands
Optional color: Of the above quantities, the following amounts may be dyed, or purchased in colored form.
   #2 reed: 1 ounce of longest strands

PREPARATION
From #5 reed, cut:
   4 base spokes, each 10″ long
   7 base spokes, each 7″ long
   34 side spokes, each 21″ long
From #8 reed, cut:
   2 handles, each 18″ long

Base: With weavers of natural #2 reed, work the *basic oval base* to a measurement of 8¾″ by 6½″.

Preparing to weave the sides: *Bi-spoke* with 34 side spokes. With #3 reed, work a *three-rod arrow* to separate the side spokes. Turn the base over and pinch the spokes.

Upsett: With #4 reed, work a locked *four-rod coil*. With natural #2 reed, work seven rows in *three-rod waling.*

Sides: With dyed #2 reed, work ten rows in *double chasing weave.* With #4 reed, work two *three-rod arrows.* It's not necessary to cut off the weavers when you have completed the first arrow. Just bring the weavers to the outside after you have completed the interlacing at the first three spokes and work the second arrow from there. With dyed #2 reed, work eight rows in *double chasing weave.* With natural #2 reed, work seven rows in *three-rod waling.*

Border: Soak and pinch the spokes for the border. Work the basic *four-row rolled border.*

Row 1: *Behind one and out.*

Row 2: *In front of two and in.*

Row 3: *Over two and down.*

Row 4: *Over two and down.*

Handles: Taper the ends as shown in 7.6. To find the place to insert the handles, count to the right from the central spoke on the side, which will be marked 1. (That's the side spoke inserted alongside the central short base spoke.) Insert the ends of the handles alongside spokes 7 and 12 on one end, and spokes 24 and 29 on the other end. The measurement of the exposed handle is 8″.

Wrap the handles with narrow medium cane. The leader is dyed #2 reed, doubled. The leader pattern is *under two, over two.*

11 Oval Basket with Beads and Handle

9.15 Oval basket with beads and handle

This basket combines elements from previous patterns in a new form. Familiar techniques include the oval base, decorative beads, rolled border, and roped handle.

TECHNIQUES
    The Basics (page 91), plus:
    Four-row rolled border (variation 5, 6.23)
    Roped handle (7.5, 7.7, 7.18–7.22, 7.29)
DIMENSIONS
    Dimensions of base: 9½″ by 7½″
    Height with handles: 13½″
    Top dimensions: 13″ by 11½″
MATERIALS
    #5 reed (3.50 mm) for spokes: 4½ ounces
    #2 reed (1.75 mm) for base weavers: 1 ounce
    #3 reed (2.25 mm) for weavers: 7 ounces
    #4 reed (2.75 mm) for four-rod coil: ½ ounce
    #5 reed (3.50 mm) (smoked) for three-rod arrows on side: 1½ ounce
    24 beads, 22 mm by 13 mm
    #10 reed (8.00 mm) for handle: 28″
PREPARATION
From #5 reed, cut:
    4 base spokes, each 10″ long
    7 base spokes, each 7″ long
    34 side spokes, each 22″ long

Base: With weavers of #2 reed, work the *basic oval base* to a measurement of 8¾″ by 6½″.

Preparing to weave the sides: *Bi-spoke* with 34 side spokes. With #3 reed, work a *three-rod arrow* to separate the side spokes. Turn the base over and pinch the spokes.

Upsett: With #4 reed, work a locked *four-rod coil*. With #3 reed, work nine rows in *three-rod waling*. Since this basket flares out from the base, weave with the spokes at a 45-degree angle from the base until you've completed the nine rows.

Sides: Continue waling, but begin to shape the basket in at this point. Work until the weaving measures 5″ from the four-rod coil. You will next work *three-rod arrows* with smoked #5 reed, incorporating the beads in the process. Work a complete arrow. Do not cut off the ends of the weavers. Put the beads on the twelve spokes at each end. Work the second complete arrow over the beads. With #3 reed, work three rows of *three-rod waling*.

Border: Soak and pinch the spokes for the border. Work a *four-row rolled border* (variation 5).
    Row 1: *Behind two and out.*
    Row 2: *In front of three and in.*
    Row 3: *Over two and down.*
    Row 4: *Over two and down.*

Handle: Taper the ends as shown in 7.5 and 7.7. Insert the handle at the side spokes which correspond to the center short spoke of the base. Work the *roped handle*.

12   Sewing Basket with Lid

This is a wonderful sewing basket. Doubled spokes give the sides strength while keeping the basket light. Work the basket, stopping short of the handle. Then work and fit the lid, and finish up by adding the wrapped double handle to the basket.

Both the basket and the lid have double-spoke trac borders. The lid fits on a ledge which is woven from the ends of the basket border. The double-spoke trac border is not exactly like any of the versions described in Chapter 6; for reference, see 6.2, 6.3, and 6.4.

The lid has a unique loop-and-ring handle, and the large wrapped double handle makes the completed set easy to carry.

9.16 Sewing basket with lid

TECHNIQUES
    The Basics (page 91), plus:
    Doubled side spokes (page 90)
    Chasing weave (3.9)
    Randing (3.2)
    Japanese weave (3.23)
    Double-spoke trac border (described here)
    Ring-and-loop handle (described here)
    Wrapped double handle with decorative leader (7.5, 7.8, 7.35)
    Pegged handle (7.10–7.12)
DIMENSIONS
    Diameter of base: 7¼″
    Height of basket: 6″
    Height with handle: 12″
    Top diameter: 10¼″
MATERIALS
    #5 reed (3.50 mm) for base and lid spokes:
1 ounce
    #4 reed (2.75 mm) for side spokes and lid

border: 6 ounces
    #3 reed (2.25 mm) for three-rod arrows: 2 ounces
    #2 reed (1.75 mm) for weavers: 5 ounces
    ¼″ flat reed for weavers: 6 feet
    narrow medium (2.75mm) cane for wrapping
handle: several strands
    #8 reed (6.00 mm) for handles: 56″
Optional color: Of the above quantities, the following amounts may be dyed, or purchased in colored form.
    ¼″ flat reed (all): *cocoa brown*
    #3 reed: 6 long strands *cocoa brown*
PREPARATION
From #5 reed, cut:
    8 base spokes, each 7½″ long
    10 lid spokes, each 10″ long
From #4 reed, cut:
    32 side spokes, each 18″ long
    32 supporters, each 16″ long
    40 lid border spokes, each 10″ long
From #8 reed, cut:
    2 handles, each 28″ long

BASKET

Base: With weavers of #2 reed, work a four-through-four *split-spoke base* to a diameter of 6½".

Preparing to weave the sides: *Bi-spoke* with the thirty-two 18" #4 side spokes. With #3 reed, work a *three-rod arrow* to separate the side spokes. Turn the base over and pinch the side spokes.

Upsett: With #4 reed, work a locked *four-rod coil.* With #2 reed, work seven rows in *three-rod waling.* Insert the 16" supporters, one to the right of each spoke, working their ends down to the four-rod coil.

Sides: With #2 reed, work 1¼" in *chasing weave.* With #3 reed, work a *three-rod arrow.* With dyed ¼" flat reed, work two rows in *randing.* With #3 reed, work a *three-rod arrow.* With #2 reed, work ½" in *chasing weave.* With #2 reed, work seven rows in *three-rod waling.*

Border and inside ledge: Work double-spoke *trac border* variation 1: *behind one, in front of two, and in.*

Form the inside ledge by working two rows of *three-rod waling* around these border ends. Separate the pairs of spokes into 64 single spokes. The pairs lie inside the basket, one on top of the other. Weave around the lower spoke of each pair first, then around the upper spoke. Look at the outside of the border frequently to make sure of the sequence in which you're weaving the ends. It will be noticeable if they're not woven right. Keep the waling tight against the border.

Work the final border edge on this ledge as *over three and down.* See illustration 9.18 for finished border and ledge.

Handle: Work the basket handle after you have made and fitted the lid, below. Taper the ends of the two handles as shown in 7.5 and 7.8. Position the handles so they follow the line of the base spokes. Mark one of the side spokes as spoke 1. Insert the handles to the left of the double spokes as you look at the basket from the outside. Insert the first ends of the two handles beside spokes 1 and 3. Count to the right and insert the other ends beside spokes 14 and 16. Run them down into the basket about 5". The exposed handle measures 18".

Work a *double wrapped handle.* Wrap each end for 4" before wrapping the two cores together. The pattern with the medium fine cane leader is *under two, over two.*

Peg the handles below the border. See illustration 9.19 for the arrangement of the handle.

LID

Base: With weavers of #2 reed, work the lid as a five-through-five *split-spoke base.* The lid is domed, just like the base. With the #2 reed, work *Japanese weave* to a diameter of 4". With the dyed #3 reed, work one *three-rod arrow.* With #2 reed, work in *Japanese weave* to within ½" of the edge of the ledge. (That will be approximately 1⅜" of Japanese weave. Turn the lid upside down inside the basket to determine just where the edge of the lid is in relation to the ledge.) With dyed #3 reed, work one *three-rod arrow.*

Border: *Bi-spoke* with the 10" #4 spokes. Work the basic double-spoke *trac border: behind one, in front of one, and in.*

Fitting the lid: If the lid doesn't quite fit in the basket, try to manipulate the basket border so that it tips outward more. The border tends to head inward, and may prevent the lid from lying in place. Make sure, too, that the basket is round.

The lid border can be pushed down if it's too large, or pulled up if it's too small. The border can also be rewoven if the lid is too small, using this variation: *in front of one, behind one, in front of one, and in.*

9.17 Sewing basket with lid

9.18 Sewing basket with lid: Inside border ledge

Handle: The handle for the lid consists of a ring through a small loop (9.20). To make the twisted *ring*, use a 24" piece of dyed #3 reed. Tie the ends in an overhand knot so one of the ends is only 2" long. Pull the circle in until it measures 2" in diameter. Twist the long end through the circle two more times until it meets the short end. Continue threading the long end through the center of the circle following the groove established by the first row. Overlap the ends so that they brace against each other, then trim them both on a slant to make a smooth join.

Make the *loop* by threading the ends of a 12" piece of dyed #3 reed up through two corners of the slath so they protrude from the top of the lid. Twist them twice, run them through the ring, then thread the ends through the opposite corners of the slath to the underside. To get rid of the ends, run them under the four rows of reverse pairing weave which tie the slath on the underside of the lid.

9.20 Sewing basket with lid: Loop and ring handle on lid

9.19 Sewing basket with lid: Trac border and pegged handles

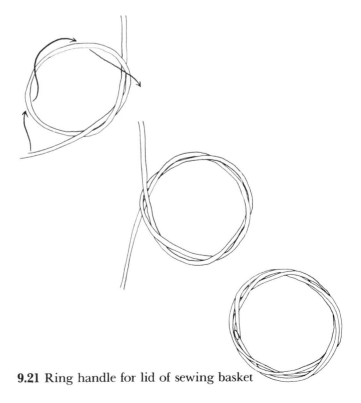

9.21 Ring handle for lid of sewing basket

13 Oval Basket with Packed Ends and Roped Handle

9.22 Oval basket with packed ends and lengthwise handle

Packing is often used as a shaping technique. Here it both serves that purpose and provides decoration. The reed used to pack the ends of the basket is colored, and the packed area is set off with rows of four-rod coil.

The four-row rolled border is not exactly like any of the versions in Chapter 6; it's a combination of variations 3 and 5 (see 6.23).

TECHNIQUES
  The Basics (page 91), plus:
  Randing (3.2)
  Packing (3.21)
  Four-row rolled border (described here)
  Roped handle (7.5, 7.8, 7.18–7.21, 7.29)
  Binding (7.23)
DIMENSIONS
  Dimensions of base: 9½" by 7½"
  Top dimensions: 13" by 11½"
  Height with handle: 13"
MATERIALS
  #5 reed (3.50 mm) for spokes: 5 ounces
  #2 reed (1.75 mm) for base weavers: 1 ounce
  #3 reed (2.25 mm) for weavers: 5 ounces
  #5 reed (3.50 mm) (flexible) for four-rod coils:

2 ounces
  #10 reed (8.00 mm) for handle: 29"
Optional color: Of the above quantities, the following amounts may be dyed, or purchased in colored form.
  #3 reed: 1 ounce *gray*
PREPARATION
From #5 reed, cut:
  5 base spokes, 11" long
  8 base spokes, 7" long
  38 side spokes, 24" long
  Base: With weavers of #2 reed, work the *basic oval base,* using five long spokes in the spine instead of four. Work to a measurement of 8½" by 6¾".

Preparing to weave the sides: *Bi-spoke* with 38 side spokes as shown in 9.23. With #3 reed, work a *three-rod arrow* to separate the side spokes. Turn the base over and pinch the spokes.

Upsett: With flexible #5 reed, work a locked *four-rod coil.* With #3 reed, work nine rows in *three-rod waling* with the spokes at a 45-degree angle to the base.

Sides: Continue working three-rod waling and begin to shape the basket in at this point. Work to a height of 5¾". With flexible #5 reed, work a *four-rod coil.* Finish it with a *step-up,* but do not lock it. Cut off the weavers.

Using gray #3 reed, doubled, *pack* the ends of the basket, following the packing variation shown in 3.21. Mark the 2 middle spokes on each side. To begin the first row, place a double set of #3 gray weavers behind one of the middle side spokes. Work in *randing* all the way around, ending at the spoke where you began. Cut off. Lay in the next set of double weavers behind the spoke to the right of the marked middle spoke. Weave around to one spoke to the left of the other middle spoke, and cut off. Weave six more rows on this end, leaving out a spoke at each end of the weaving on each row. The last row will be worked around only three spokes. Repeat this sequence at the other end.

With flexible #5 reed, work another *four-rod coil.*

Border: Soak and pinch the spokes for the border. Work a *four-row rolled border.*
Row 1: *Behind two and out.*
Row 2: *In front of two and in.*
Row 3: *Over two and down.*
Row 4: *Over two and down.*

Handle: Taper the ends of the handle as shown in 7.5 and 7.8. Insert the handle 5½″ into the basket at each end, alongside the center end spokes. The exposed handle measures 18″. *Rope the handle* with #3 reed, and add *binding.*

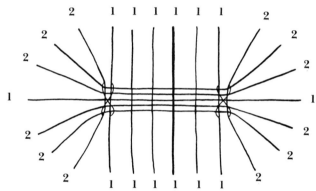

9.23 Bi-spoking for oval basket with packed ends and lengthwise handle

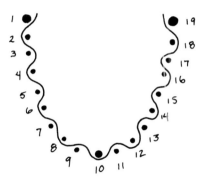

9.24 Pattern for packing one end of the oval basket.
Row 1: Completely randed.
Row 2: Pack spokes 2–18.
Row 3: Pack spokes 3–17.
Row 4: Pack spokes 4–16, and so forth.

14   Large Shopping Basket with Double Handle

9.25 Large shopping basket with double handle

This is a very large, sturdy oval basket. It introduces the large oval base. The techniques are the same as for the other oval baskets but are worked on a grander scale. Be sure you feel comfortable making smaller oval baskets before attempting this one.

Hong Kong seagrass adds texture to the basket's sides, and the herringbone pattern is worked along the double handle after it has been completely wrapped. The four-row rolled border is not exactly like any of the variations in Chapter 6; it's closest to variation 1 (see 6.10–6.22).

TECHNIQUES
The Basics (page 91), plus:
Chasing weave (3.9)
Four-row rolled border (described here)
Wrapped double handle (7.31–7.35)
Herringbone handle pattern (7.41–7.44)
Pegged handle (7.10–7.12)

DIMENSIONS
Dimensions of base: 17½″ by 10¾″
Height of basket: 9½″
Height with handle: 15″
Top dimensions: 23½″ by 15½″

MATERIALS
#6 reed (4.50 mm) for spokes: 1⅓ pounds
#3 reed (2.25 mm) for weavers: 4 ounces
#4 reed (2.75 mm) for weavers: 8 ounces
#5 reed (3.50 mm) for weavers: 8 ounces
#3 Hong Kong seagrass: 18 yards
#12 reed (10.00 mm) for double handles: 74″
#10 reed (8.00 mm) for filler between handles: 10″
medium (3.00 mm) cane for wrapping handle: several strands

PREPARATION
From #6 reed, cut:
5 base spokes, each 17″ long
16 base spokes, each 11″ long
42 side spokes, each 30″ long
From seagrass, cut:
3 strands, each 6 feet long
From #12 reed, cut:
2 handles, each 37″ long

Base: With #3 reed, work the *large oval base* until it measures 14¼″ by 7½″. With #4 reed, weave one more inch; the final dimensions will be 15¼″ by 8½″.

Preparing to weave the sides: *Bi-spoke* with the 42 side spokes, as shown in 9.25. With #4 reed,

work a *three-rod arrow* to separate the side spokes. Turn the base over and pinch the side spokes.

Upsett: With #5 reed, work a locked *four-rod coil.* Continuing with #5 reed, work five rows in *three-rod waling.*

Sides: With #4 reed, work 1¾″ (18 rows) in

chasing weave, followed by one *three-rod arrow* with #5 reed.

With seagrass, work four rows in *three-rod waling.* It's best not to get the seagrass wet before you weave with it, because the ends unravel. (Don't worry if it gets wet when you soak it to work the border. After trimming, use a dab of clear craft glue on the ends to keep them neat on the inside of the basket.)

With #5 reed, work another *three-rod arrow.* With #4 reed, work 1¼" (14 rows) in *chasing weave.* With #5 reed, work five rows in *three-rod waling.*

Border: Soak and pinch the spokes for the border. Work a *four-row rolled border.*

Row 1: *Behind one and out.*
Row 2: *In front of three and in.*
Row 3: *Over two and down.*
Row 4: *Over two and down.*

Handle: Insert the handles on each side of the central short base spoke. The exposed handle length is 23". Work a wrapped double handle.

Wrap each end separately for 6½". Insert a 10" piece of #10 reed between the handles and wrap all three together. Wrap seven times before inserting the narrow medium cane leader. The leader pattern is *under one, over one.*

Make a *wrapped handle.* Work the *herringbone design* after the handle has been completely wrapped. *Peg* the handle ends underneath the border.

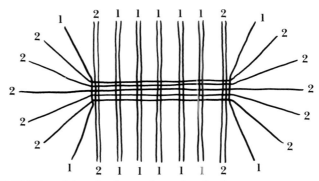

9.26 Bi-spoking for large shopping basket

CHAPTER 10
Baskets in Color

For the baskets in the last chapter, the use of color was optional. You can make the following baskets in naturals as well, but you'll be missing more than half the fun. They have been designed to give you experience with the color effects which can be produced easily with the weaves that should be familiar by now. Whether you buy dyed reed or use the instructions in Chapter 8 to color your own, don't miss the pleasure of discovering what happens when you combine structure and pattern.

In particular, you'll see a lot of three-rod waling in this chapter: in its various forms, it can produce a wide range of effects. Baskets 15 through 21 depend on combinations of three-rod waling, reverse three-rod waling, three-rod arrow, and three-rod arrow chasing weave.

With a good background in the possibilities of one weave, you can experiment with others. Braid weave is another rich possibility, demonstrated in baskets 22 and 23. Pairing makes a brief appearance in basket 20, and the final basket gives a sample of what can be done with double double Japanese, chasing weave, another application of braid weave, and diamond weave.

15   Spiraling Basket

This attractive basket, shown in color photo 12, is much simpler to weave than it looks. It is worked in three-rod waling, using three different colors. The number of spokes (divisible by three minus

one) makes the design spiral. This is called the "outside spiral" in Chapter 8, and it's also a design element in the basket in color photo 5.

TECHNIQUES
The Basics (page 91), plus:
Four-row rolled border (basic, 6.10–6.22)
DIMENSIONS
Base: 7½"
Height: 4½"
Top diameter: 11"
MATERIALS
#5 reed (3.50 mm) for spokes: 4½ ounces
#2 reed (1.75 mm) for base weavers: 1 ounce
#3 reed (2.25 mm) for weavers: 4 ounces

#4 reed (2.75 mm) for four-rod coil: small amount
Color required: Of the above quantities, the following amounts should be dyed, or purchased in colored form.
#3 reed: 1½ ounces *cocoa brown*
#3 reed: 1½ ounces *pink*
PREPARATION
From #5 reed, cut:
8 base spokes, each 7½" long
32 side spokes, each 20" long

Base: With weavers of #2 reed, work the four-through-four *split-spoke base* to a diameter of 6½".

Preparing to weave the sides: *Bi-spoke* with 32 side spokes. With #3 reed, work a *three-rod arrow* to separate the side spokes. Turn the base over and pinch the spokes.

Upsett: With #4 reed, work a locked *four-rod coil.*

Sides: With #3 reed, and three weavers of different colors, weave 4½" in *three-rod waling.*

Border: Soak the spokes and pinch for the border. Work the basic *four-row rolled border.*
Row 1: *Behind one and out.*
Row 2: *In front of two and in.*
Row 3: *Over two and down.*
Row 4: *Over two and down.*

16   Reversing Spirals

To reverse a pattern means weaving in the opposite direction, or, for most people, to the left. Working in one of the directions will probably come more naturally to you than working in the other; the spectacular design that results from combining the two directions makes the effort worthwhile.

This basket is shown in color photo 11. It also has a braided border—another challenge that's worth practicing.

TECHNIQUES
  The Basics (page 91), plus:
  Waling to the left (3.41, 3.45)
  Braided border (6.55–6.65)
DIMENSIONS
  Base: 11½″
  Height: 3″
  Top diameter: 14½″
MATERIALS
  #6 reed (4.50 mm) for base spokes: ½ ounce
  #5 reed (3.50 mm) for side spokes: 3 ounces
  #3 reed (2.25 mm) for weavers: 4 ounces
  #2 reed (1.75 mm) for starting the base: three long, flexible strands

#4 reed (2.75 mm) for four-rod coil: ½ ounce
Color required: Of the above quantities, the following amounts should be dyed, or purchased in colored form.
  #3 reed: 2½ ounces *rust*
  #3 reed: 1 ounce *gray*
PREPARATION
From #6 reed, cut:
  10 base spokes, each 12″ long
From 5 reed, cut:
  40 side spokes, each 18″ long

Base: With weavers of #2 reed, work a five-through-five *split-spoke base* to a diameter of 3″. With rust #3 reed, work a *four-rod coil*. Work a *step-up* at the end of the row, but don't lock it.

With one weaver each of #3 reed in gray, rust, and natural, begin the *three-rod waling*. Work to a diameter of 7¼″, ending with the weavers coming from behind the three beginning spokes. Cut the weavers off and place them behind the same spokes, over the same colors but going in the opposite direction. Don't tuck in the ends. Weave counterclockwise (to the left) to a diameter of 10¼.″

Preparing to weave the sides: *Bi-spoke* with the 40 side spokes. With natural #3 reed, work a *three-rod arrow* to separate the side spokes. Turn the base over and pinch the spokes.

Upsett: With #4 reed, work a locked *four-rod coil.*

Sides: With rust #3 reed, work 3″ in *three-rod waling.*

Border: Soak and pinch the spokes for the *braided border.* Work the two-rod, three-stroke braided border.

17   Spiraling Arrows

Regular and reverse waling combined in a specific sequence result in three-rod arrow chasing weave. This basket and the next produce two different designs by varying the number of spokes over which this combination is worked. Spiraling arrows, worked over a number of spokes divisible by three minus one, create a dramatic design. The basket is shown in color photo 13.

The two weaves are worked with two separate sets of three weavers each. You'll need to be careful to remember which set is being used for regular waling and which for reverse waling, and to keep the sets separated enough so you don't accidentally use a weaver from the wrong set. Keep in mind that regular waling slants upward to the right, reverse waling upward to the left.

TECHNIQUES
    The Basics (page 91), plus:
    Three-rod arrow chasing weave (3.46)
    Three-rod plain border (6.39–6.45)
        with follow-on trac #1 (6.46–6.48)
        and an extra trac row (6.18–6.21)
DIMENSIONS
    Base: 7½″
    Height of basket: 5″
    Top diameter: 10″
MATERIALS
    #5 reed (3.50 mm) for spokes: 4 ounces

    #3 reed (2.25 mm) for weavers: 4½ ounces
    #2 reed (1.75 mm) for base weavers: 1 ounce
    #4 reed (2.75 mm) for four-rod coil: ½ ounce
Color required: Of the above quantities, the following amounts should be dyed, or purchased in colored form.
    #3 reed: 1½ ounces *blue*
    #3 reed: 1½ ounces *rust*
PREPARATION
From #5 reed, cut:
    8 base spokes, each 7½″ long
    32 side spokes, each 20″ long

Base: With weavers of #2 reed, work a four-through-four *split-spoke base* to a diameter of 6½″.
    Preparing to weave the sides: *Bi-spoke* with 32 side spokes. With #3 reed, work a *three-rod arrow* to separate the side spokes. Turn the base over and pinch the side spokes.
    Upsett: With #4 reed, work a locked *four-rod coil*.
    Sides: With #3 reed in blue, rust, and natural, work *three-rod arrow chasing weave* until the basket reaches a height of 4¾″. Be sure to end with a reverse waling row, and end both sets of weavers over their corresponding beginning spokes.
    Border: Soak and pinch the spokes for the border. Work a *three-rod plain border* with *follow-on trac #1.* Work one row of *over two and down* on the inside.

18 Bargello Design

Three-rod arrow weave worked with a number of spokes divisible by three gives an entirely different effect from that of spiraling arrows; Chapter 8 calls this variation "vertical arrows." In both cases, the combination of weaves is worked in exactly the same way; the number of spokes makes all the difference. The design for this basket, shown in color photo 14, imitates the needlepoint stitch for which it is named.

The four-row rolled border is a combination of variations 3 and 6; refer to 6.9–6.14.

TECHNIQUES
    The Basics (page 91), plus:
    Three-rod arrow chasing weave (3.46)
    Four-row rolled border (described here)
DIMENSIONS
    Base: 7½″
    Height: 7½″
    Top diameter: 11″
MATERIALS
    #5 reed (3.50 mm) for spokes: 4½ ounces
    #4 reed (2.75 mm) for four-rod coils: 1 ounce
    #3 reed (2.25 mm) for weavers: 6 ounces
    #2 reed (1.75 mm) for base weavers: 1 ounce
Color required: Of the above quantities, the following amounts should be dyed, or purchased in colored form.
    #3 reed: 1½ ounces *gray*
    #3 reed: 1½ ounces *dusty rose*
PREPARATION
From #5 reed, cut:
    8 base spokes, each 7½″ long
From #5 reed, cut:
    33 side spokes, each 23″ long

Base: With #2 reed, work a four-through-four *split-spoke base* to a diameter of 6½″.

Preparing to weave the sides: *Bi-spoke* with 33 side spokes; double up spokes 32 and 33 in the same space. With #3 reed, work a *three-rod arrow* to separate the side spokes. Turn the base over and pinch the spokes.

Upsett: With #4 reed, work a locked *four-rod coil*. With natural #3 reed, work 2¼″ in *three-rod waling*.

Sides: With #4 reed, work a *four-rod coil*. Work a *step-up* but don't lock it. Cut off the weavers. With #3 reed in gray, dusty rose, and natural, work 3″ of *three-rod arrow weave*. With #4 reed, work a *four-rod coil*. Work a *step-up* but don't lock it. Cut off the weavers. With natural #3 reed, work 1½″ in *three-rod waling*.

Border: Soak and pinch the spokes for the border. Work a variation of the *four-row rolled border*.

    Row 1: *Behind two and out.*
    Row 2: *In front of two and in.*
    Row 3: *Over two and down.*
    Row 4: *Over two and down.*

19   Dart Pattern Basket

This basket, in color photo 15, combines several attractive color patterns, all developed from three-rod waling. The bottom spirals move into reversing spirals, then into darts. The top returns to regular spirals, then ends in zigzags. Because the number of spokes is divisible by three minus one, the patterns appear clearly on the outside of the basket.

The three-row rolled border is similar, but not identical, to variation 4 (see 6.10–6.14).

TECHNIQUES
The Basics (page 91), plus:
Waling to the left (3.41)
Three-row rolled border (described here)

DIMENSIONS
Base: 7½″
Height: 8½″
Greatest diameter: 12″
Top diameter: 7″

MATERIALS
#5 reed (3.50 mm) for spokes: 5½ ounces
#2 reed (1.75 mm) for base weavers: 1 ounce
#3 reed (2.25 mm) for weavers: 10 ounces

#5 reed (3.50 mm) (flexible) for three-rod waling on the side: ½ ounce
#4 reed (2.75 mm) for four-rod coil: ½ ounce
Color required: Of the above quantities, the following amounts should be dyed, or purchased in colored form.
#3 reed: 4 ounces *purple*
#3 reed: 4 ounces *blue-gray*
#5 reed (flexible): ½ ounce *purple*

PREPARATION
From #5 reed, cut:
8 base spokes, each 7½″
32 side spokes, each 24″

Base: With weavers of #2 reed, work a four-through-four *split-spoke base* to a diameter of 6½″.

Preparing to weave the sides: *Bi-spoke* with 32 side spokes. With #3 reed, work a *three-rod arrow* to separate the side spokes. Turn the base over and pinch the side spokes.

Upsett: With #4 reed, work a locked *four-rod coil.*

Sides: Mark spoke number 1. All weaving on the sides is *three-rod waling* or *reverse three-rod waling.* All weavers not otherwise designated are #3 reed. Work five rows in *three-rod waling* with three strands of natural, then six rows with two strands of natural and one strand in blue-gray. (Change the natural weaver to blue-gray at spoke 1.) Work six more rows with one strand of natural and two strands of blue-gray. (Change the second natural weaver to blue-gray at spoke 2.) Wale five rows to the left with two blue-gray weavers over their same colors and a purple weaver over the natural. Then work five rows in regular *three-rod waling* with two purple weavers and one blue-gray over their same colors, followed by three rows of regular waling with three purple strands.

To make the first half of the dart, change the purple weaver to natural at spoke 1 on each of the next three rows. The third row will be entirely in natural color.

To make the second half of the dart, wale to the left. Place a blue-gray weaver behind spoke 1 and two natural weavers behind the two spokes to the left of spoke 1. On each of the next two rows, change one of the natural weavers to blue-gray at spoke 1.

Wale four rows to the left with blue-gray. Trim off the weavers behind the first three spokes.

Pinch the spokes as you would for the base, to make the basket go inward at this point.

With the flexible purple #5 weavers, work a row of *three-rod waling* over the bend. Work a *step-up* but do not lock it. Cut off the weavers. With purple #3 reed, work six rows in *three-rod waling.* At the beginning of each of the next three rows, change one weaver to blue-gray at spoke 1. Weave two rows of blue-gray. At the beginning of the next three rows, change to natural at spoke 1. Weave two rows of natural.

Border: Soak and pinch the spokes for the border. Work a variation of the *three-row rolled border.*
Row 1: *Behind two and out.*
Row 2: *In front of three and in.*
Row 3: *Over three and down.*

20 Step-Up to Stripes

The inspiration for this basket (color photo 19) came from a woven pattern in a piece of fabric. Two different weaves, pairing and three-rod waling, form the vertical and horizontal stripes and add textural contrast as well.

The techniques are described as "vertical stripes or blocks" in Chapter 8. Vertical stripes call for pairing or chasing weave worked over an even number of spokes. In this case, the three-rod waling is worked with all three weavers in the same color, to produce horizontal stripes. Each stripe ends sharply with a step-up. Three-rod waling can be used this way over any number of spokes. For blocks, which require a specific spoke arrangement, see the next basket.

TECHNIQUES
The Basics (page 91), plus:
Pairing weave (3.26)
Randing (3.2)
Four-row rolled border (basic, 6.10–6.22)
Roped handle (7.5, 7.8, 7.18–7.21)
Binding (7.23)
DIMENSIONS
Base: 8″
Height of basket: 12″
Height with handle: 18″
Top diameter: 12″
MATERIALS
#5 reed (3.50 mm) for spokes: 5 ounces

#2 reed (1.75 mm) for base weavers: 1 ounce
#3 reed (2.25 mm) for weavers: 12 ounces
#10 reed (8.00 mm) for handle: 32″
#4 reed (2.75 mm) for four-rod coil: ½ ounce
½″ flat reed for sides: 7 feet
Color required: Of the above quantities, the following amounts should be dyed, or purchased in colored form.
#3 reed: 4 ounces *gray*
#3 reed: 4 ounces *mauve*
PREPARATION
From #5 reed, cut:
8 base spokes, each 8″ long
32 side spokes, each 28″ long

Base: With weavers of #2 reed, work a four-through-four *split-spoke base* to a diameter of 7″.

Preparing to weave the sides: *Bi-spoke* with 32 side spokes. With natural #3 reed, work a *three-rod arrow* to separate the side spokes. Turn the base over and pinch the side spokes.

Upsett: With #4 reed, work a locked *four-rod coil*. With gray #3 reed, work three rows in *three-rod waling*.

Sides: With ½″ flat reed, work one row in *randing*.

From this point on, each row of three-rod waling ends with a *step-up*. After the step-up, either resume regular three-rod waling, or cut off the weavers behind each of the three beginning spokes, whichever the pattern calls for.

With gray #3 reed, work three rows in *three-rod waling*. With natural #3 reed, work five rows in *pairing weave*. With one strand each of mauve and natural #3 reed, work five rows in pairing weave. With gray #3 reed, work four rows in *three-rod waling*. With natural #3 reed, work one row in *three-rod waling*. With gray #3 reed, work one row

in *three-rod waling*. With natural #3 reed, work one row in *three-rod waling*. With gray #3 reed, work four rows in *three-rod waling*. With one strand each of mauve and natural #3 reed, work five rows in *pairing weave*. Match the colors with the same pairing pattern below.

With natural #3 reed, work five rows in *pairing weave*. With gray #3 reed, work three rows in *three-rod waling*. With ½″ flat reed, work one row in *randing*. With gray #3 reed, work three rows in *three-rod waling*.

Border: Soak and pinch the spokes for the border. Work the basic *four-row rolled border*.

Row 1: *Behind one and out.*
Row 2: *In front of two and in.*
Row 3: *Over two and down.*
Row 4: *Over two and down.*

Handle: Taper the ends of the handle. Run one end into the basket about 5″, then count around to the sixteenth spoke and insert the other end the same distance. The exposed handle measures 22″. *Rope the handle* with gray #3 reed, and add *binding*.

21 Block Design Basket

The block-like designs in this basket (color photo 16) are achieved with three-rod waling worked over a number of spokes divisible by three.

The four-row rolled border is a combination of techniques (see 6.10–6.22).

TECHNIQUES
The Basics (page 91), plus:
Four-row rolled border (described here)

DIMENSIONS
Base: 8½″
Height: 8½″
Greatest diameter: 13″
Top diameter: 8½″

MATERIALS
Note: Dye the reed to be used for spokes before cutting it.
#5 reed (3.50 mm) for spokes: 6 ounces
#2 reed (1.75 mm) for base weavers: 1½ ounces
#3 reed (2.25 mm) for weavers: 12 ounces
#4 reed (2.75 mm) for four-rod coil: ½ ounce

Color required: Of the above quantities, the following amounts should be dyed, or purchased in colored form.
#2 reed: 1½ ounces *gray*
#3 reed: 5 ounces *gray*
#4 reed: ½ ounce *gray*
#5 reed: 6 ounces *gray*
#3 reed: 4 ounces *pink*
#3 reed: 3 ounces *rust*

PREPARATION
From #5 reed, cut:
10 base spokes, each 8½″ long
39 side spokes, each 25″ long

Base: With weavers of gray #2 reed, work a five-through-five *split-spoke base* to a diameter of 7½″. (The base can be dyed after it has been woven.)

Preparing to weave the sides: *Bi-spoke* with 39 side spokes. One base spoke will get only one side spoke. With gray #3 reed, work a *three-rod arrow* to separate the side spokes. Turn the base over and pinch the side spokes.

Upsett: With gray #4 reed, work a locked *four-rod coil.*

Sides: Work *three-rod waling* with #3 reed: seven rows all gray, six rows with two gray and one pink, four rows with all pink, five rows with two pink and one rust. The rust stripe follows the gray stripe below.

Work three rows with two gray and one rust; the two gray replace the two pink. Work five rows in all rust. Work three rows with two pink and one rust; the rust continues in the same position. Work two rows with two pink and one gray; the gray replaces the rust. Work one row in all gray.

Pinch the spokes as you did for the base to make them bend inward. Continue with ten more rows of gray, shaping the basket inward.

Work three rows with two gray and one rust; the rust follows the rust stripe below. Work two rows with two pink and one rust; the pink replaces the gray. Work two rows in all rust.

Border: Soak and pinch the spokes for the border. Work a variation of the *four-row rolled border.*

Row 1: *Behind three and out.*
Row 2: *In front of three and in.*
Row 3: *Over three and down.*
Row 4: *Over three and down.*

22 Braid Weave Basket I

Some of the design potential in braid weave is demonstrated in the next two baskets, and makes another brief appearance in basket 24. In each case, you will work with three sets of three weavers each. While all the weavers in a single set will be the same color, each set will be a different color.

Dramatic arrows are created when braid weave is worked over an uneven number of spokes divisible by three. The Japanese call this design "pine needles"; it is referred to as "giant arrows" in Chapter 8. The basket is shown in color photo 17.

TECHNIQUES
    The Basics (page 91), plus:
    Braid weave (3.51–3.54)
    Four-row rolled border (basic, 6.10–6.22)
DIMENSIONS
    Base: 8″
    Height: 6″
    Top diameter: 12½″
MATERIALS
    #5 reed (3.50 mm) for spokes: 4½ ounces
    #3 reed (2.25 mm) for weavers: 5 ounces
    #2 reed (1.75 mm) for base weavers: 1 ounce
    #4 reed (2.75 mm) for four-rod coil: ½ ounce

Color required: Of the above quantities, the following amounts should be dyed, or purchased in colored form.
    #2 reed: 1 ounce *wine*
    #3 reed: 1 ounce *wine*
    #4 reed: ½ ounce *wine*
    #5 reed: 5 ounces *wine*
    #3 reed: 2 ounces *dusty rose*
    #3 reed: 2 ounces *gray*
PREPARATION
From #5 reed, cut:
    8 base spokes, each 8″ long
    33 side spokes, each 23″ long

Base: With weavers of wine #2 reed, work a four-through-four *split-spoke base* to a diameter of 7″. (The base can be dyed after it has been woven.)

Preparing to weave the sides: *Bi-spoke* with 33 side spokes; double up spokes 32 and 33 in the same space. With wine #3 reed, work a *three-rod arrow* to separate the side spokes. Turn the base over and pinch the spokes.

Upsett: With wine #4 reed, work a locked *four-rod coil*. With gray #3 reed, work nine rows of *three-rod waling*.

Sides: Work two rows of *braid weave:* use #3 reed in three sets of three strands each—one set each of gray, wine, and dusty rose. With dusty rose #3 reed, work twelve rows in *three-rod waling*. Work a *step-up* at the end of each row. With gray #3 reed, work two rows in *three-rod waling*. Work a *step-up* at the end of each row.

Border: Soak and pinch the spokes for the border. Work the basic *four-row rolled border*.
    Row 1: *Behind one and out.*
    Row 2: *In front of two and in.*
    Row 3: *Over two and down.*
    Row 4: *Over two and down.*

23 Braid Weave Basket II

The colors in this braid weave basket (color photo 18) produce vertical stripes because the number of spokes is divisible by six.

TECHNIQUES
The Basics (page 91), plus:
Braid weave (3.51–3.54)
Four-row rolled border (variation 5, 6.23)

DIMENSIONS
Base: 8″
Height: 7″
Top diameter: 9¼″

MATERIALS
#5 reed (3.50 mm) (smoked) for spokes: 4½ ounces
#3 reed (2.25 mm) (smoked) for weavers: 4 ounces
#3 reed (2.25 mm) for weavers: 2 ounces
#2 reed (1.75 mm) (smoked) for weavers: 1 ounce

Color required: Of the above quantities, the following amounts should be dyed, or purchased in colored form.
#3 reed: 1 ounce *gray*
#3 reed: 1 ounce *rust*

PREPARATION
From #5 smoked reed, cut:
8 base spokes, each 8″ long
30 side spokes, each 24″ long

Base: With weavers of #2 smoked reed, work a four-through-four *split-spoke base* to a diameter of 7″.

Preparing to weave the sides: *Bi-spoke* with 30 side spokes. Two base spokes opposite each other will get only one side spoke each. With #3 smoked reed, work a *three-rod arrow* to separate the side spokes. Turn the base over and pinch the side spokes.

Upsett: With #5 smoked reed, work a locked *four-rod coil*. With #3 smoked reed, work eight rows of *three-rod waling*.

Sides: Work two rows of *braid weave:* use #3 reed in three sets of three strands each—one set each of gray, rust, and smoked. With #3 smoked reed, work eight rows in *three-rod waling*. Work a *step-up* at the end of each row.

With gray #3 reed, work one row in *three-rod waling*. Work a *step-up* at the end of the row.

With rust #3 reed, work one row in *three-rod waling*. Work a *step-up* at the end of the row. With #3 smoked reed, work four rows in *three-rod waling*. Work a *step-up* at the end of each row. Work one row *braid weave*, matching the colors in the first braid weave section. End as in 3.55–3.59. With #3 smoked reed, work five rows in *three-rod waling*. Work a *step-up* at the end of each row.

Border: Soak and pinch the spokes for the border. Work variation 5 of the *four-row rolled border*.
Row 1: *Behind two and out.*
Row 2: *In front of three and in.*
Row 3: *Over two and down.*
Row 4: *Over two and down.*

24 Sampler Basket

A sampling of weave variations is included in this tall round basket (color photo 20). Braid weave is here worked over a number of spokes divisible by three minus one, and produces the "random pattern" discussed in Chapter 8. A number of other weaves are briefly introduced. Bands of three-rod waling separate the different weaves, and an arrow border completes the basket.

TECHNIQUES

The Basics (page 91), plus:
Double double Japanese (3.24–3.25)
Chasing weave (3.9, 3.11–3.12)
French randing (3.13–3.16)
Diamond weave (3.63–3.66)
Braid weave (3.51–3.54)
Arrow border (6.34–6.38)

DIMENSIONS

Base: 8″
Height: 10¾″
Top diameter: 11″

MATERIALS

#5 reed (3.50 mm) for spokes: 5½ ounces
#2 reed (1.75 mm) for base weavers: 1 ounce
#3 reed (2.25 mm) for weavers: 7 ounces
#4 reed (2.75 mm) for four-rod coil: ½ ounce
¼″ flat reed for weavers: 2 ounces

Color required: Of the above quantities, the following amounts should be dyed, or purchased in colored form.
#3 reed: 1 ounce *blue-gray*
¼″ flat reed: 1 ounce *blue-gray*
#3 reed: 1½ ounces *turquoise*
¼″ flat reed: you will need approximately 32 pieces, 10″ long, in a variety of colors in the pink/purple/blue/gray range

PREPARATION

From #5 reed, cut:
8 base spokes, each 8″ long
32 side spokes, each 28″ long
From ¼″ flat reed, cut:
32 pieces, each 10″ long

Base: With weavers of #2 reed, work a four-through-four *split-spoke base* to a diameter of 7″.

Preparing to weave the sides: *Bi-spoke* with 32 side spokes. With natural #3 reed, work a *three-rod arrow* to separate the side spokes. Turn the base over and pinch the side spokes.

Upsett: With #4 reed, work a locked *four-rod coil*. With natural #3 reed, work six rows of *three-rod waling*.

Sides: Work *double double Japanese* with two sets of two #3 weavers each, in turquoise and blue-gray, as follows. Begin *double Japanese weave* with the turquoise set at spoke 2. Work all the way around to within three spokes of spoke 2. Add the blue-gray set of weavers behind spoke 1 (the spoke to the left of spoke 2). Work the two sets as you would for chasing weave (3.9, 3.11). Weave nine rows, ending the sets of weavers behind their corresponding beginning spokes.

With natural #3 reed, work three rows in *three-rod waling*. Work a *step-up* at the end of each row.

With ¼″ blue-gray flat reed and turquoise #3 reed, work five rows in *chasing weave*. Taper the end of the ¼″ flat reed for 6″. Start the flat weaver behind spoke 2 and the #3 weaver behind spoke 1. The final row will be woven with the flat weaver.

Taper the end of the flat reed for 6″. End the #3 weaver behind spoke 1 and the tapered end of the flat weaver behind spoke 2.

With natural #3 reed, work three rows in *three-rod waling*. Work a *step-up* at the end of each row. With the 10″ pieces of ¼″ flat reed, work three rows of *French randing*.

With natural #3 reed, work three rows in *three-rod waling*. Work a *step-up* at the end of each row. With ¼″ flat reed and turquoise #3 reed, work three rows in *diamond weave* with alternating rows. For the first and third rows, use blue-gray flat reed; for the second row, use natural flat reed.

With natural #3 reed, work three rows in *three-rod waling*. Work a *step-up* at the end of each row. Work three rows in *braid weave* with #3 reed in three sets of two weavers each: one set each in natural, turquoise, and blue-gray.

With natural #3 reed, work six rows in *three-rod waling*. Work a *step-up* at the end of each row.

Border: Soak the spokes for the border and pinch them ¼″ above the weaving. Work the *arrow border*.

Row 1: *In front of two, behind two, and out.*
Row 2: *In front of two and in.*
Row 3: *Over two and down.*
Row 4: *Over two and down.*

CHAPTER 11
How to Design a Basket

Now that you've made some baskets from the directions in the book, you'll want to go on to design your own. The prospect of starting from scratch may feel a little daunting. But as you gain confidence in your ability by working through the designs in Chapters 9 and 10, you'll get the urge to branch out.

Look over this chapter once in a while, and you'll begin to see that making your own designs is not so complicated after all. The most critical information you'll need is the size, number, and length of the spokes. There are logical ways to think this through before you start, and that's what this chapter is about.

Give it a try! There's nothing as exciting as making a basket that's all your own.

PLANNING YOUR BASKET

As a resource for your own designs, keep a notebook of ideas gleaned from books and magazines, and make sketches of shapes that interest you. These will give you an idea of proportions, textures, combinations of different weaves, and kinds of handles and borders you might like.

When you begin a basket design, first decide on the size and shape: will the basket be small or large, round or oval? Draw the shape of the basket on a piece of graph paper, letting each square equal one inch. I like to use paper with four squares to the inch, so the drawing is of a reasonable size. Drawing it to scale allows you to see the overall proportions of the basket and where design elements can be placed. The drawing will also give you the measurements of the base and the top of the basket.

SIZES OF REED

An important part of designing is knowing what size reed to use in the different parts of the basket. Sizes of reed are selected in relation to each other; I use the following guidelines.[1]

- Begin by selecting a size for the side spokes. I prefer to work with sizes #4 and #5 as a general rule, or #6 for large baskets.
- Base spokes are most often the same size as or one size larger than the side spokes. This often turns out to be size #4, #5, or #6.
- Weavers are two or three sizes smaller than the spokes. Unless the spokes are doubled, using a weaver in the same size as the spokes can bend them and distort the basket. The weaver should do all the bending; the spokes should hold their shape.
- The size of reed for the three-rod arrow separating the bi-spokes depends on whether you are making a large or a small base. On a small base which uses the same size weaver throughout, use reed one size larger than the base weavers. On a large base, use reed the same size as the final weaver.
- For a four-rod coil, I often select reed one or two sizes larger than that used for the side weavers.

---

[1] The Small Interwoven Base Basket, which appears as the first project in Chapter 9, is an exception to several of these principles. The small-size reed is malleable enough to avoid the problems which appear when you work with larger sizes.

DESIGNING A ROUND BASKET

The first steps in designing a round basket are the same, whether you plan to weave a separate base or to have continuous base and side spokes. Once you have done your scale drawing, you can start with the dimensions either of the top or the bottom of the basket.

One way to design a basket is to start with the base and determine the size of the basket from there. I've made many baskets, and I find this is the easiest way for me. One chart on page 156 gives specifications for round baskets: the size of the base, the size and number of side spokes, and the maximum top diameter of the basket. These are approximate measurements and should be used only as guidelines.

Another way to design is by starting from the top and working down to the base. Your diagram will give you the basket's diameter: simply count the squares across the top of your scale drawing to get the planned diameter in inches. From this dimension, you first determine the number of side spokes you'll need. Then you compute the number of base spokes.

To decide *how many side spokes* are required, start by finding the circumference of the top of the basket: multiply the diameter by 3.14. Decide what size the side spokes should be. Their size should suit the size of the basket and give it necessary strength (see guidelines under "Sizes of Reed," above).

See the chart on page 156 which gives approximate distances between different sizes of spokes. Divide the circumference of the top by the estimated distance between the spokes; the number you get will be an approximate count of the side spokes. Remember, though, that these numbers can be juggled to fit the requirements of your design or weaving pattern.

Next, figure out *how many base spokes* you will need. For a round base, this is easy: divide the number of side spokes by four. Four is the magic number because each base spoke has two ends (each end turns into a separate side spoke) and because when you bi-spoke, you usually add an extra side spoke at each end of the base spoke. So each single base spoke becomes four side spokes as the basket takes shape. (Oval baskets have different principles, described below.)

At this point, you need to determine the *lengths of the spokes*. Your measurements will depend upon whether you are weaving a separate base or an all-in-one basket. For a separate base, you will end up with a base-spoke measurement and a side-spoke measurement. For an all-in-one

basket, you will need a starting-spoke measurement and a side-spoke measurement.

Before you start to calculate, decide on the shape of the sides. Will your basket be short and squat, or tall and thin? Will it be rounded or straight? Also decide what border is appropriate to your design.

Separate Base

The *length of base spokes* for a separately worked base can be figured in two ways. If you will *not* be working a three-rod arrow and coil, cut the spokes to a length equal to the finished diameter of the base plus 1 inch for good measure. If you do plan to work the arrow and coil, cut the spokes to a length which equals the finished diameter (no extra inch). When you weave this base, work until the woven area is 1 inch short of the desired diameter. Then bi-spoke. By the time you work the arrow and coil, the base will reach its intended size.

To determine the *length of the side spokes*, add together the following:

- the *basket's height* from base to border, plus an inch or two for curves and ease of working,
- the *height of the border*,
- the *length of each spoke* that is worked into the base. The side spokes usually will extend into the base between 2½ and 3 inches on a 7- or 8-inch base, or up to 4 inches on a larger base.
- an *allowance for working the border*; see Chapter 6 for information on the spoke length required for the border you have in mind.

Continuous Base and Side Spokes

When the side spokes are a continuation of the base spokes, each starting spoke will equal two side spokes and one base spoke. The following calculations will give you the length for the starting spokes:

Add together:

- the *basket's height* from base to border, plus an inch or two for curves and ease of working,
- the *height of the border*,
- an *allowance for working the border*; see Chapter 6 for information on the spoke length required for the border you have in mind.

Multiply the result by two. Add that number to:
- the diameter of the base.

The length of the additional spokes which you add when bi-spoking will be determined according to the formula for side spokes used with a separate base.

A Sample Round Basket

Perhaps you want to make a fruit basket for your dining room table. You can make it with a separate base for more strength. The basket doesn't need to be too high, but it should be wide at the top, so the fruit can be nicely displayed without being crushed. You plan to use the three-rod arrow to separate the spokes, and a four-rod coil for the upsett.

Draw your design on graph paper. The basket in Fig. 11.1 has a base diameter of 5 inches and a top diameter of 11 inches. To find the circumference of the basket's top, multiply the 11 inches by 3.14: 34.5 inches. To make the basket sturdy, #5 reed would be a good choice for spokes. With #5 reed the distance between spokes at the top will be about 1 inch (according to the chart on page 156).

Divide the circumference by the distance between the spokes to get the number of side spokes: 34.5 inches divided by 1 inch = 34.5 side spokes. (We'll deal with the half-spoke in a minute.) Now divide the number of side spokes by 4 to determine the number of base spokes: 34.5 divided by 4 = 8.6. Round off the numbers to 32 side spokes and 8 base spokes.

You plan to work a three-rod arrow and coil. For a 5-inch-diameter base, cut 8 base spokes 5 inches long and weave the base to a 4-inch diameter. Next, figure the length of the side spokes.
- 2″ to be inserted into the base,
- 5″ for the height of the basket, plus
- 1″ for ease, and
- 14″ for the four-row rolled border (14 × distance between spokes at top of basket).

The total length of each side spoke in this example will be 22″.

The three-rod arrow and four-rod coil will require about an inch of the total diameter of the base (keep this in mind for any basket on which you use them). Lay out and secure the slath, separate the spokes, and weave until you have 4 inches of completed base. Bi-spoke, work the three-rod arrow, and add the four-rod coil for the upsett. You should have reached the 5-inch finished diameter. Weave 5 inches for the sides, and work the border. Done!

DESIGNING AN OVAL BASKET

The set-up of an oval base is much different from that of a round one. You'll need to think both of the half-circles at the end and of the connecting area of short, parallel spokes. The ends actually control the shape of the basket, so the base must be planned carefully.

The Base

The first step is to determine the kind of oval you want, whether long and narrow, short and wide, or long and wide. The number of long spokes which make up the spine can vary from three to five. The fewer there are, the narrower the base.

The number of short cross spokes will depend on the length of the basket, the size of the spokes, and how far apart they should be. The chart on page 156, which tells appropriate spacings for side spokes, also can be used to determine the spacing, and therefore number, of cross spokes in an oval base. The process will be demonstrated more fully in a moment.

Think ahead about your basket design before you become too firmly committed to a particular number of base spokes. The design of your handle or handles, if any, and the weave you use for the base will affect the number and arrangement of spokes.

If you plan to use a handle or handles, see the information on adding handles to oval bases on page 69. The handle design can affect either short or long spoke requirements.

If you want to use Japanese weave on the oval base, the number of spokes cannot be divisible by three. If the number of spokes *is* divisible by three, chasing weave is an alternative. Never

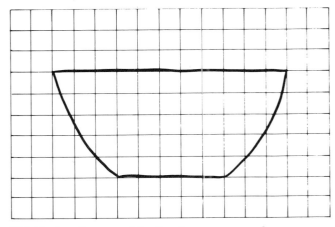

11.1 Design for round basket drawn on graph paper

use regular pairing weave exclusively on an oval base; the weave will warp the base. Pairing arrows can be used, because each row of regular pairing is countered with reverse pairing.

Calculating the numbers and lengths of the spokes. Because of the complexities of shaping, an oval base is most easily constructed as a separate base. A graph-paper diagram of the basket will be extremely helpful as you figure out how many spokes you need and how long to cut them.

First you need to know how long and wide your base will be, and to decide the size of base spokes you will use. As an example, let's plan a base that is 12 inches long and 7 inches wide, constructed with spokes of #5 reed. The basic oval on graph paper will be 12 squares long and 7 squares wide.

This is considered a narrow oval base, because the width is less than ⅔ of the length. As a general rule, the spine of an oval basket contains between three and five spokes; this narrow basket will have a spine consisting of three 12-inch-long spokes.

According to the chart on page 156, we want the cross spokes to end up between ⅝ inch and 1 inch apart, because we are working with #5 reed. In order to determine how many cross spokes will be required, we need to determine the length of the slath—that is, the rectangular center area of the base which connects the two half-circle ends. To get this number, we need to know how much of each end of the long spokes will be part of the woven area of the base, and to subtract that amount from the total length.

The woven amount at each end will be equal to the woven amount along each side, so we'll start by figuring that amount. The cross spokes are 7 inches long—the desired width of the base. The area where the long spokes and cross spokes intersect cannot be woven; the size of this area can be determined by laying the long spokes next to each other and measuring their combined width. For three spokes of #5 reed, this is ½ inch.

Subtract the width of the spine from the length of the cross spokes to determine the full amount of cross spoke available for weaving (the open spoke not involved in the slath): 7 inches – ½ inch = 6½ inches. Half of this will be on each side, so divide by 2: 6½ ÷ 2 = 3¼ inches of weaving along each side.

Therefore, there will also be 3¼ inches of weaving at each end of the long spokes. With a spine length of 12 inches, minus 3¼ inches for each of two ends, we get: 12 inches – (3¼ inches × 2 = 6½ inches) = 5½ inches. The amount of the spine involved in the slath—and crossed by cross spokes—is 5½ inches.

Now we can determine how many cross spokes we need. For #5 spokes, spacing will be ⅝ to 1 inch. To get the basic number of intersections, divide the length of the slath by the spacing. At the closer spacing, 5½ inches ÷ ⅝ inch = 8.8 intersections. At the wider spacing, 5½ inches ÷ 1 inch = 5.5 intersections. On the first number, you could round up slightly to 9 intersections. On the second number, you could round up slightly to 6 intersections. Each modification would keep the placement of the spokes within the spacing guidelines for this size of spoke. I prefer the closer spacing, for a stronger basket.

You'll need one spoke for each intersection, and an extra spoke at each end (the ends have paired spokes). So add 2 to your numbers: either 11 or 8 cross spokes. Which of these you choose will depend upon your handle design and weave selection (see pages 68–69).

Say you have selected the first possibility. The 11 short spokes are split and the 3 long spokes are threaded through them. Two pairs of short spokes are set 3¼ inches in from each end of the long spokes. The spine is wound with #2 reed for eight wraps between the single short spokes, to space them evenly at ⅝ inch apart.

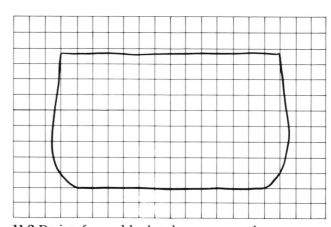

11.2 Design for oval basket drawn on graph paper

Bi-Spoking an Oval Base

The second consideration in the design of an oval basket is the shape of the sides: straight, flaring, or rounded. A straight-sided basket will need fewer side spokes inserted at the ends, while one that flares out from the base will need more.

There is no set formula for determining exactly how many side spokes should be added at the ends. This decision is often made during bi-spoking. Once you have made some sample baskets, you'll be able to decide how many spokes to add through a combination of instinct, visualization of the desired finished shape of the top of your basket, and the spoke spacing guidelines in the chart on page 156. The sample basket will take you through this process.

A Sample Oval Basket

Let's say that you want to make a narrow oval basket good for carrying handwork projects. It will flare at the bottom so it can hold a good amount, then slant in toward the top so nothing will fall out. An end-to-end handle will make the basket easy to carry and won't be in the way when you put things in or take them out. To make the basket sturdy without adding bulk, you'll use #5 spokes. For simplicity, we'll use the base we planned above, which is 12 inches long and 7 inches wide.

At the top, the basket's length will be 13½ inches and its width will be 8½ inches. The height of the basket's sides will be 8½ inches. The side spokes will flare out from the base at a 45-degree angle for 1½ inches, then slant inward slightly from that point to the top.

There are two ways to figure the circumference of the top. The first is a quick method which works when the length and width are not substantially different. For a quick number, add the length and width of the top, divide by 2, then multiply by 3.14. In this example the circumference will be 34½". The other method works on any basket. If L = length and W = width, the circumference is [(L − W) × 2] + (W × 3.14). For a basket 13½ inches by 8½ inches, [(13.5 − 8.5 = 5) × 2 = *10*] + (8.5 × 3.14 = *26.69*) = *36.69*, which can be rounded off to 36 inches.

To determine how many side spokes are needed, divide the circumference by the distance between the spokes. The spokes in this basket are a little closer than the round basket example, because the basket tapers in at the top, so the distance between them will be about ⅞ inch. A circumference of 36 inches ÷ spacing of ⅞ inch = 41, or 40 side spokes (an even number) for this basket.

The length of the side spokes is determined just as it was for the round basket example. This basket will also have a four-row rolled border. Add together:

- 2″ to be inserted into the base,
- 8½″ for the height of the basket, plus
- 1″ for ease, and
- 12¼″ for the four-row rolled border (14 × distance between spokes at top of basket).

The total length of each side spoke in this example will be 23¾″, which can be rounded off to 24″.

You now know that this basket requires approximately 40 side spokes, each 24″ long. You also know that a central side spoke is needed at each end, because the handle runs from end to end. For each of the 9 parallel short spokes in the

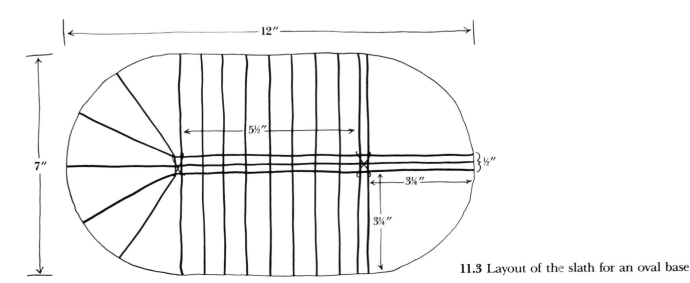

11.3 Layout of the slath for an oval base

base, you will add a single spoke on each side, for a total of 18 spokes. Each end will have 5 spokes, 3 of which were originally part of the spine and 2 of which came from the paired short spokes at the ends of the slath. These five will be bi-spoked, for 20 more spokes. Each central long spoke will have a third spoke inserted into it after it has been split for about 1½ inches (see 5.5) to give two more. The total number of side spokes, then, is 40.

Weave to 1 inch less than the desired finished diameter, bi-spoke, and work the three-rod arrow and four-rod coil.

When you weave up the sides, be sure to keep the central end spoke in the correct position so the handle will be symmetrical when it's inserted.

A good reed for the handle is #10—double the size used for the side spokes (see Chapter 7). Now the handle length has to be determined. The principles are explained in Chapter 7, but we'll run through the specific example here.

Half the circumference of the basket top is 17 inches, and the measurement from border to border, going under the basket, is 29 inches. The length of the exposed handle will fall between these two measurements. Since the height of the handle need not be more than 7 inches above the border, the exposed handle will be 20 inches long. The handle will be inserted into the basket about 6 inches at each end, so add 12 inches to the exposed handle length. The complete handle core will measure 32 inches. Choose whether you will make a roped or a wrapped handle, and proceed.

Approximate distances between spokes

Size	Approximate distances between spokes at sides and top of basket
#3	⅜–½″
double #2	½–⅝″
#4	½–¾″
double #4	⅝–⅞″
#5	⅝–1″
#6	1¼–1½″

This chart will be helpful in figuring how far apart spokes should be in the sides of a basket, or how to space the short spokes on an oval base.

Designing a round basket

Size of finished base*	Base spokes		Size of weavers	Side spokes		Approximate maximum top diameter
	Number	Size		Number	Size	
4″–5″	8	#4	#2	32	#4	8″
6″–7″	8	#5	#2	32	#5	10″
6″–7″	10	#4	#2	40	#4	9½″
7″–8″	10	#5	#2 and 3	40	#5	13″
8″–9″	8	#6	#2 and 3	32	#6	15″
9″–10″	10	#6	#2 and 3	40	#5	13″
9″–10″	12	#5	#2 and 3	48	#5	15″
11″–12″	10	#6	#2, #3 and 4	40	#6	19″

*This measurement does not include a three-rod arrow or coil.

Translating from distance-between-spokes to open-spoke requirements

Although these measurements seem exact, basket-making is an art, not a science. Take them as guidelines, add an extra inch or so for a fudge factor, and experiment.

If the distance between spokes at the top of the basket is:	And the instructions ask you to multiply that distance by:	The amount of open spoke required to work the border is:
⅝″	4	2½″
	6	3¾″
	7	4⅜″
	8	5″
	9	5⅝″
	10	6¼″
	11	6⅞″
	12	7½″
	14	8¾″
¾″	4	3″
	6	4½″
	7	5¼″
	8	6″
	9	6¾″
	10	7½″
	11	8¼″
	12	9″
	14	10½″
1″	4	4″
	6	6″
	7	7″
	8	8″
	9	9″
	10	10″
	11	11″
	12	12″
	14	14″
1½″	4	6″
	6	9″
	7	10½″
	8	12″
	9	13½″
	10	15″
	11	16½″
	12	18″
	14	21″

Summary of border techniques and required open-spoke factors

This chart lists the borders for which instructions are given in chapter 6, along with the number of rows required to complete them. To determine how much open spoke is required to weave a given border, begin by measuring the distance between spokes at the top of the basket. From the righthand column below, find the number by which you will multiply that measurement in order to figure how much open spoke is needed. Unless double spokes are specified, all numbers are for a border worked with single spokes. Either a calculator or the chart at left will give you the open-spoke measurement.

Type of border	Number of rows	Multiply by
Basic Trac Border	1	6 (double)
Trac Variation 1	1	5; 7 (double)
Trac Variation 2	1	7; 10 (double)
Trac Variation 3	1	6; 9 (double)
Trac Variation 4	1	8; 12 (double)
Basic Rolled Border	4	14
Rolled Variation 1	2	6
Rolled Variation 2	3	10
Rolled Variation 3	2	10
Rolled Variation 4	3	10
Rolled Variation 5	4	14
Rolled Variation 6	3	12
Rolled Variation 7	3	14
Japanese Braided Border	2	6
	3	10
Arrow Border	4	14
Three-Rod Plain Border	1	7
Follow-On Trac 1	1	4
Follow-On Trac 2	1	4
	2	8
Follow-On Trac 3	2	8
Braided Border	1	11 (double)

Appendix

GLOSSARY

This list of definitions includes both words used in the text of this book and words you may find undefined in your reading of other texts. The vocabulary of basketweaving has not been standardized. Both British and American terms are in use, and one technique may have several names. Once you get your hands on the materials and are familiar with the possibilities, these confusions clear up. While you are learning, however, make good use of this section.

Arrow – two rows of weaving which converge at each spoke. The first row is regular pairing or waling; the second, reverse pairing or waling.

Awl – a pointed tool, similar to an ice pick, used for making holes in spokes or creating spaces in the weaving. The British term is bodkin.

Back trac border – a second border woven in the opposite direction from the first border.

Base – the bottom of a basket, which can be round, oval, square, or rectangular.

Binder cane – wider and thicker version of natural strand cane.

Bi-spokes – spokes inserted on each side of a base spoke to form the framework for the sides.

Bodkin – the British term for awl.

Border – the finished edge at the top of a basket or lid formed by the interweaving of the spokes.

Breaking down – dividing or separating a group of spokes into smaller groups or single spokes.

Button – the center of slath of a round base.

Bye-spoke or bye-stake – the British term for a second spoke inserted next to a side spoke for added strength. Also known as a liner or supporter.

Cane – natural strand cane used for chair seating made from the inner bark of rattan. The bark is cut by machine to uniform widths.

Cane – the British term for reed. Also called pith cane, centre cane, pulp cane, or rattan core.

Cane – when rattan is classified by size for commercial use (such as for furniture frames, walking sticks, and the like), *cane* refers to those rattan sticks which are 9 feet long and at least 20 mm in diameter.

Center – the start or slath of a base.

Chain pairing – pairing arrows

Chair cane – natural strand cane used for weaving chair seats.

Changing-the-stroke – a step-up.

Chasing weave – also called chase weave or chasing. Continuous randing over any number of spokes with two weavers, each weaver weaving one round and chasing the other but never overtaking it.

Coil – one row of waling, resembling a rope twist, woven around a basket to strengthen it or to create a pattern, ending with a step-up and sometimes a lock.

Cross – the center of the slath on a round base.

Crown, crowning – the British term for dome and doming. Crowning is also called working the crown.

Datu rattan – a variety of rattan used in its natural state with only the outer bark removed. Size ranges from 2.5 to 4.5mm.

Diagonal cutting pliers – also called dikes or side cutters. Used for cutting reed.

Doming – shaping the base so that it resembles an upside-down saucer. Makes the basket stand on the outer rim of the base.

Double weaving – weaving with two weavers as one, as in double Japanese or slewing.

Fitching – a band of openwork, either straight or crossed, held in place on the top edge with reverse or fitch pairing.

Flow or spring – the angle the sides of the basket take.

Follow-on border – a second border woven in the same direction as the first border.

Foot – a coil worked over the bend of the spokes where they are pinched to go up the sides. Also called footing.

Foot border – a border added at the outer edge of the base, or a border worked on the underside of a wooden base.

French randing – a willow technique in which a weaver is placed in each space between spokes and randed on an angle.

French slewing – French randing with two weavers worked together as one.

Glossy cane – the British term for whole rattan which has not had its hard outer covering removed.

Glossy wrapping cane – the British term for natural strand cane.

Grin – the British term for spaces occurring in a rope handle.

Hairpin marker – Both ends of one piece of reed placed in the weaving or border to mark two consecutive places, thereby forming a hairpin shape.

Handle bow – the British term for the core of a handle.

In-and-out weave – randing.

Indian weave – continuous randing over an even number of spokes; adjusted each round by going under two or over two spokes before resuming the regular pattern. This creates a spiral on the inside or the outside of the basket.

Japanese weave – over two spokes and under one. The British terms are rib randing or Chinese randing.

Join – the addition of a new weaver. Also called joining in.

Joining spoke – the spoke behind which an old weaver ends and a new weaver begins.

Kind – the character of user-friendly materials.

Kooboo rattan – also spelled kubu rattan. A variety of rattan used in its natural state with just the outer bark removed. Size ranges from 5mm to more than 8mm. Too heavy for basketmaking, except in the Orient where it is available green.

Lapping – the British term for wrapping a handle with a flat weaver. Also called wrapping.

Leader – a round or flat weaving element laid across a wrapped handle and wrapped over and under to make a pattern.

Locking a coil – a method of ending a coil in which the ends are inserted into the same channel as their own beginnings.

Mellowing – the process of letting damp materials cure over a period of time to make them more flexible. Mellowing is not necessary with the light forms of reed used in this book; it becomes essential with less pliable materials, like willow.

Over-and-under weave – over one spoke and under one spoke. Also called plain weave, simple weave, randing, in-and-out weave, and single weave.

Packing – a way of building up or filling in areas by randing in a series of short turns.

Pairing – a weave in which two weavers are used alternately in a twisting pattern, in front of one spoke and behind one spoke. Also called twining.

Palembang – a variety of rattan used in its natural state with only the outer bark removed. The size ranges from 3mm to 8mm. It is, in general, too heavy for the basketry we are discussing.

Pegging – inserting a short piece of reed into a hole made in a handle with an awl just under the border to prevent the handle from being pulled out of the basket.

Plain rod border – the most common type of closed border, also called plain or rod border, or named by the actual number of turn-downs such as 3 behind 1, 4 behind 2, etc. Sometimes referred to as a commercial border.

Plain weave – randing.

Plaited border – the British term for a braided border. A strong decorative border which looks like a braid. Less commonly called a vale border.

Puloet rattan – also spelled pullet. A variety of rattan used in its natural state with only the outer bark removed. The size ranges from 3mm to 5mm.

Randing – the weaving of a single strand alternately in front of one spoke and behind the next single spoke, over an uneven number of spokes. Also called over-and-under weave, plain weave, simple weave, in-and-out weave, or single weave.

Rattan – the vine-like palms which grow in the tropical climates of southeast Asia. They are used in the manufacture of furniture and baskets. In Japanese basketry, the equivalent word is used to mean reed.

Reed – the flexible strands cut from the core of the long, slender stems of the rattan palm. Types of reed include round, flat, flat oval, oval oval, half round, and spline.

Rope handle – a handle wrapped with round weavers and resembling a rope twist.

Round – interchangeable with row.

Row – movement of a weaver one time completely around a base or basket.

Sadori binder cane – binder cane with a strip of bark removed from the center.

Scallop border – a fancy open border used for small baskets where strength is not necessary.

Simple weave – randing.

Slab rattan – like binder cane, but wider, thicker, and more roughly cut.

Slath – the arrangement of the spokes used to start a round or oval base.

Slewing – randing with two or more weavers used together as one.

Slype – British term for a long, slantwise cut.

Spine – the long spokes used in the slath of an oval base.

Spiral randing – weaving over two spokes and under two spokes with one weaver over a number of spokes divisible by 4 plus 1, or 4 minus 1.

Spiral slewing – weaving over two spokes and under two spokes with two weavers used together as one, over a number of spokes divisible by 4 plus 1, or 4 minus 1.

Splay – to spread out or apart.

Spokes – the elements which form the rigid framework of the base and sides of a basket.

Stake-and-strand – the British term for wicker baskets.

Stakes – the British term for side spokes.

Step-up – a stroke used at the end of each round of waling to make each row look complete in itself and to avoid a spiral. Also called change-of-stroke, changing the stroke, reversing, and change-over.

Staking up – the British term for adding side spokes to the base.

Sticks – the British term for the short, heavy spokes used in a base.

Stroke – one movement of the weaver; can be compared to a stitch in knitting or sewing.

Taper – to cut a piece of flat reed on an even gradual slope so that it comes to a point at the end.

Three-rod wale – a weaving pattern in which the left weaver of a set of three is woven, in turn, in front of two spokes, behind the third and out. Also called triple weave, triple twist, or three-strand twining.

Top diameter – the space across the basket measured from the outside edge of the border.

Trac border – a border in which each spoke is turned down in sequence, completing its movement entirely before the next spoke is worked.

Triple weave – three-rod waling.

Twining – a weave worked with 2 or more strands with the left weaver always being woven over the other weaver(s) in a twisting pattern.

Tying the slath – winding the center of a round or oval base to tie the spokes together before they are opened out. Also called tying in the slath.

Turning a basket – upsetting.

Unkind – the character of basketry materials which makes them difficult to work.

Upsett – several rows of weaving which serve to reorient the spokes at the correct angle and spacing before the sides are woven.

Upsetting – the pinching, bending and weaving of the several rows which set the shape of the basket. The techniques used for upsetting vary with different basketry traditions. English basketmakers traditionally use waling for this task, while the Japanese often use randing or pairing.

Vale – a braided or plaited border.

Wale – a weaving pattern in which the left weaver of a set of three, four, or more weavers is woven in turn in front of a varying number of spokes, behind one and out.

Weaver – a flexible round or flat material used for weaving in and out of the rigid framework formed by the spokes.

Whole cane – whole rattan which has not had its hard outer covering removed.

Wicker – a broad term for baskets made with round materials such as willow, oak rods, rattan, reed, and so forth. This type of basket consists of a rigid frame work for the bottom and sides, horizontally interwoven with pliable materials. The British term is stake-and-strand.

BIBLIOGRAPHY

Basketry Books

A.C.I. Craft Leaflets. *Basketry*. New York: Alnap, n.d.

———. *Home Basketry*. New York: Alnap, n.d.

Allbon, Leonard D. *Basic Basketry*. London: Max Parrish, 1961.

Basketry. New York: Woman's Home Companion, n.d.

Bindon, Eyleen. *Basic Basketry*. New York: Drake, 1977.

Blanchard, Mary Miles. *The Basketry Book*. New York: Charles Scribner's Sons, 1916.

Bobart, H. H. *Basketwork through the Ages*. London: Oxford University Press, 1936. Republished by Singing Tree Press, Book Tower, Detroit, 1971.

Boy Scouts of America. *Basketry*. North Brunswick, New Jersey: Boy Scouts of America, 1968.

Brown, Margery. *The Complete Book of Rush and Basketry Techniques*. London: B. T. Batsford, 1983.

Butcher, Mary. *Willow Work*. London: Dryad Press, 1986.

Cary, Mara. *Useful Baskets*. Boston: Houghton Mifflin, 1977.

Christopher, F. J. *Basketry*. New York: Dover, 1952.

Crampton, Charles. *Canework*. Leicester: Dryad Press, 1969.

———. *The Junior Basket Maker*. Leicester: Dryad Press, 1969.

Crooke, Edith M. *Artistic Cane Basketry up to Date*. London: The School of Basketry, 1918.

Daugherty, Robin Taylor. *Splintwoven Basketry*. Loveland, Colorado: Interweave Press, 1986.

Decorative Items for the Advanced. #7813. Japan.

Deutch, Yvonne, editor. *Cane, Rush and Straw*. New York: Excalibur Books, 1977.

Dyer, Anne. *Basketry*. London: Berkeley, 1979.

Firth, Annie. *Cane Basket Work: A Practical Manual on Weaving Useful and Fancy Baskets*. Second series. London: L. Upcott Gill, n.d.

Fitzgerald, Sallie G. *The Priscilla Basketry Book No. 1*. Needlecraft Publishing Company, 1911.

Gill, Anna A. *Practical Basketry*. Philadelphia: David McKay, 1916.

Hart, Carol, and Dan Hart. *Natural Basketry*. New York: Watson-Guptill, 1976.

Harvey, Virginia. *The Techniques of Basketry*. New York: Van Nostrand Reinhold, 1974.

Hasegawa. *Basic Rattan*. #7808. Japan.

———. *Furniture Made with Rattan*. #5759. Japan.

———. *Rattan Baskets*. #7761. Japan.

———. *Rattan Items: Baskets, Home Accessories*. #7788. Japan.

Hasluck, Paul N., editor. *Basket Work of All Kinds*. London: Cassell and Company, 1912.

Heseltine, Alastair. *Baskets and Basketmaking*. U.K.: Shire Publications, 1982.

Hosking, Phyllis. *Basket-making for Amateurs*. London: G. Bell and Sons, 1960.

Jacot, R. M. *Useful Cane Work, Parts I and II*. London: Charles and Dible, n.d.

Johnson, Kay. *Canework*. London: Dryad Press, 1986.

Kirmeyer, Maxine. *A Materials Guide for the Basket Maker*. San Jose, California: Kirmeyer Publications, 1987.

Klickman, Flora, editor. "Stitchery, No. 48," *Woman's Magazine*. London, n.d.

Knock, A. G. *Willow Basket Work*. Leicester: Dryad Press, 1970.

Kroncke, Grete. *Weaving with Cane and Reed*. New York: Van Nostrand Reinhold, 1968.

Lang, Mrs. Edwin. *Basketry: Weaving and Design*. New York: Charles Scribner's Sons, 1925.

Lasansky, Jeannette. *Willow, Oak and Rye*. University Park, Pennsylvania: Pennsylvania State University Press, 1979.

Lee, Martha L. *Basketry and Related Arts*. New York: D. Van Nostrand, 1948.

Legg, Evelyn. *Country Baskets*. London: Mills and Boon, 1960.

Maki, Masako. *Rattan Work*. Tokyo: Ondorisha, 1986.

Maynard, Barbara. *Modern Basketry from the Start*. New York: Charles Scribner's Sons, 1973.

Morse, T. Vernette. *Basket Making*. Chicago: Art Craft Supply, 1903.

Obata. *Advanced Rattan Crafts*. #5717. Japan.

———. *Basic Rattan Making*. #5893. Japan.

———. *More Rattan Baskets*. #7809. Japan.

———. *Rattan for the Advanced*. #5775. Japan.

Okey, Thomas. *An Introduction to the Art of Basket-Making*. England: The Basketmakers' Association, 1986.

Parkin, Doug, and Eleanor Zimmerman. *Creating with Reed and Other Natural Fibers*. Salt Lake City, Utah: Zim's, 1980.

Polkinghorne, R. K. *Weaving and Other Pleasant Occupations*. Ann Arbor, Michigan: Gryphon Books, 1971.

Roffey, Mabel. *Simple Basketry for Homes and Schools*. New York: Pitman, n.d.

Rossbach, Ed. *The Nature of Basketry*. Exton, Pennsylvania: Schiffer, 1986.

Roth, Vreni. *Flechten Mit Peddigrohr*. Horgen, Austria: Herausgegeben im Selbstverlag, n.d.

Schanz, Joanne E. *Willow Basketry of the Amana Colonies.* Iowa City, Iowa: Penfield Press, 1986.

Schiffer, Nancy. *Baskets.* Exton, Pennsylvania: Schiffer, 1984.

Scott, O. R. *Basketry Step by Step.* London: Sir Isaac Pitman and Sons, 1958.

Seed, T. Rutherford. *Basket Work: A Practical Handbook.* London: Oxford University Press, n.d.

Sekijima, Hisako. *Basketry: Projects from Baskets to Grass Slippers.* New York: Kodansha International/USA, 1986.

Stephenson, Sue H. *Basketry of the Appalachian Mountains.* New York: Van Nostrand Reinhold, 1977.

Tanigawa. *New Rattan Baskets.* #7777. Japan.

————. *Rattan Baskets.* #5770. Japan.

————. *Rattan Gift Items.* #5760. Japan.

Three Cane-Work Borders. Leicester: Dryad Press, n.d.

Tinsley, Laura Rollins. *Practical and Artistic Basketry.* New York: A. S. Barnes, 1904.

Tod, Osma Gallinger. *Earth Basketry.* New York: Crown, 1972.

Tod, Osma Gallinger, and Oscar H. Benson. *Weaving with Reed and Fibers.* New York: Dover, 1975.

Turner, Luther Weston. *The Basket Maker.* New York: Mentzer, Bush, 1909.

White, Mary. *How to Make Baskets.* New York: Doubleday, Page, 1902.

————. *More Baskets and How to Make Them.* New York: Doubleday, Page, 1912.

Will, Christoph. *International Basketry.* Exton, Pennsylvania: Schiffer, 1985.

Wright, Dorothy. *A Caneworker's Book for the Senior Basket Maker.* Leicester: Dryad Press, 1970.

————. *The Complete Book of Baskets and Basketry.* North Pomfret, Vermont: David and Charles, 1983.

————. *The Complete Guide to Basket Weaving.* New York: Drake, 1972.

Books about Dyeing and Color Theory

Adrosko, Rita J. *Natural Dyes and Home Dyeing.* New York: Dover, 1971.

Bliss, Anne. *North American Dye Plants.* Boulder, Colorado: Juniper House, 1980.

Blumenthal, Betsy, and Kathryn Kreider. *Hands On Dyeing.* Loveland, Colorado: Interweave Press, 1988.

Brooklyn Botanic Garden. *Dye Plants and Dyeing: A Handbook.* Brooklyn, New York: Brooklyn Botanic Garden, 1964.

Chijiiwa, Kideaki. *Color Harmony.* Rockport, Massachusetts: Rockport, 1987.

Knutson, Linda. *Synthetic Dyes for Natural Fibers.* Loveland, Colorado: Interweave Press, 1987.

Proctor, Richard M., and Jennifer F. Lew. *Surface Design for Fabric.* Seattle: University of Washington Press, 1984.

Stockton, James. *Designer's Guide to Color.* San Francisco: Chronicle Books, 1984.

Vinroot, Sally, and Jennie Crowder. *The New Dyer.* Loveland, Colorado: Interweave Press, 1981.

Books about Rattan

Blatter, E. *Palms of British India and Ceylon.* 1926.

Burkhill, Isaac Henry. *Dictionary of Economic Products of the Malay Peninsula.* London: Crown Agents for the Colonies, 1935.

Dransfield, John. *A Short Guide to Rattans.* Indonesia: Biotrop, 1974.

Jordon, Don. "The Rattan Industry," *The Malay Forester,* April 1965.

Keeney, Allen. "Rattan, The Wonderful Plant," *Allen's Basketworks Newsletter,* Winter 1988. Vol. 2, No. 1.

Ramaswami, S. "Indian Canes (Rattan)," *Indian Forester,* Vol. 76.

Whitmore, T. C. *Palms of Malaya.* London: Oxford University Press, 1973.

Magazines of Interest to Basketmakers

American Craft. American Craft Council, 40 W. 53rd Street, New York, NY 10019.

The Basketmaker Magazine. MKS Publications, Inc., P.O. Box 340, Westland, MI 48185-0340.

The Crafts Report. 700 Orange Street, P.O. Box 1992, Wilmington, DE 19899.

Fiberarts. 50 College Street, Asheville, NC 28801.

Handwoven. Interweave Press, 201 East Fourth Street, Loveland, CO 80537.

Shuttle Spindle and Dyepot. Handweavers Guild of America, 2402 University Avenue SE, Suite 702, St. Paul, MN 55114.

SUPPLIERS OF MATERIALS AND TOOLS

ACP Inc., P. O. Box 1426, Salisbury, NC 28144. (704) 636-3034. *Wholesale/retail.*

Allen's Basketworks, 8624 SE 13th, P. O. Box 02648, Portland, OR 97202. (503) 238-6384. *Wide assortment of basketry materials; classes; newsletter. Very sharp Chinese basketry scissors. Wholesale/retail.*

Alliance Trading Co., 1021 R. St., Sacramento, CA 95814. (916) 442-9225. *Wholesale only.*

The Basket Works, 4900 Wetheredsville Road, Baltimore, MD 21027. *Wide assortment of basketry materials; classes.*

Cane and Basketry Supply Co., 1283 S. Cochran Ave., Los Angeles, CA 90019. *Wholesale/retail.*

The Canery, 236 S. Liberty St. Annex, Winston-Salem, NC 27101.

The Caning Shop, 926 Gilman St., Berkeley, CA 94710. *Wide assortment of basketry materials, tools, and books; classes. Carries Japanese trimming shears.*

Carol's Canery, Route 1, Box 48, Palmyra, VA 22963. (804) 589-4001.

Commonwealth Manufacturing Co., 5-05 48th Ave., Long Island City, NY 11101. *Wholesale only.*

Connecticut Cane and Reed Co., P. O. Box 762, Manchester, CT 06040. *Wide selection of basketry materials and tools, including the bone awl.*

The Country Seat, Box 24, RD 2, Kempton, PA 19529. (215) 756-6124. *Wide selection of basketry materials. Carries brass gauge, Platoshears. Excellent selection of books.*

Crooked River Crafts, P. O. Box 917, LaFarge, WI 54639. (608) 625-4460. *Dyed reed.*

W. Cushing Co., P. O. Box 3513, Kennebunkport, ME 04016. *Cushing "Perfection" dyes.*

Dianne Stanton, 365 High Street, Pembroke, MA 02395. *Spring-loaded diagonal cutting pliers.*

English Basketry Willows, RFD 1, Box 124A, South New Berlin, NY 13843-9649. (607) 847-8264. *Five-inch thin bodkin (awl).*

Fibers and Reed, 504 41st Street N., Great Falls, MT 59401. *Procion MX dyes, dyed reed samples, dye information booklet.*

Frank's Cane and Rush Supply, 7252 Heil Avenue, Huntington Beach, CA 92647. (714) 847-0707. *Wide assortment of basketry materials; newsletter. Wholesale/retail.*

Goldblatt Tool Co., 511 Osage, P. O. Box 2334, Kansas City, KS 66110. *Seven-inch flower and fruit shears.*

The H. H. Perkins Co., 10 S. Bradley Rd., Woodbridge, CT 06525. (203) 389-9501. *Wide assortment of basketry materials, books, European cut reed, and Hamburg cane. Wholesale/retail.*

Linda Snow Fibers, 3209 Doctors Lake Drive, Orange Park, FL 32073. *Dyed reed samples of Cushing and Comcraft Basketry Dyes, for reference purposes.*

Ozark Basketry Supply, P. O. Box 56-H, Kingston, AR 72742.

Plymouth Reed and Cane Supply, 1200 W. Ann Arbor Rd., Plymouth, MI 48170. (313) 455-2150.

Pro Chemical and Dye, Inc., P. O. Box 14, Somerset, MA 02726. *Fiber reactive dyes, Procion MX dyes.*

Rio Grande Albuquerque Inc., 6901 Washington NE, Albuquerque, NM 87109. *Roundnose pliers in tools catalog.*

Rit Consumer Service, Dept. CC-1, P. O. Box 21070, Indianapolis, IN 46221. *Dye chart.*

Royalwood, Ltd., 517 Woodville Road, Mansfield, OH 44907. (419) 526-1630. *Assorted supplies and books, including microtweezers which can substitute for roundnose pliers.*

Wooden Porch Books, Rte. 1, Box 262, Middlebourne, WV 26149. (304) 386-4434. *Out-of-print basketry books.*

The Woven Warp, KC Sibert, 7712 Gromwell Court, Springfield, VA 22152. (703) 644-1045. *Assortment of supplies and tools, including roundnose pliers.*

BASKETRY GUILDS AND ASSOCIATIONS

Association of Michigan Basketmakers (AMB), 28 Faculty Way, Bloomfield Hills, MI 48013.

Basket Artisans of Arizona (BAA), c/o Barbara Gronemann, President, 6440 Presidio Road, Scottsdale, AZ 85254.

The Basket Weavers Guild of Florida, 10412 Ebbit Rd., Jacksonville, FL 32216.

The Basketmakers' Association (England), Betty Whitehead, Membership Secretary, Martins, Lee Common, Great Missenden, Bucks HP16 9JP, England.

Basketmakers Guild of Fort Wayne (BGOFW), c/o Karen Peak, Forest Downs Drive, Fort Wayne, IN 46815.

The Basketmakers of Victoria (Australia), Jean Stone, President, 3 Loudon Rd., Burwood, Victoria 3125, Australia.

The Basketweavers Guild of Georgia (BWGG), Patricia Alexander, P.O. Box 1309, Roswell, GA 30077.

Bay Area Basket Makers (BABM), Cheryl Provost, President, 115 Melrose Avenue, San Francisco, CA 94127.

Desert Basketry Guild (DBG), c/o Alice Kotzen, 43100 Tennessee, Palm Desert, CA 92660.

Great Basic Basketmakers (GBB), c/o Mary Lee Fulkerson, 5055 Twin Springs Road, Palomino Valley, NV 89510.

Gulf Coast Weaver's Guild (GCWG), Sally Brown, President, 2332 Bayshore Road, Gulf Breeze, FL 32561.

Gwinnett County Basketweaver's Guild (GCBG), c/o Tracey Barnhart, 5188 Aberdeen Ct., Lilburn, GA 30247.

High Country Basketry Guild (HCBG), P.O. Box 1102, Fairfax, VA 22030-1102.

Houston Area Basket Guild (HABG), Lynn Gammon, 14627 Wind Hollow Circle, Houston, TX 77040.

Iowa Basket Weavers Guild (IBWG), Kathy Kellenberger, RR 1, South Amana, IA 52334.

Los Angeles Basketry Guild (LABG), Judy Mulford, 2098 Mandeville Canyon Rd., Los Angeles, CA 90049.

Long Island Basketmakers Guild (LIBG), P.O. Box 1433, Melville, NY 11746.

New Jersey Basketweavers (NJB), P.O. Box 224, Short Hills, NJ 07078.

North Carolina Basketmakers Association (NCBA), Judy Wobbleton, 305 Chanute Rd., Goldsboro, NC 27530.

North Country Basketmakers' Guild (NCBG), c/o Lynn Thorp, Corresponding Secretary, Box 183, Franconia, NH 03580.

Northeast Basketmakers Guild (NBG), P.O. Box 125, Staffordville, CT 06077.

Northwest Basket Weavers (NBW), Vi Phillips, Basketry Guild, P.O. Box 5657, Lynnwood, WA 98046-5657.

Prairie Basketry Guild (PBG), c/o Barb Hantschel, 1355 Deane Blvd., Racine, WI 53405.

Trinity Arts Basket Guild (TABG), c/o Jayne Stirpe, 3708 Whitefern Dr., Fort Worth, TX 76137.

Venetian Society of Basket Weavers (VSBW), P.O. Box 1013, Nokomis, FL 33555.

Westchester Area Basketmaker's Guild (WABG), c/o Nancy Slye, 36 Chestnut Ridge Road, Mount Kisco, NY 10549.

Wildwood Basketry Guild (WBG), Jackie Freeman, 1076 West Jackson St., Painesville, OH 44077.

Index